T0367150

A New Generation of African Writers

A New Generation of African Writers

Migration, Material Culture & Language

BRENDA COOPER

Professor, Centre for African Studies &
Department of English
University of Cape Town

James Currey

University of KwaZulu-Natal Press

© Brenda Cooper 2008

All Rights Reserved. Except as permitted under current legislation
no part of this work may be photocopied, stored in a retrieval
system, published, performed in public, adapted, broadcast,
transmitted, recorded or reproduced in any form or by any means,
without the prior permission of the copyright owner

First published 2008
Reprinted in paperback 2013

ISBN 978 1 84701 507 5 hardback
ISBN 978 1 84701 076 6 paperback

James Currey www.jamescurrey.com
is an imprint of Boydell & Brewer Ltd
PO Box 9, Woodbridge
Suffolk IP12 3DF, UK
and of Boydell & Brewer Inc.
668 Mt Hope Avenue, NY 14620-2731, USA
website: www.boydellandbrewer.com

University of KwaZulu-Natal Press
Private Bag X01
Scottsville, 3209
South Africa
www.ukznpress.co.za

The publishers have no responsibility for the continued existence or
accuracy of URLs for external or third-party internet websites referred
to in this book, and do not guarantee that any content on such
websites is, or will remain, accurate of appropriate.

A CIP catalogue record of this publication is available from the
British Library

Typeset in 9.5/11.5pt Melior by forzalibro designs, Cape Town

Printed in Great Britain by
CPI Group (UK) Ltd, Croydon CR0 4YY

For Martin, Adam,
Sara & Nerissa

Contents

Acknowledgements

The financial assistance of the National Research Foundation, South Africa, towards this research is acknowledged. The opinions and conclusions are mine.

A version of Chapter Two appeared as 'Parallel Universes and Detonating Words: The Brixton Wonderland of Biyi Bandele's *The Street*', *Journal for the Study of Religion*, Vol. 19, Number 2, 2006, 17–40.

A version of Chapter Three appeared as 'Look Who's Talking? Multiple Worlds, Migration and Translation in Leila Aboulela's *The Translator*', *The Translator*, Vol. 12, No. 2, 2006, 323–44.

A version of Chapter Six entitled 'Resurgent Spirits, Catholic Echoes of Igbo and Petals of Purple: The Syncretised World of Chimamanda Ngozi Adichie's *Purple Hibiscus*' will appear in *African Literature Today* (ALT 27): *New Novels in African Literature* (forthcoming).

1 Introduction
Multiple Worlds, Material Culture & Language

'What sort of form would a story that escapes the Symbolic have?
(MacCannell, 1983: 916)

This is a book about African fiction, published within the last decade, by a younger generation of exciting new talent. They are Biyi Bandele, Leila Aboulela, Jamal Mahjoub, Moses Isegawa and Chimamanda Ngozi Adichie. Their novels are *The Street* (1999), *The Translator* (1999), *The Carrier* (1998), *Abyssinian Chronicles* (2000), *Purple Hibiscus* (2004) and *Half of a Yellow Sun* (2006). They are all writers who have either migrated, or who have spent time studying and writing outside of the African countries in which they were born or grew up. These countries are Nigeria (Bandele and Adichie), Sudan (Aboulela and Mahjoub) and Uganda (Isegawa). I examine how these novelists, from across Africa, who have migrated away, find ways of manipulating the English language in order to depict the realities of their multiple worlds and languages.

I have included two novels by Adichie for two reasons. Firstly, she has created a stir on the literary scene with her talent and originality. Her second novel, especially, has been widely publicised and read and has won the prestigious Orange Broadband Prize for fiction. In a book that examines new fiction by young writers, both of her novels deserve a place. Secondly, and more importantly, the contrast between the two novels vividly illustrates the point that I make in this book. I will be demonstrating the difficulties that *Half of a Yellow Sun* gets into, as it increasingly fights its battles on a metaphoric front. This is so because the English language is steeped in imperialist and patriarchal tropes and symbols. The writers are challenged to find an English into which to translate their more than one culture, language and knowledge base without being sucked into some of those older tropes and imperial metaphors. The solution that these writers sometimes craft is to become quite concrete and literal, including focussing on the shape and rhythm of words themselves as objects, or by incorporating words and wisdoms from their indigenous languages. In so doing, they rely quite heavily on the enabling potential of the rhetoric of metonymy whose function I will be enlarging upon.

Although the following chapters are organised more or less chronologically in terms of the date of publication of the novel under discussion, I begin with Bandele in the next chapter and then move on to Aboulela, both of whose novels were published in 1999, albeit that Mahjoub's appeared a year earlier in 1998. This is because the issues raised by Bandele and Aboulela assist us in deciphering Mahjoub's rather more dense and coded work. I will be tracking the journeys undertaken by these African writers, their protagonists and their daily lives, and the material culture and the solid objects

1

that populate their fictions, and which translate into language. Arjun Appadurai (1986), in his *The Social Life of Things*, has suggested that objects have 'life histories' (41) and that they may 'accumulate an idiosyncratic biography or enjoy a peculiar career' (42). Appadurai describes how these objects, or commodities, leave their designated paths and find themselves 'in unlikely contexts' (27). These 'diversions' are, however, 'meaningful only in relation to the paths from which they stray' (Appadurai, 28). The paths that the fictional objects encountered in this book take and leave, are multiple and global. The writers carry intriguing baggage from across North, East and West Africa, arriving in England (Bandele), Scotland (Aboulela), Denmark (Mahjoub) Holland (Isegawa) and the USA (Adichie).

And so, this book has excavated a wealth of weird and wonderful solid objects and their life histories, which entwine with the protagonists of the novels in interesting, and sometimes unpredictable, ways. In Biyi Bandele's *The Street*, we find bizarre objects, like a corkscrew, which is a portal to a parallel universe, a land of dreams, in which objects disappear the second one looks away and words materialise as commodities, sold on average for ten pence each. In Leila Aboulela's *The Translator*, there is a winter coat with toggles instead of buttons and perfume 'from heaven via Paris'. That coat and this perfume are benign translation objects, which contrast with the plundered toxic relics on display at the museum, in Aboulela's prize-winning short story entitled 'The Museum' from her collection, *Coloured Lights*. There is the quest for a telescope and the discovery of a brass box, nearly four hundred years old, and perplexingly buried in a remote corner of the Danish peninsula, in Jamal Mahjoub's epic novel, *The Carrier*. There are objects invested with the power of Family, State and Church in Moses Isegawa's *Abyssinian Chronicles*. These are, respectively, the bobbin stolen from a dictatorial mother, the headboard and the television, which smells of fish, expropriated from Ugandan Asians expelled by Idi Amin, and the boat, *Agatha*, doomed darling of the expatriate priest. In *Purple Hibiscus*, there are ceramic figurines, an incomplete painting, furniture inhabited by spirits and, not least of all, the purple flowering bushes that give Chimamanda Ngozi Adichie's first novel its title. Finally, there is the bronze casting of a roped pot, which is hundreds of years old, a pair of leather slippers and the decapitated head of a child in a wooden calabash in Adichie's second novel, *Half of a Yellow Sun*. All of these comprise a universe of solid objects, which become the luggage on intriguing journeys, as these material things become props in the social practices and rituals of writers re-enacting their new and old identity formations.

The argument I will be developing in the book, and which will structure this introduction, begins with an examination of the social and psychological consequences for African writers of the dominance within the English language of Western symbols and colonial metaphors. Linked to this, I examine Bourdieu's concept of symbolic capital, which many postcolonial migrants lack. I go on to analyse how this symbolic lack relates to the literal and material realities of daily life, which some migrant writers portray. The issue of language permeates all of this discussion and I will demonstrate that many postcolonial writers, and African writers among them, have drawn on the potential of the rhetoric of metonymy to contest the dominance of metaphor. This cuts to the quick of the nature of the politics of language in recent African fiction.

At the same time, it is critical not to set up false polarities, as for example, between metaphor and metonymy. I am mindful of this as I dismantle the literal and the figurative, the spiritual and the material, metaphor and metonymy, and do so in the knowledge that these dimensions are syncretised and blended and, in practice, operate together. Finally, therefore, I bring us back in this introduction to the multiple, hybridised worlds simultaneously inhabited by African migrant writers. Disaggregating these worlds for a moment, however, enables us to see how they operate and the complexities involved in bringing about transformation – in language, in the psyche and in society.

What we must also remember is that these writers are as different as they are similar. They come from different parts of Africa, have different life histories and religious beliefs. For example, there is the overt religious passion of Aboulela and Adichie, by comparison with the others. This similarity, buttressed by their shared gender, is qualified by the difference between Aboulela's Islam and Adichie's indigenised Catholicism. Then again, differences in gender manifest most powerfully in relation to the material culture on which we are focussing – the way in which the public and private division mediates and determines everyday lives. While woman have entered the workplace and men have stormed the kitchen, it is still the case that conventional gender roles remain significant. As Highmore puts it 'it is the street rather than the home that is seen as the privileged sphere of everyday life' (2002: 12). We may take as symptomatic of this male site Biyi Bandele's cacophony of Brixton High Street, where black and poor men mingle and rave and recite and smoke dope and booze up and dream and speak in tongues. This contrasts with the use to which Leila Aboulela puts the loving preparation of her translated soup in *The Translator*, where she has to search the supermarkets of Aberdeen for her Sudanese ingredients, or their closest equivalents. We will explore these differences as socially and aesthetically constructed, based on the daily experiences of writers, whose genders open them up to different arenas in the new cities they inhabit and represent in manipulated Englishes.

Subjectivity, symbolic capital & the dominance of metaphor

The language issue continues to be fundamental to African writers who are contesting colonial power and its bequests. Subjectivity, and indeed the language gift it carries, is double edged. We become individuated and also socialised as members of families and communities. We also become subject to social laws and prohibitions and inherit a language saturated with dominant power. This process occurs at the site of what Lacan has termed the Symbolic. As Frosh puts it: 'Lacan sees the Law of the Father as identical with the law of language, the symbolic order ... which structures all interactions' (1999: 218). Language, therefore, comprises what Deleuze and Guattari call 'order-words'. They suggest that 'language is made not to be believed but to be obeyed, and to compel obedience' (1987, 76). These order-words buttress the status quo, ensuring the perpetuation of the balance of power. What this means is that 'we constantly pass from order-words to the "silent order" of things, as Foucault puts it, and vice versa' (Deleuze and Guattari, 1987: 87).

Lacan's concept of the Symbolic is invaluable, for all the impenetrability of his theory, given that we are exploring the nature of language, and particularly of its figurative dimensions, as it works on the deepest recesses of the human psyche. In other words, the Symbolic must be understood here in two crucially interlocking ways. Firstly, there is the Symbolic with a capital 'S', which is the rather specialised Lacanian site where subjectivity is constituted in language via the gateway of the dominant structures of the Law. This relates to the more conventional understanding of the term, 'symbolic'. The link between the two forms of the S/symbolic becomes obvious, given that symbols, tropes and metaphors are steeped in the Law and contribute to subject formation in the interests of dominant cultures and classes. Or, as Anika Lemaire puts it, 'the human being acquires his individuality only on condition of being inserted into the symbolic order which governs and specifies humanity' (1977: 67). This is why Deleuze and Guattari propose an alternative to this route of becoming human in their search for 'a *nonfigurative* and *nonsymbolic* unconscious' (1983: 351, my emphases). This is why they wage a fierce battle against the tyranny of psychoanalysis, which now aspires to be 'a master of ... metaphor' (27). To be master of metaphor is to be fully constituted in the dominant language and Law of society. Opposing Oedipus, Father, Doctor, Imperialist, is the schizo, nomad, migrant, the marginalised person, who 'scrambles all the codes' (35). Instead of the figurative, they proffer what they call 'partial objects', fragmented, concrete things, leftovers, shards of glass or bits of brick (42). These bits and pieces 'unquestionably have a sufficient charge in and of themselves to blow up all of Oedipus' (44). The partial object resists symbolisation, 'is not representative' (47). In being outside of the arsenal of cultural, buried meaning, it is not part of the coded language from which strangers and nomads are excluded.

This exclusion is what migrant writers often depict when their protagonists find themselves perplexed in strange, hostile climates and settings, where they do not get the joke, understand the irony, the pun or the analogy and where their accented English and their dress, food and manners, are not quite right. They are gesturing towards a politics of lack, of the absence of safe entry through those portals of the Law. The bewilderment in the face of the dominant culture, for all the migrant's education and schooling in the European language, could be summed up when Homi Bhabha quotes V.S. Naipaul as bemoaning the fact that 'the English language was mine; the tradition was not' (Bhabha, 1984: 95). This 'tradition' is the deep meanings, metaphors and associations that the dominant culture shares with insiders. What these migrants lack, is 'symbolic' or 'cultural capital', as Pierre Bourdieu would put it, which is 'inherited from the family or acquired at school' (1984: 13). This concept of cultural capital encapsulates both meanings of the S/symbolic, relating as it does both to subjectivity and to figurative meanings available to native speakers of the language. Bourdieu integrates this symbolic value into material life in that it is 'intellectual stock in trade' that belongs to a person 'as if it were a house or money' (1). This is not crude, given that it becomes solid material advantage. It becomes a house or money, bestowed on those who go to the right schools and are raised in 'good' families, who read books, listen to music and go to the theatre. It provides 'both a head-start and a credit' (70); it is symbolic in the sense that it does so 'in the most unconscious and impalpable way' (71) and yet 'nothing more rigorously distinguishes the different classes' (40).

For our purposes, we may add that nothing so much distinguishes the postcolonial, black migrant from the European citizen. This migrant, as much as an aspiring member of an underclass, is trapped in what Bourdieu dubs the dilemma of 'parvenus', the uneasy, in-between people, who have to choose between conforming to, or ostentatiously rebelling against, the mores of the upper class to which they aspire (Bourdieu, 1984: 95). If parvenus are social upstarts, with newly acquired wealth or education, who do not quite properly exhibit the exquisitely and supposedly instinctive style of inherited behaviour, then migrants, in their attempts to become citizens, are quintessential parvenus. This point has been made quite poignantly by Zygmunt Bauman, who says that 'wherever they come and dearly wish to stay, the nomads find themselves to be parvenus. Parvenu, *arriviste*; someone already *in*, but not quite *of*, the place' (1997: 72, his emphasis). Moses Isegawa marks this moment of entry right at the end of *Abyssinian Chronicles* when his wily protagonist, Mugezi, storms the invisible barricades of Amsterdam and declares that albeit it is a 'Herculean task for Abyssinians to get their foot in the door, but once in, they never budge. I was in' (462).

This image emphasises that the power of the Law is always fractured, partial and available for contestation. The site of culture and language is unstable and full of alternative strategies and possibilities. Isegawa enacts through Mugezi precisely how resistance to being excluded, be it from the city or language, becomes possible. And so

> when Lacan pronounces that all there is is the symbolic and that this wears the phallic veil of the name-of-the-Father, a space is created into which others rush, saying no, this is not so, we can imagine something else within which your imagined structure looks arbitrary and oppressive'. (Elliott and Frosh, 1995: 4)

The politics may go either way in this migrant site, which carries opportunities, and also pitfalls, for challenging the Law. The writers craft a language, which sometimes confronts and sometimes colludes with the dominant S/symbolic. What is certain is that 'the father's rule is threatened whenever the subject plays with words, with tropes, and the combinatory power of language' (Stoltzfus, 1996:14). What this book is exploring is how writers play with the combinatory power of metaphor and metonymy in order to threaten the imperial father's surviving rule. I am pointing to the cultural politics of favouring a combination in which metonymy is used in order to represent the rich and concrete realities of material culture. What this may enable is a challenge to some of the deep stereotypes invested in the stubborn and surviving metaphors that have always falsely represented Africa.

Material culture, the rhetoric of metonymy & the resistance to the law

The mundane daily-ness of life lacks the drama of quests deep into jungles, where drums beat to the rhythm of Africa's dark heart. At the same time, capturing the multiplicity and repetitiveness of the everyday poses an aesthetic challenge, which is to make the ordinary the subject of compelling fiction. Njabulo Ndebele's essay, 'The Rediscovery of the Ordinary', which provides the title of a collection of his essays on South African literature and culture, makes this point precisely when he confronts what he sees as the failure *in method* of much of South African 'protest' literature. He identifies this failure as the result of its adherence to 'an artistic convention', a 'complex system of aesthetics' which 'involves the transformation of objective reality into conventional tropes which become the predominant means by which that objective reality is artistically ritualised' (1991: 44). This form of writing, ironically, for all its resistance to Apartheid racism, remains stuck in the paradigm of symbolic stereotype and sweeping generalisation of the nature of African lives, loves and longings. Ndebele searches for new work that breaks 'with this tradition of spectacle' (47) and the alternative method he poses is in the title – 'the rediscovery of the ordinary' attention to the detail of ordinary people's complex, yet everyday lives, for 'the struggle involves people not abstractions' (55).

The challenge of distilling the dull routines of the everyday into aesthetically satisfying and compelling works of art could be captured by Lefebvre's use of the term, the quotidian. He explains that the English translation of '*la quotidienne*, which really refers to repetition in daily life', is imperfect (1988: 78). He struggles to define the quotidian, given the contradictory project of capturing the quintessential nature of something vast, slippery and random. He does so by seeing it politically as 'lived experience', which is 'elevated to the status of a concept and to language' in order to bring about social transformation (80). In an attempt to pinpoint this elusive quotidian, Lefebvre in his book, entitled *Everyday Life in the Modern World*, charts the everyday in France in such a way as to 'expose its ambiguities – its baseness and exuberance, its poverty and fruitfulness – and by these unorthodox means release the creative energies that are an integral part of it' (1984: 13). It is base and poor in its weight of repetition; it is exuberant and utopian in its mundane possibilities of ordinary lives attaining heroic, joyful, exceptional moments of achievement, of sensuality, of empowerment.

What we will see throughout this book, is how postcolonial parvenus attempt to explore their mixed cultures and identities in Europe or America through the everyday of material reality. This is what postcolonial migrant writers seek to document and enact in their fictions, when they set them on the pavements, in the kitchen, on an archaeological dig or in a garden blooming with purple flowers. Globalisation has ensured that European and North American capitals include increasing numbers of inhabitants from parts of the world that were colonised; the 'man in the street' is no longer necessarily white and maybe not a man. Perhaps it is Shadia, Aboulela's student in Aberdeen, from Khartoum, as she makes her fateful visit to the museum to look at objects plundered from Africa. What we will see is how the nature of the Western everyday itself has become an amalgam of different cultures and languages. Travellers from Africa, India, Sri Lanka, Pakistan, the Caribbean and elsewhere have arrived and are walking in Aboulela's supermarket in Aberdeen, or waiting for the train in Isegawa's Central Station in Amsterdam, or walking along Bandele's High Street in Brixton, where they have transformed the goods in the shops, the food in the restaurants, the fashions and the feel of these places. These travellers, in their turn, have themselves metamorphosed and they write the changes in their kaleidoscopic fictions. They see the Africa in which they were born, and where they grew up, through the lenses of their experiences far from home.

The quotidian becomes even more interesting if it is understood as not merely a reflection of the material realities of daily life, but as linked to power and to the concept of cultural capital. Cultural capital operates at every level and is part of 'everyday choices of everyday life' (Bourdieu, 1984: 40), which Bourdieu spells out as 'matters like cosmetics, clothing or home decoration' (57). One of the mechanisms for capturing the paradox of the deep significance of the trivia of routine is by fixing on concrete objects, through which interactions with the environment and with other people take place. The massive weight of little events, small solid possessions and apparently insignificant happenings, are what embed one in one's time and place. A visit to the supermarket, the bus ride to work, the tea break, the preparation of meals – the list is infinite and the details may be minute – and yet, this is the fabric that comprises social lives and identities. The daily-ness of life becomes part of new realities, invested with past experiences remembered from other places, spaces, landscapes and climates.

What these writers are doing, as Laura Marks puts it in relation to intercultural cinema, is 'to sort through the rubble created by cultural dislocation and read significance in what official history overlooks' (2000: 28). The 'rubble', the rubbish, is a codeword for the solid objects of everyday life – the bits and pieces, the paraphernalia of existence, which are as significant as they are ordinary. For 'official history' read the dominant culture of colonial metaphors and 'the rubble' as the history and culture that was rubbished by the 'civilising mission' and Imperial plunder. Moreover, these objects link to daily lives by having real 'physical contact' with an original (80). In other words, in being linked to everyday life, they 'are not only discursive productions; their meaning cannot be separated from their materiality' (92); they are metonyms rather than metaphors.

In addition, by being 'transnational', they embody or relate to more than one culture. In their transnational status, they broker translation between cultures. Marks defines 'transnational objects' as 'created in cultural translation and transcultural movement' (78). Another way of conceptualising this role of translation across cultures of these objects is to refer to them, as Bowker and Star do, as 'boundary objects'. Boundary objects are 'a means of translation' or 'they are working arrangements that resolve anomalies of naturalization' between different cultures. And so, 'the creation and management of boundary objects is a key process in developing and maintaining coherence across intersecting communities' (Bowker and Star, 1999: 297). In other words, through the rituals of material exchanges, translations and transactions, different cultures, which have become neighbours, learn to negotiate, with greater or lesser success, each other's differences. We will see this most especially in Aboulela's fiction, where a bottle of perfume or a painting of Khartoum by an expatriate artist, act as portals uniting individuals from different worlds.

This negotiation is not always successful and Bowker and Star caution us against assuming too harmonious a process whereby objects provide safe passage between the worlds of the former Empire and the Postcolony. They suggest that while boundary objects manage tension between divergent worlds (292), they are less effective in situations of inequality, such as imperialism and its aftermath (297). They propose that where there is a lack of naturalisation or integration of these objects into their new environments, then 'marginal people and monsters' (300), or parvenu, arise. Again, we will see toxic objects, like Aboulela's displays of African objects in a museum, acting as barriers to cross-cultural relationships.

Furthermore, the quotidian is visceral; it is bodies jostling, queuing, competing and collaborating, within the world of unequal access to comforts and possessions. It is physical, human bodies that encounter solid objects. Privilege ensures a comfortable home, car, food on the table, along with all the other comforts and benefits. These comforts act directly upon bodies, which are fleshy realities, which experience pain, visibly age, contract dread illnesses, including those induced by lack and poverty. This has been emphasised by Elaine Scarry, who demonstrates a 'profound link between bodies and objects' (Scarry, 1985: 254). In fact, 'a made object is a projection of the human body' (281). What happens is that

> human beings project their bodily powers and frailties into external objects such as telephones, chairs... and then those objects in turn become the object of perceptions that are taken back into the interior of human consciousness where they now reside as part of the mind or soul'. (256)

These objects that Scarry lists, the telephones, chairs and tables, are corporeal and concrete, rather than being metaphors for the human condition.

Having insisted upon this materiality, however, Scarry simultaneously recognises the social construction of bodies, alongside their concrete reality. She suggests that those who have wealth and comfort are, as it were, insulated by layers of objects outside the body 'like shelter, furniture, and food'. This contrasts with bodies, which are prone to 'the disease and accident and exhaustion to which those who are shelterless, furnitureless, foodless, are immediately subject' (262). This brings her to the difference between 'belonging to the people who are disembodied and belonging to those who are radically embodied' (262). Or, as Judith Butler has it, in her *Bodies that Matter*, alongside the production of 'intelligible bodies' there lies 'a domain of unthinkable abject unlivable bodies'. These are bodies 'that do not matter in the same way' (1993: xi) and her study fundamentally interrogates 'which bodies come to matter – and why?' (xii). Butler's emphasis is on 'hetero-sexual hegemony' (xii), but she herself recognises how race works in the same way producing white bodies that matter (18). The apparently trivial questions posed by daily lives, and the things that people do or do not have access to, turn out to be the big questions of politics and quality of life. We will see in Chapter Four, how Rashid, Mahjoub's carrier, has a body which is at one point reproduced as animal, metamorphosing him into a lizard; he is dispossessed of all he owns as part of the ritual stripping process.

In fact, the relationship between bodies and things, as they shape the narratives, is foregrounded in just about all the chapters that follow. This relationship is particularly intense in Chapters Four, Five and Six, focusing on Mahjoub's *The Carrier*, Isegawa's *Abyssinian Chronicles* and Adichie's *Purple Hibiscus*, respectively. Mahjoub's, Isegawa's and Adichie's protago-nists are beaten and their bodies horribly abused; they find healing of these bodies, in different ways through, among other cures, their exploration of their physical environments.

The challenge, then, is for the writers to find the language of art, with which to capture and organise the barrage of detail of bodies encountering objects in their daily lives. This relates to the rhetoric of the metonymic and its potential to capture the quotidian in interesting ways. Roman Jakob-son and Morris Halle (1956) popularised the distinction between metaphor and metonymy, which has since been quite widely used and variously applied. If metaphor has been defined in terms of a comparison between different domains, then metonymy consists of the relationship within the same domain (Lakoff and Johnson, 1980: 36). In other words, there is a real, concrete connection between elements within metonymy, either in terms of spatial closeness, or as in the part standing for the whole. That is to say, in metonymy 'we are using one entity to refer to another *that is related to it*' (Lakoff and Johnson, 35, my emphasis). This is also known as synecdoche, or the part for the whole, such as reference to his stool or her crown as actu-ally being the chief or the queen, respectively. The chief being likened to a lion is metaphorical and draws on two different categories and links them, whereas his stool has a real connection to the chief and is a shorthand way of identifying him.

Metonymy, thus, is grounded in the material world and linked to the real-ity of dimensions within the experience of the subject. Metonymy (unlike metaphor) 'usually involves direct physical or causal associations' (Lakoff and Johnson, 39). This means that 'experience with physical objects provides the basis for metonymy' (59). Metonymic connections are real and concrete in another sense, although, paradoxically, this reality comes about through chance, rather than organic connection. Happenstance, such as the strangers who find themselves on a train or in a queue, or the relationship between words that do not share meaning but sound similar, or set up a rhythm. This is referred to as contiguity, i.e. those elements that find themselves next to each other, rather than the deep, symbolic, figural and imaginary bonds of metaphor. Rhymes and jangles, the concrete and coincidental are, therefore, all metonymic. Or, as Ronald Schleifer puts it: 'metonymy articulates a world in which things happen without any touchstones of transcendental meaning, where absolutes of history and meaning and tonality take their places contingently' (1990: 9).

Such touchstones of deep meaning are created through metaphors; where these become tropes, or master metaphors, entwined recurrently in the dominant culture's ability to make sense of ex-colonised places and people, they potentially become exploitative. This exploitation may be able to be challenged by prising open the deeply figurative tentacles with the concrete, material realities of these places and people; it may be confronted by playfulness or chance, instead of design or master plans and enterprises.

This is what Deborah Durham and James Fernandez mean when they assert that 'the structure of the world, sustained by an authoritative and legitimating metaphor' may be challenged 'through the use of the metonymic' (1991: 209). Metonymy 'is a trope most suitable for either asserting or challenging established hierarchies and conventions – for asserting and/or challenging worldviews indeed!' (198). This is so because whereas metonymy is characterised by its 'volatility' and is therefore more 'highly individualised' and 'freely assembled and dissembled according to particular experience and circumstance', metaphor, by contrast, is part of 'the 'inner storehouse' of a culture and its sets of cultural assumptions or models' (195).

Bill Ashcroft is the postcolonial theorist who has drawn most overt attention to the potential of metonymy as a tool of resistance. In an early paper, subtitled 'Language as Metonymy in the Post-Colonial Text', he foregrounds the metonymic devices with which postcolonial writers introduce a different language and knowledge system in the undertow of their English. This occurs when 'texture, sound, rhythm and words are carried over from the mother tongue to the adopted literary form' (1989: 4). Ashcroft enlarges upon the many metonymic devices that are deployed in order to construct 'an english discourse according to the rhythm and texture of a first language' (5), to bring out this infusion of 'a certain cultural experience', which is not reproduced but 'whose difference is at least validated in the new situation' (6).

What Ashcroft perceptively points out, and which cannot be over-emphasised, is that the use of those variants of English is not the involuntary eruption of an indigenous culture; this device does 'not embody the essence of the African world view, but as a contiguous trope it proposes an ability to negotiate that cultural distance of which it is itself a sign' (1989: 7). The medium is the message, given that this parallel universe, which is installed within the dominant English text, is itself an example of these other worlds, knowledge bases and languages. And so 'the texture, the sound rhythm and syntax of the original language determine the "shape" and mode of the English variant' (9).

In his later writing, Ashcroft has focussed on one particular phenomenon,

what he has called 'the metonymic gap' (2001: 75). He continues to emphasise how cultural differences of experience are 'actually *installed* in the text
in various ways' (75, his emphasis). The metonymic gap, by means of which
this installation of difference is accomplished, occurs when postcolonial
writers 'insert unglossed words, phrases or passages from a first language, or
concepts, allusions or references which may be unknown to the reader' (75).
What then happens is that

> Such words become synecdochic of the writer's culture – the part that stands for the
> whole ... Thus the inserted language 'stands for' the colonized culture in a metonymic
> way, and its very resistance to interpretation constructs a 'gap' between the writer's
> culture and the colonial culture. (75)

Ashcroft also observes that this harnessing of metonymy flies in the face of
the Law of the powerful, Western centre – 'in the European tradition the
contiguous and accidental, those characteristics which seem to accrue to the
metonymic, will never have the power of truth' and truth, of course, 'is the
province of the metropolitan' (75). Ashcroft, in fact, describes this 'metonymic gap' as 'a crucial feature of the transformative function of post-colonial
writing' (75) and goes so far as to suggest that it is '*the* distinguishing feature
of post-colonial literature' (76). This explains Jamal Mahjoub's warning –
'never trust a novel with a glossary; we don't have to understand everything'
(2002: 8). In other words, the inclusion of untranslated bits of language other
than English, among other devices, is a signal, on the part of these writers,
that Western readers may not understand everything about the daily lives
and material cultures of people from other parts of the planet. This is what
Marks, still poking about in the rubble of the moment after deconstruction,
refers to as 'incomprehension' – 'the interstitial space of the fetish produces
meaning, lots of meanings, but they are built on incomprehension' (2000:
90) or why she insists that 'an acceptance of untranslatability [is] part of the
postcolonial experience' (116). This explains why Doris Sommer, otherwise
perplexingly, calls for readers to embrace their 'partial deafness' or 'incompe-
tence' as a kind of 'modest-making goal' (1996: 89). Certain postcolonial texts
announce 'limited access' to their readers and 'demarcate' their 'constitutive
gaps' (92). These are, in other words, 'uncooperative texts' which 'declare
their intransigence' (94). Ultimately, this is not an act of hostility, but rather
an invitation to readers at home in their cosy worlds, places to which some
postcolonial writers have migrated, 'to listen attentively' (104).

As we shall see, there are other devices for inserting another language and
culture into English, devices that also act as metonymic gaps, in addition to
the inclusion of 'foreign' words. These include jingles and rhymes, rhythms
and references to oral traditions, transformed words, made up words, nonsense and stuttering. More recently, still focussing on the possibilities of
postcolonial resistance, of the 'refusal to be absorbed' through altering the
weapons of the dominating power and turning them into tools, Ashcroft
embeds this resistance in the 'everyday', given that this politics is mostly 'a
pragmatic and mundane array of living strategies' (2003: 385). This attempt
to render into art the concrete texture of their multiple lives and layered

experiences, through the manipulation of English, is at the nub of what I am hoping to capture in this book.

However, what also becomes apparent is that the inclusion of words from indigenous languages and oral tales, proverbs and wisdoms, do not necessarily, by definition, enable the portrayal of complex realities; it does not always contest the stereotypes regarding African culture and heterogeneity. It may do the opposite and contribute to buttressing old symbols and constructing new figurative distortions about the continent and its history. For example, in a recent essay, Eileen Julien has contested the politics of this alternative language inclusion. She suggests that it results from the pressure on African novelists to 'authenticate' their writing as genuinely African by dressing up their European structures of thought in the garb of African 'oral traditions, national languages, and folklore' (2006: 674). For this she coins the word 'ornamentalism' (669). She finds this pressure on writers, who use European languages, to prove their authenticity highly problematic. In their felt obligation to capture quintessential African pre-colonial accomplishments, they tend to essentialise them. This works against the reality that 'the categories of orality and writing that have governed criticism of African literature are primarily ideological constructs' (676). Julien links this tendency to migrancy where novelists who are often 'living beyond their countries' borders' means that they 'speak outward and represent locality to nonlocal others' (684).

This critique is as compelling as the transformative possibilities invested in the rhetoric of the metonymic gap, which this book is emphasising. We need to understand the relationship between them. By becoming symbolic of a static, authentic, homogenised Africa, the use of Igbo or Yoruba words and wisdom may transform from being concrete manifestations of other languages and cultures into fetishes, metaphors and tropes and in the process become ornamental in Julien's sense. This is the danger inherent in Afrocentrism, that in its desire to confront European denigration of African culture as frozen in a long night of primitivism, it is vulnerable to freezing Africa in the glorious light of civilisation. In what becomes an intra-metaphoric battle, the paradigm of freezing Africa in the first place is retained, and even strengthened.

Along these lines, I have written elsewhere about Isidore Okpewho's *Call Me By My Rightful Name* (Cooper, 2007). I suggested that Okpewho's novel operates on the level of the symbolic, the spiritual and the metaphorical, rather than within the flesh and blood of the everyday and its concrete objects and bodies. Its abundant use of Yoruba words, the wisdom of Ifa, the reference to proverbs and stories taken from the oral tradition, perform the function of metonyms turned metaphor of a mythic Africa as the nurturing source for all black people living in the diaspora. In other words, African spirituality, rituals, culture and language become a phantasmagoria through which black people everywhere may find their identities. Okpewho, in fact, defends this essentialism and in his introduction to *The African Diaspora: African Origins and New World Identities*, he explicitly rejects the fact that 'essentialism' has emerged as an 'ugly label' in 'recent Diaspora discourse'

(2001: xv). What we will see is that something similar operates in Adichie's second novel. In fact, what most often occurs is a continuum back and forth between metonymic and metaphorical functions and it is perhaps in *Half of a Yellow Sun*, more than any of the other novels that we will discuss, that we will see the tensions that arise from these rhetorical swings.

This is the context in which to understand the recurrence of attempts on the part of writers discussed in this book to reverse metaphors and to return them to their literal concreteness. When the magical, holy grail of the telescope is eventually acquired in Jamal Mahjoub's novel, its power is reduced by profound anti-climax. It becomes a useless heavy burden to the hunted protagonist, who has to flee travelling light. It is, therefore, jettisoned later in the novel. It is why Bandele takes metaphors that have become so commonplace in English that they are now stereotypes and by returning them to their literal meanings, he exposes the extent of the figurative network of the language. This is why the burglar alarmed door becomes a stressed out door which is actually alarmed and worried in Bandele's chapter two. This explains Moses Isegawa's emphasis on de-fetishising household stuff, like a bobbin for a sewing machine and a headboard for a bed in his chapter five. These demonic objects, which are toxic and puffed up, become potentially new and oppressive symbols. The task of Isegawa's protagonist is to expose their evil power and bring them back to reality.

The subversiveness of this de-fetishisation is a cornerstone of the politics of Achille Mbembe's *On the Postcolony*, where he acknowledges his debt to Bakhtin. Mbembe demonstrates the particular way de-fetishising carries transgressive power in the postcolony. By stripping the shiny magnificence of the dictator down to his smelly, ordinary, physical, grossness, the nature of illegitimate power is naked for all to see and to poke fun at and potentially to overturn. Ordinary people, in this way, 'tear apart the gods that African autocrats aspire to be' such that 'the presidential anus is brought down to earth; it becomes nothing more than a common garden-variety arse that defecates like any other' (2001: 112). These everyday aromas, bodily smells and orifices contest, in the language of texture, rhythm and the ordinary, the trappings of power, privilege and exploitation. The deployment of rhetoric, therefore, is not a matter of art unhinged from social, historical and political life, but it is deeply implicated in it.

Then there are blended tropes, as the material morphs into metaphor, in new, old and mixed ways. We will see how the flesh and blood woman disappears in flames in chapter four of *The Carrier*, and how mother as demon rears her ugly head in *Abyssinian Chronicles*, chapter five. Stereotypes of African blood-letting savagery are let loose in *Half of a Yellow Sun*. Perhaps this is not surprising, given all we know about how tenacious certain metaphors for representing Africa are, and how embedded they are in the English language, unless a special effort is made to release their hold. Adichie's latest novel bears the signs of its struggle to achieve this release. However, it is worth enlarging upon the transformative possibilities of the use of metonymy by reference to some relevant comparative cases.

The metonymic weapon: some case studies

While Edouard Glissant does not use the term 'metonymy', his description is replete with how it works within Caribbean Creole. He emphasises how the slave camouflaged the language of the *békés*, the whites, the masters, in order to find a voice. And so 'slaves camouflaged the word under the provocative intensity of the scream' (Glissant, 1992: 124). In this way 'the dispossessed man organized his speech by weaving it into the apparently meaningless texture of extreme noise' (124). What developed was 'a specialized system of significant insignificance' (124). What evolves is that 'the meaning of a sentence is sometimes hidden in the accelerated nonsense created by scrambled sounds. But this nonsense does convey real meaning to which the master's ear cannot have access' (124). This 'verbal delirium' (128) is 'the outer edge of speech' and defines 'the counterpoetics practiced by Creole' (128). As Celia Britton puts it, Creole 'developed as a subversive language whose purpose from the start was not simply to communicate but also to conceal its meanings, thereby turning the master's language against him' (1999: 25). This strategy employed by Caribbean Creole has also been identified in relation to Alejo Carpentier's baroque style, which 'moves him to name one thing after another' (Benitez-Rojo, 1999: 183). This style is not 'a will toward ornamentation' (183), but 'it is vertical, *metonymic*, a linear sum of aggregates' (184, my emphasis). Carpentier is a consummate master of the linguistic construct and in the excesses of his baroque he is insisting on asserting the marvellous, complex and unassimilated reality of his history.

Emily Apter provides other examples, ranging from Salmon Rushdie's *The Satanic Verses*, where 'Anglo-Indian prose rhythms collide with the alien vocabulary of American product lines, British brand names, global community fetishes' (2002: 191) to the Nigerian, Ken Saro-Wiwa's novel, *Sozaboy*, which he himself sub-titled *A Novel in Rotten English*'. In this novel, 'rotten English is used to flush out monolingualism as the linguistic superego whose interpellative force "hails" the subject, bending him to ordinance' (192). This captures succinctly the politics of damaging standard English in order to enable our growth into becoming differently socialised human beings. Saro-Wiwa's language is devastatingly concrete, rather than figurative, and bears 'the stress marks and psychic cavities of starvation, violence, humiliation, and colonial mimicry' (194). And so 'the spirit of a lost African language gene runs amok in the syntactic corridors of Standard English' (195). This gene may run amok, but in the amalgam of Standard English, pidgin, indigenous words and made up vocabulary, Saro-Wiwa has crafted a route for this language mayhem, which is as constructed as apparently out of control.

Apter provides a further example in the Martinican writer, Raphaël Confiant, who in his *La Savane*, crosses 'Creolisms ... with Anglo advertising jingles' (196) along with his 'unpronounceable loan words, verbal calques, and warped grammaticalities' (198). This especially echoes the language gymnastics of Biyi Bandele, as we shall see in Chapter Two.

Apter, following Deleuze and Guattari on Kafka, calls this kind of subcultural, combative writing a 'minor literature' (188). This naming is unfortunate, appearing to collude with the hegemony of more mainstream, and presumably, 'major literature'. However, Deleuze and Guattari explain that 'minor' does not refer to a minor language but is 'that which a minority constructs within a major language' (1986: 16). Specifically, with regard to Franz Kafka, there is 'the situation of the German language in Czechoslovakia, as a fluid language intermixed with Czech and Yiddish' (20). They describe Kafka's language as a 'mélange', 'a Harlequin costume in which very different functions of language and distinct centers of power are played out' (1986, 26). The challenge, they say, is how 'to become a nomad and an immigrant and a gypsy in relation to one's own language?' (19).

The answer to their question appears to lie in writing stories that bravely attempt to escape dominant metaphors and meanings, and so, write Deleuze and Guattari, Kafka depicts a character, like Gregor, as 'warbling' in 'blurred words'; Kafka foregrounds 'the whistling of the mouse, the cough of the ape' (21). This created a 'language torn from sense, conquering sense, bringing about an active neutralization of sense' (21). Like jingles and nonsense rhymes, 'at the beginning of *The Castle*, the schoolchildren are speaking so fast that one cannot understand what they are saying' (21). This is the language of metonymy, one that is opposed to the deep cultural tentacles of metaphor. In fact, Deleuze and Guattari quote Kafka as declaring in his *Diaries* of 1921, that 'metaphors are one of the things that makes me despair of literature' (22). They elaborate that 'Kafka deliberately *kills all metaphor*, all symbolism' (22, my emphasis).

While metaphor cannot, and should not, be killed, the goal and purpose of this statement of murderous intent is the desire to find a way of speaking in 'an other tongue' as a defence against treacherous tropes. This *An Other Tongue* is the title of a collection edited by Alfred Arteaga (1994), and also the title of his own paper in the collection. The 'minor literature', with which he is concerned, is that of Chicano poetry, which falls 'in the interface between Anglo and Latin America' (10) and where hybrid words are constructed which mix English and Spanish and create a kind of 'double voicing' and where in one case 'even the typeface speaks difference' and provides Ashcroft's metonymic gap given that 'the poems are printed in the script of barrio graffiti' (11).

The strategy of the metonymic is one to which women writers have sometimes turned in order to contest dominant stereotypes and metaphors. For example, Barbara Johnson analyses Zora Neale Hurston's novel in a paper entitled 'Metaphor, Metonymy and Voice in *Their Eyes Were Watching God*'. Johnson describes Hurston's play between metaphor and metonymy in the novel as a politics of resistance, in her conviction that Hurston was aware of the problem of 'metaphor as privileged trope and trope of privilege' (208). Johnson points out that Hurston's novel incorporates the everyday life of its protagonist, Janie, which results in Richard Wright's review of it as carrying 'no theme, no message, no thought' (215). Johnson's retort is apt and relevant to us – 'No message, no theme, no thought: the full range of questions and experiences of Janie's life are as invisible to a mind steeped in maleness as Ellison's Invisible Man is to minds steeped in whiteness' (215). We have seen that the everyday, linked to concrete objects and material realities, expressed through the trope of metonymy, is potentially a powerful tool in the hands of postcolonial writers in general, and black women writers in particular.

Still focussing on case studies that gesture towards the combative possibilities of the use of the device of metonymy, in a paper, entitled 'Echo' Gayatri Spivak discovers a woman, Echo, who converses with Narcissus. Given that 'Echo is obliged to echo everyone who speaks', her language is metonymic; she does not speak the symbolic, figurative language of the Law, but 'her desire and performance are dispersed into absolute chance' (1993: 27). What then, asks Spivak, does Echo offer us, 'us' being 'the worldwide collectivity of conscientized feminists of color from bourgeois origins...?' (27). What she offers African women writers, like Leila Aboulela and Chimamanda Ngozie Adichie, who are examples of Spivak's bourgeois feminists of colour, is an alternative language that enables them to give voice to their female protagonists, and to transform their silences and their stuttering. This they do within a different site, where subjects may be constituted outside of Lacan's Symbolic and the successful resolution of Oedipus.

Spivak suggests that 'Asia and Africa are always supposed to have had trouble with Oedipus' (17). She points to the consequences of the fact that she, and women like her, like the Algerian Muslim writer, Assia Djebar, like the Indian writer Mahasweta Devi and, I would add, like Leila Aboulela and Chimamanda Ngozie Adichie, have been 'culturally banished from Oedipus' (24). Terms like banishment and homelessness have to be understood more as ways of framing alternative sites of speech, home and power, rather than that these writers, and notably Spivak herself, are sad, speechless victims. Spivak is expressing the now familiar critique of the patriarchal space of the Symbolic, where women are conceptualised as voiceless subjects. For Spivak, the Imaginary, Lacan's earlier phase, the space of Echo, of chance and metonymy, is a potentially productive, alternative space. It is a radical site where language and subjectivity, other than the male Law of Oedipus, might be ritually and dramatically enacted. It is a space that inspires her question of: 'Why, in spite of so many hard lessons to the contrary – not the least from the vicissitudes of many cultural and gender-inscriptions – do we still cling to the rotarian epistemology of *advancing* from the Imaginary to the Symbolic?' (Spivak, 35, her emphasis). This is why Jane Gallop privileges metonymy, as associated with the female and celebrates 'a new, feminine metonymic reading' (132). This is in opposition to the situation where Lacan charts 'a radical shift from metonymy to metaphor' (Fleck, 1998: 269). What Fleck is emphasising is that, according to Lacan, it is with the metamorphosis from the accidental of metonymy to the meaningfulness of metaphor, that subjectivity becomes constituted in the fullness of significant language, a subjectivity that Gallop and Spivak suggest could be inimical to gender equality. This is what Radhakrishnan refers to as the politics of 'a number of feminists' who resist 'total interpellation by the Symbolic' (2000: 62).

However, while women writers may have particularly positioned themselves in opposition to the Symbolic, I have been demonstrating that this opposition occurs quite broadly in postcolonial language. What Radhakrishnan most admires, for example, about Amitav Ghosh's *The Shadow Lines*, is that it is 'interested in the overthrow of the mighty Symbolic by the Imaginary' (2000: 62). He sees that 'the attempt to shore up one's self in the imaginary of the mirror ... could well be a powerful attempt to interrogate the tyranny of the Symbolic' (2002: 793). According to Radhakrishnan (2000: 58), this is necessary in order to foreground other knowledges, worlds and cultures.

It is worth repeating that these devices are constructed, self-conscious, contrived and political; they are not the earthy pre-logical noises of a primitive people – 'it is a deliberate ploy' or 'craftiness' (Glissant, 1992 [1981]: 126). This cautionary note is particularly pertinent to strategies that are often devised by women writers and intellectuals in order to oppose the dominant patriarchal culture and the language associated with it. Destructive stereotypes to be avoided are that women's or the postcolonial's language is earthy, bubbling poetry, bodily instinct and primitive signing. This playing with metonymy, battling with loaded metaphors, struggling with new forms of expression, is no return to some pre-linguistic Edenic and archetypal African Mother's womb. Writers in the chapters that follow produce carefully constructed narrative Molotov cocktails in which they take the English language and subject it to their wills in a cultural political battle that began with colonialism and which has not ended.

To emphasise this constructedness, Sandhya Shetty warns that readings which 'seek only to re-materialize and ground the mother in a body' (1995: 51) might precisely replicate the stereotype linking women to visceral instincts. In her paper entitled '(Dis)figuring the Nation: Mother, Metaphor, Metonymy', Shetty wishes to avoid laying that body open to being appropriated by the opportunistic, nationalist metaphor, which is always waiting for its moment, that of Mother India. Her solution to this danger is to craft a way of writing, a rhetoric, which will move 'the site of materiality from the body to language' (52). This language she identifies as that of metonymy, given its better access to the material and the concrete. And so, 'it is the metonymic functioning of mother ... that breaks the back of the nationalist-patriarchal allegory' (53). How does Shetty's 'subversive metonymic thrust of signification' (61) work? It works against the grain of the stereotype of woman as corporeal, pre-linguistic and instinctive and takes us into the realm of the considered construction of a language enabling women to be empowered.

Besides the vulnerability to essentialism, to which I have referred already, there is the danger that these torrents of words fail to communicate at all. As Michael Dash, translator of Glissant's *Caribbean Discourse*, points out in his introduction to this collection of essays, writers, like Glissant, are 'precariously poised' in the 'attempt to voice the unvoiced ... particularly so in multilingual postplantation societies' (1992: xxvi). And, of course, 'there is something forced about this kind of writing in its striving to avoid the trap of eroded forms and self-consciously reaching for the realm of the unsaid and perhaps the unsayable' (xxvi). The fact that it is forced is another way of recognising Glissant's own point about the 'counterpoetics', the politics of language. The question arises as to whether this writing achieves its purpose, as both politics and aesthetics, or does the babble remain just that – a blur of noise unable to communicate?

In other words, metonyms are not always revolutionary. We will see in Chapter Two the knife edge on which verbal gymnastics, apparent nonsense, endless lists and jokes, word games and narrative screaming, balance in *The Street*. We will negotiate the abyss through a stream of words in Moses Isegawa's *Abyssinian Chronicles* in Chapter Five. While there are dangers and pitfalls inherent in these endless lists, torrents of words and depictions of kitchens, toilets, streets and yards, we do need to understand them as political and strategic. At the same time, metaphor is never murdered; there is no perpetual anarchy of either language or subjectivity and the Law, along with its deeper meanings, quests and Order words wielding power, reasserts itself in one form or another, as we will see especially powerfully in Chapter Seven. The form may not be what we expect; the blending of dimensions acting simultaneously is always as potentially regressive as it is transformative.

Multiple worlds & knowledges: metonymy & metaphor

For the purposes of analysis it has been important to separate the literal from the figurative, metonymy from metaphor and the Imaginary from the Symbolic. No such clean cut separation exists, of course. Old and new tropes rub shoulders and bump into concrete objects, which are both old weapons and new tools. A cleansed metonymic, concrete language, flying free of culture and discourse does not exist. Maria Ruegg emphasises 'the impossibility of separating the two imaginary axes of "similarity" and "contiguity" given 'the inevitable mimetic *play* between a multiplicity of codes, texts, context: play which implicates *all* discourse in a complex, ambiguous, undecidable web' (146, her emphases). While confronting the tyranny of the symbols that uphold the Law, we should also avoid 'misplaced concretism' (Bowker and Star, 1999: 307) and the worship of solid objects, which may become dominating. Or as Jane Gallop cautions, 'it would be yielding to simply another "amputated unipolar schema" to choose the metonymic dimension and neglect the metaphoric' (1985: 132). Metonyms do not, by definition, contest power, and the binaries set up by simplistically constrasting metonymy and metaphor are themselves distorting.

Metaphor and metonymy always work together, forming a relationship, which determines the style and also the content of literature. While the distinction between metaphor and metonymy is important in this study, we should not succumb to the fallacy of fake binaries. Hayden White's (1999) study of the implications of rhetoric, *Figural Realism*, emphasises that the distinction between the literal and the figurative is purely 'conventional(ist)' and should be understood 'by its relevance to the sociopolitical context in which it arises' (vii). This sociopolitical context is what drives the search in this book for an understanding of the use of language as a form of resistance. Johnson (1984), who emphasises Hurston's metonymic language, also insists that both metaphor and metonymy are 'continually operative' and what emerges is that 'under the influence of a cultural pattern, personality, and verbal style, preference is given to one of the two processes over the other' (206). The cultural pattern for the writers under discussion is the heritage of imperial domination, deeply vested in the English language, which they may contest by altering the weight from the figurative, to the concrete material realities of daily life.

There is, in fact, traffic back and forth between these tropes and their politics, given that not all metonyms are transformative and not all metaphors are imperialist and that the literal and the figurative work together, albeit with different strengths and emphases. What this multiplicity demands is new kinds of poetic troping, within a syncretism of the literal and the figurative. This syncretism could be precisely what Lakoff and Johnson (1980) refer to when they use the concept of 'symbolic metonymies' as syncretising the 'critical links between everyday experience and the coherent metaphorical systems that characterize religions and cultures' (40). These symbolic metonymies are figurative and also 'grounded in our physical experience' (40).

In other words, while I am illustrating how and why some postcolonial writers favour the metonymic as a political tool, I am also suggesting, again with Hayden White, that other modes (and he includes irony and synecdoche, along with metaphor and metonymy) always come into play as well. That is to say, rhetorical modes always interact in a rich language web, but where metaphor or metonymy dominate, this will have the effect of determining 'the structure of the discourse' (White, 1999: 11). Furthermore, which trope dominates will provide an entry point into the nature of the 'historical discourse' that is being represented. We see this concretely when we compare Adichie's two novels in Chapters Six and Seven. She moves between metonymy and metaphor in both, but whereas the material and metonymic dominates in *Purple Hibiscus*, the metaphoric becomes more dominant in *Half of a Yellow Sun*, which does indeed have the effect of determining the nature of the discourse.

What is the case, however, is that metonymy has tended to be underestimated and demoted in the hierarchy of what constitutes great literature. This 'great literature' is the canon of predominantly male, Western writing, whose metaphors have often worked, deeply, subtly and invisibly, to caricature, conquer and colonise, through belittling the cultures it encounters. What I am examining in this book is the particularly strong role that material culture, and its representation through the rhetoric of metonymy, plays in some postcolonial migrant novels, in order to contest this history and this strategy of conquest.

This combination of the literal and the figurative, metonymy and metaphor, and the political and aesthetic consequences of their interaction, have been conceptualised in different ways. Antonio Barcelona (2000) explores 'the metonymic basis of metaphor' (1) and Gunter Radden (2000) , struggling somewhat with these definitions, says that 'metaphors which are grounded in metonymy are more basic and natural than those which do not have a metonymic basis' (93). However, he emphasises that the distinction between the two is 'notoriously difficult' and that therefore 'instead of always separating the two we may much rather think of a metonymy-metaphor continuum' (93). Along the same lines, Mark Turner and Gilles Fauconnier, in a paper called 'Metaphor, metonymy, and binding' talk about the 'dynamic integration processes which build up new "blended" mental spaces' (133).

Blended mental spaces, as well as blended spiritual and material circumstances, is what African writers in London or Amsterdam are grappling with, and searching to express in an appropriate language, one that relates to their experiences of Africa, as well as to their other inheritances. This resounds with Achille Mbembe's attempts to capture African imaginary worlds with what he has called 'simultaneous multiplicities' (2001: 145). I do not wish to tread the minefield of the nature of a 'traditional' African spirituality, with all the essentialisms and stereotypes waiting to blow up here. This question of African pre-colonial traditions is, of course, as much about beliefs in the past as about the use to which these beliefs have been put in the strategic cultural battles that African writers wage against cultural imperialism in the present. As Mbembe himself puts it, 'these networks of meaning have not remained wholly untouched'; they have been altered by 'colonization and christianization' (146).

What, nonetheless, are these 'simultaneous multiplicities'? Mbembe suggests that it would be to misunderstand the complexity of different dimensions if 'the visible' and 'the occult' are regarded as opposed to each other. They need to be interpreted simultaneously. These dimensions were 'governed by relations of similarity, relations far from making the one a mere copy or model of the other' (144). Mbembe enlarges that 'the invisible was not only the other side of the visible.... The invisible was in the visible and vice versa' (145). These worlds were 'part and parcel' of each other (145) and provide the basis for 'the inseparability of ... the being and the nonbeing of persons and things' (145). What is being abolished is 'the distinction between being and appearance, the world of the living and the world of spirits' (145). The porousness between these worlds is especially palpable in both *The Street* and *Purple Hibiscus*, as discussed in Chapters Two and Six respectively.

This focus on the everyday, the material and the concrete, which is imbricated with the spiritual and the unseen, links to my earlier work on magical realism in a West African context (Cooper, 1998). There I described how, by definition, magical realism renders the magical/supernatural religious worlds as mundane and ordinary – as part of the daily lives of ordinary people. Similarly, it is the attempt to come to grips with the parallel worlds of the living and the spirits, of the animate and the inanimate, within an understanding of history, politics and strategic interventions, that motivates Harry Garuba's use of the concept of 'animist materialism' (2003: 268) in which everyday objects are 'the physical and material manifestations of the gods and spirits' (267). This entails an interrogation of binaries and hierarchies, given that we have 'the "locking" of spirit within matter or the *merger of the material and the metaphorical,* which animist logic entails' (267, my emphasis). This is the blended language, giving rise to alternative subjectivities, which a refusal of the binary between the Imaginary and the Symbolic, the metaphorical and the metonymic, would entail. The animist intertext, which Garuba suggests often informs African literature, is not about an intrinsic, magical or religious view of the world. It is profoundly political and linked to institutional power. In the world of fiction, with which we are dealing, it becomes a narrative device, 'a representational strategy that involves giving the abstract or metaphorical a material realization' (284). What this book attempts to uncover is the nature of the cultural politics invested in the narrative strategies of messing with metaphor in a variety of ways, including embedding it in the material. Without this embeddedness, writers run the danger of reproducing the dominant language, or what Julien, as discussed earlier, called 'ornamentalism'. What we will see in the chapters that follow is how metaphors are reduced and exposed, how old tropes prevail and new symbols are minted.

The prospect of a cunning tale: conclusion

The kind of resistance with which we are dealing in this book is always piecemeal and disorganised. It has been described by Michel de Certeau, in his *The Practice of Everyday Life* as operating 'from the wings' of dominance, where fractions of society resist being 'reduced' to the grid of power, as conceptualised by thinkers such as Foucault, who de Certeau challenges (1984: xiv). This grid of power resounds with Lacan's Symbolic structure of social reproduction of dominance. The subject of de Certeau's book is 'the clandestine forms taken by the dispersed, tactical, and makeshift creativity of groups and individuals' (xiv). In other words, de Certeau's politics of the everyday, 'doesn't offer solutions, nor does it offer to overthrow oppression'. Rather it 'puts its faith in the everyday as a means for its own transformation' (Highmore, 2002: 173). The nature of this politics needs to be understood quite subtly. These migrant writers are not political radicals, who propose revolutionary change in the balance of power of the world of their novels. They are privileged, mobile, middle-class intellectuals, whose lives are at a far remove from the majority of their African countrymen and women. Their perch of privilege and their insights gleaned from their travels across cultures, however, qualify them to capture their own struggles, as strangers, parvenus, diasporics. Their daily lives are complex, full of potential and of pitfalls. They play out the tug of war between resisting absorption into European cultures and codes, and resenting their exclusion from them.

The question of the nature of the politics of migrant writers is the site of quite combative postcolonial debate. Marxist critics, such as Aijaz Ahmad (1992) and Benita Parry (2004), berate the dominance in postcolonial studies of attention to these privileged, mobile migrants. Parry, for example, decries their blindness to the issues of exploitation and poverty, to the enormous struggles and achievements of liberation movements and their discourses

(2004: 8–9, 71, 75). This insight is important, but it is also quite narrow and judgemental. How far can Parry's criticism take us? It is true that poor communities 'do not share in the free-wheeling pleasures of commuting between cultures available to the privileged postcolonial' (Parry, 2004: 71). It is also true that these writers commute more readily between cultures and are blessed with material possessions, food and shelter. But this does not necessarily mean that their writing is merely self-indulgent, warped and uncommitted.

The more interesting and subtle point that Parry makes is that by throwing binaries into the trash heap and by embracing only the liminal, the hybrid and the ambiguous, we construct smokescreens that conceal and perpetuate significant differences arising out of exploitation and oppression, with which our global twenty-first century has not dispensed (Parry, 2004: 8). The recognition of social and economic disparities, however, is not in contradiction with the acknowledgement of porousness, perplexity and collusion. What we need to be aware of throughout this book, is that the everyday worlds that the writers under discussion examine are indeed particular to their circumstances; we should know that they are not spokespeople of the worlds and circumstances of the majority of people from the countries from which they come; but we should examine their lives and struggles, within the particular angle from which they write, with respect and interest, for they deliver powerful insights into struggles and dilemmas, politics and transformations that are part of the structures of globalisation and the mobility that comes with it. In playing with language, they engage in the deadly serious work of culture, identity and resistance to the current of homogenisation of worlds in the image of the American shopping mall. Love–hatred for European languages, along a porous scale, constitutes the paradox of identity and language. This way of conceptualising the world explains efforts on the part of African writers and intellectuals to find a language with which to express their complex traditions and experiences, their differing alliances and allies, the different contexts and histories between which they switch and operate.

And so, it is in interrogating the discourse, in which Western imperialism found its language, its rationale and its poetry, that postcolonial writers confront their nemesis. The narrative consequences of this interrogation are what Juliet MacCannell is asking us to conceive of with her question: 'what sort of form would a story that escapes the Symbolic have?' What is the alternative? MacCannell describes the 'basis for a post-Oedipal condition' as lying 'in the Real; but finding the Real is no simple task'. This is so because 'it demands an impossible attempt to think form beyond Oedipal narrative conventions' (916). She challenges us to imagine '"tropes" that do not themselves blindly gravitate toward the Sun' (929). She asks whether we can 'see the prospect of a tale, a "cunning" tale ... to counter our (white) mythology constructed of these tropes?' (929–30).

Could these cunning tales, these seeing tropes, ground themselves to the Earth by way of history and of everyday objects, which make up daily, lived reality? It is here, at the surface, on the tarmac, that deterritorialised, wily migrants try to situate their narratives and to see a way of steering them clear of the blinding power of the Symbolic Sun. After the fetish has been de-fetishized, or the symbol reduced to its fleshy ordinariness, the African writer, the refugee, stranger, parvenu, exile or nomad, might construct a new metaphorical language liberated from the tentacles of imperial power. Perhaps there is only a fleeting moment of clarity, 'a moment of suspension that occurs in these works after the official discourse has been (if only momentarily) dismantled and before the emerging discourse finds its voice' (Marks, 2000: 25). This pause, this moment, however, 'is also enormously suggestive' (25–6). At the end of the day, our writers are Latour's wily Daedalus, innovative engineer, 'using any expedient at hand, *in the cracks and gaps of ordinary routines*, swapping properties among inert, animal, symbolic, concrete and human materials' (190, my emphasis). This is the space Ronald Schleifer refers to as 'the hesitations of narrative' – '*hesitation* is a complex figure, a confusion of the literal and the figurative' (1983: 885). This is, perhaps what Walter Mignolo means by 'the crack ... between local histories and global designs' induced by playing with multiple languages (2000: 250). It is what Deleuze suggests by the poetic operation of making the language stutter (1997: 107). In this potent moment, there is perhaps only a hesitation, a crack, a pause, between old symbols of Imperial power and new tropes, symbols and metaphors. Nonetheless, here, at this suggestive, dangerous, site, knowledges embedded in the objects lying in the rubble of history, knowledges other than those of the dominant, official discourse, may be excavated.

2 Virtual Objects & Parallel Universes
Biyi Bandele's *The Street*

The street referred to in Biyi Bandele's novel of the same name is Brixton High Street. At the same time, the novel occupies parallel universes – the worlds of the living and the dead, the lands of reality and of dreams, the Nigeria of Bandele's birth and growing up and the London of his chosen home. In the process of spanning these universes, of mixing and mingling these dimensions, Bandele Africanises Lewis Carroll's *Alice in Wonderland* mode of nonsense writing and flies Amos Tutuola's West African oral tradition of *The Palm-Wine Drinkard* to London.

When Diez-Tagarro suggests to Bandele 'So you could say that your writing is a mixture of these Nigerian experiences and your life in London' (1995: 58), he replies:

> Yes. If you have seen I have written TV films which I always set here. ... they are all set in London. For me, this is my way of responding to this environment that surrounds me and was not part of my life some years ago, but it is now. I felt I had to do this. There are writers who would not respond to a society that is not their own, but I do. It is my choice, I am here. At the same time I want to stop writing about Nigeria because I prefer this gipsy aspect of my life. (58)

What Bandele is acknowledging is that this response to his new home might only be accomplished through the intersection between his many lives – in Africa and in Europe, in the material and the spiritual dimensions. There are, therefore, many viewpoints in *The Street* and a veritable profusion of narrators and protagonists to express them. There is a central narrator, Dada, who is in many ways most suggestive of Bandele himself. However, there are two other characters whose life trajectories will deliver the most insight into Bandele's forays into London life. There is Dada's cousin, 'Biodun, otherwise known as 'The Heckler', and Ossie Jones, an immigration lawyer from Nigeria. We will look at each of them more closely. There is also Ossie's daughter, Nehushta, who was Dada's girlfriend for a time. Another persona of Bandele might be found in a strange, floating protagonist narrator, Mr Bill, who is a word peddler – he literally collects, buys and sells words.

Through these multiple viewpoints, many worlds and word games, Bandele is seeking, playing and hiding his identity, as a Nigerian living in London. He is doing so by means of the here and now of daily life on the High Street of Brixton. He is not seeking it in the depths of his psyche, his roots in the past of deep symbols, metaphors and figurative language. He wishes to discover a language and an urban landscape in all its concrete reality, such that he might find a solid place, as a writer and an artist, in the environment in which he lives and works. He is playful, full of nonsense, reacting against the heavy political responsibilities that he inherited from his

Nigerian tradition of anti-colonial struggle, in the form of literary giants, like Chinua Achebe. This is why he says – contradicting Achebe's famous words – 'I do not see the writer as a teacher' (in Diez-Tagarro, 1995: 59).

The action takes place midst exploding words – words, which detonate the boundaries between worlds and dimensions, words in all their metonymic, fleshy, powerful and solid materiality. As we shall see, Bandele draws up bizarre and lengthy lists, returns the figurative into the literal, indulges in rhymes, songs and ditties, invents a weird and wonderful portmanteau vocabulary and delights in the randomness of contiguity. To what purpose all these detonating words? They clear the dross and carve out a reality in which the writer becomes a gipsy, instead of an exile hankering after a nostalgic motherland. As Bandele says, 'writers should be careful with words; because they can explode' (Diez-Tagarro, 59). This they indeed do in *The Street.*

For example, the rhythm of the language in *The Street* is metonymically drummed out through a pastiche of non-sequiturs, as in this conversation between Dada and Nehushta:

> They talked about Luddites and the digital age, of misoneists and miscegenation, of *déjà vu* and tiramisu, and of deserts and the sea, and of Quentin Tarantino films, which they loved and hated. She told him about the bird that saw an aircraft and bowed in worship, he told her about the radio that went into therapy because it was hearing voices. (*The Street*, 213–14)[1]

Déjà vu and tiramisu are linked only because they rhyme; alliteration links the strange word, 'misoneists', to 'miscegenation'. There is no meaning invested in the birds which worship aeroplanes and in objects, like the radio, which is personified through the pun, where hearing voices relates literally to its being a radio, but also tells of madness, the schizophrenia, that permeates Bandele's London, as lunatics walk the street in a fug of psychosis.

The conversation between Dada and Nehushta, who talked about '*déjà vu* and tiramisu, and of deserts and the sea', echoes that between Lewis Carroll's Walrus and Carpenter, in *Through the Looking-Glass*, whose delirious topics, alliteratively entwined, likewise include random kings, cabbages, shoes and ships:

> 'The time has come,' the Walrus said,
> 'To talk of many things:
> Of shoes – and ships – and sealing-wax –
> Of cabbages – and kings –
> And why the sea is boiling hot –
> And whether pigs have wings. (1998: 161)

Flying pigs and boiling seas, worshipping birds and schizophrenic radios may appear nonsensical, but they point to the different worlds, the parallel universes, or multiple dimensions, with which these writers juggle, in the light-hearted language of play. Different and simultaneous zones organise the chaos of Bandele's novels, as he portrays the multiple sites he occupies

---

1 Page references to quotations in this chapter, unless indicated otherwise, are to The Street (London: Picador, 1999).

and explores. These are the concrete realities of daily life on a busy London
street and the echoes of Nigeria; there are the elusive dimensions of dreamland, death, the spirit world and other planets. These different worlds happily co-exist and are contiguous and the incongruous becomes the norm.
And nothing characterises the co-existence of these many worlds more than
Bandele's Brixton 'Undead', who exist between the living and the dead, blurring the boundary between them.

Parallel universes: Ossie Jones & 'the Heckler'

> Brixton High Street was, as always, busy and frenetic, packed with the ever-present
> floating cast of the walking wounded and the clinically Undead; ... damaged souls
> haunted by memories of past transgressions and paralysed with guilt for sins not yet
> committed. (11)

Floating in the space between dream and waking, hallucinatory marijuana
trip and reality, there is the netherworld of the Undead. The High Street
teems with a multitude of off-beat, liminal characters – migrants, madmen
and nomads. These underworld characters have been transposed from Nigeria, where Bandele had mingled with a variety of 'shady characters':

> [Bandele] grew up in Kafanchan in the strictly Hausa-Muslim speaking north of Nigeria,
> amidst armed robbers, pickpockets, prostitutes and smugglers.
>   His father, a Yoruba from the southwest of Nigeria, owned the property used by the
> shady characters mentioned above as their base of operation.
>   Tales of their exploits inspired the young Biyi. (Sheyin, 1995: 26)

Dada writes about the Undead for a lunatic fringe magazine; Nehushta paints
them; the Heckler is one of them. These Undead, for all their psychotic rav-
ings, paradoxically structure the anomic, chaotic, word frenzied world of the
novel. There is Mr Meletus, whom Dada interviews, whose psyche has been
rebooted inexplicably, resulting in institutionalisation, shock therapy and
now 'a permanent prescription of non-illicit happiness drugs' (125). He is
convinced that a pigeon had said 'fuck you' to him, an insult that he is sure
his mother confirmed, a mother, who has been dead for the past five years
(127–8). There is the old eccentric, who rides buses all day and the bag lady,
who 'spent over twenty years compiling a list of those not to be invited to
her funeral' (129).
    Then there is the young man, who is tormented by spirits, whose letter to
Dada's editor sounds like something straight out of Amos Tutuola: 'At least
2 or 3 spirits are around me and fly past, 1 or 2 live in my mouth and nose.
More bads: they don't let me have friends or get married till death' (130).
The language of 'more bads' manipulates an adjective and turns it into a
noun, disrespecting the boundary between parts of speech. There is the man
who was convinced that he was 'the restless soul of a Tamagochi tortured to
death by a ten-year-old apprentice psychopath' (168). Nehushta began painting them shortly after her father's death 'as a celebration of Brixton through
its used, abused and contused' (174). These rhymes, mumbo jumbo narra-

tives and testimonies, raves and rants, weave in and out of the narrative from beginning to end. There is Ras Joseph, who rambles on for about four pages, while Dada is recording him and Nehushta is sketching him (199 onwards). Later Dada will listen to his mini recorder 'from which the lyrical cadences of a somnolent voice slurred a farrago of smooth increrudition, into his ears' (199). Increrudition? Incredulity, erudition and confusion? The following is a typical, wordy wonderland of nonsense, referring to the Lonely Hearts column of Dada's magazine:

> Through which hypochondriacs sought out the company of pharmacomaniacs ..., mythomaniacs found comfort in the arms of pseudomaniacs, pyromaniacs reached out to hydromaniacs, homicidal psychopaths (homicidomaniacs) arranged candle-lit blind-dates at Sushi bars with the chronically suicidal (autophonomaniacs), and the merely pixillated received single red roses from the severely demented. (132)

Bandele asks for a great deal of leeway from his reader in order to make this point. Failure to understand his purpose could render this reader deaf from the sheer noise of the novel. These out of control lists, crazy words and insane metonymic ramblings, are at the intersection between the worlds of madness and sanity, of the living and the dead, of sense and nonsense. These porous worlds are distilled through the story within the story of Ossie's journey to dreamland, which is a powerful and extended section of the novel. It is significant that when Bandele adapted his *The Street* for the London stage in his play, *Brixton Stories*, the part that he used was Ossie's sojourn in parallel universes (Fisher, 2001: 1).

Ossie Jones had originally come to London from Nigeria for a temporary stay, to get his law degree. The civil war in Nigeria had intervened, as did his love affair with Kate, an English nurse, whom he married. Two years later 'Nehushta came calling from the land of the Unborn' (30). Nigeria and England and 'the land of the Unborn' constitute his worlds. At the outset of the novel, Ossie was convinced that his twin brother had visited from the land of the Dead. He says he saw his twin brother, Taiye, 'at St Pancras' (25). Nehushta pointed out to him that his twin had died twenty years previously in Lagos 'without having ever left the shores of Nigeria, let alone come to London' (27). This sighting of his twin in the other world presages Ossie's own impending journey into another reality. The night after Ossie's vision of his brother, he fell on a corkscrew (more about this object later) and went into a fifteen-year coma. We move seamlessly in the novel from the reality of Ossie's life in London into his dream world, which goes on for the next thirty-three pages:

> Ossie Jones drifted from a deep, drunken sleep into a dream in which he was completely sober and in his car driving *down a strange, liminal highway* that stretched from a nebulous tunnel at the soles of his feet, past the toll-gates of his soul, where he was stopped, even his passport checked, and into the boundless openness of the universe. (28, my emphasis)

That Ossie has entered another dimension is referred to more than once in the novel – 'in the parallel world, outside of this dream he was dreaming' (39). In fact, more than anything else, this world he enters resembles the limbo place of the newly dead, the same one that Tutuola's palm-wine Drinkard's tapster occupies: 'the whole people who had died in this world, did not go to heaven directly, but they were living in one place somewhere in this world' (Tutuola, 1952: 9).

In his 'dream' Ossie's car breaks down and he cadges a lift with a demonic young man called Apha, a little devil child, with overtones of Esu, the Yoruba trickster god. Apha incriminates Ossie for the murder that he had committed of his parents, whose bodies were stored in the boot of the car. Ossie is wrongly arrested for this double murder and 'his dream was in fact a nightmare' (42). He tries to wake up but 'his dream would not let go of him' (42). Ossie, like newly arrived migrants in a strange country, where the Law is hostile and punishing, loses his name and becomes an alien creature – none of his phone numbers work and everybody 'simply stood there looking at *him as if he'd just dropped in from another planet*' (43, my emphasis). He is tried for the murder of Apha's parents and is given a life sentence in the land of dreams (47).

This is an upside down world in which even bodily ageing time is different. For example, Johni, one of Ossie's fellow dream prison inmates, 'looked to be forty but was actually approaching seventy-five' (54). In this topsy turvy world, people live more than one life and even gender boundaries are porous – baby Johni returns in a pram in his next life, but this time round 'as a lass' (61). Here sleep is inverted into action and you can do all kinds of things while you 'sleep': 'although he was completely asleep, he was in fact awake' (48). Here Ossie learns 'to read while sleeping' (59) thereby obtaining a degree on Astronomy by correspondence, 'through studying while asleep' (60). The reference to the Astronomy degree is not a random one, given Bandele's multiple universes where the moon, the stars and other planets all co-exist with London, Lagos and the land of dreams. In this dreamland, backwards is forwards and 'a truth was merely a lie whose time had come; conversely, a lie was simply a truth being conceived' (52). In this moral grey area, Johni may be a homicidal psychopath, but is 'a nice guy at heart' (50).

In this Chinese box of worlds, meanings and moralities, we have Johni's story, within Ossie's story, within the story of Brixton. Johni's story is about his combative encounter with Death (49–51), which echoes Tutuola's Drinkard's own tussles with Death (Tutuola, 1952: 14–16). As with the loose, episodic structure of Tutuola's book, in which the story of the Drinkard's quest is interspersed with the multiple stories of the people and creatures he encounters, so Ossie's story becomes entwined with the stories of his fellow dream jail inmates, like those of Johni. Johni pursues Death, in order to hasten the end of his three life sentences, but 'Death crossed the road to avoid him whenever it saw him coming' (49). Johni, by chasing Death out of the town, inadvertently also 'chased Life to the city limits' because Life needed Death and it, therefore, became 'impossible to say whether the inhabitants of this one particular town in the land of dreams were dead or alive. It was said that they were neither dead nor alive' (52). Bandele's ethical world hovers between zones – neither dead nor alive, neither truth nor lies, neither good nor bad.

There are multiple worlds and realities, but also 'scientific' explanations for what was happening, in that Ossie may well have just knocked his head on the corkscrew and been in 'a coma that had lasted fifteen years' (64). In other words, there is another interesting porous boundary here between a kind of magical realism that would commit the novel to the belief in the supernatural possibility of these multiple universes, and a realism that explains strange and magical occurrences as the result of a coma or dream. Ossie himself becomes confused in that when he 'thought about the land of dreams', he 'wasn't so sure any more that what he thought had happened had actually happened' and he worries that 'the land of dreams had merely been the side effect of some esoteric drug the doctors had administered on him during his coma?' (117). However, he stands by his belief in more than one reality and for him, 'the people he felt he had met during those fifteen years ... were as real to him as anybody who had ever been a part of his life' (117). Different dimensions co-exist in Ossie's life, in his waking and sleeping and in the 'the monstrous munificence' of his thoughts:

> He thought of the slouching shadows of lonesome giants and the radiance of a shared moment, the syncopated silence of selective amnesia and the resonating infinitude of a done deed, the ticking of time and the hypothesis of immortality, the threat of rain and the beauty of a green landscape, the falling out of teeth and the serenity of a toothless smile, the numbing shock of a sudden disappointment and the lingering scream into which an orgasm erupts. (116)

This passage captures the style and the politics of *The Street* as a whole. Lagos and London, giants and a shared moment, silence and an accomplished task, time, rain, nature, ageing and teeth, a smile and an orgasm, are all able to mingle and mix in Ossie's worlds. Sukhdev Sandhu is a reader, who becomes impatient with Bandele's style, when he accuses him of digression in that 'Bandele's belief in the spectral quality of Brixton life' leads him 'to retard narrative thrust with a forty-page excursion into a coma-stricken character's dream wanderings' (1999: 23). The spectral quite precisely explodes narrative thrust, or linear progress, which is fragmented by parallel worlds. They are the touchstone of the novel's attempts to depict a Brixton that has been metamorphosed by migrant spirituality, vision and languages. But perhaps Ossie, like some readers, can no longer hold all this together, and soon after emerging from his other world, he properly leaves this one and dies, creeping 'out of his body and into the mist' (119).

Reminiscent of Ossie, who communes with the living, the dead and the inhabitants of dream land, Dada's cousin, who is known as 'the Heckler', lives in an interstitial space between the living and the dead. 'Biodun is an abiku, a spirit child that his mother had 'tried but failed three times in the past to bring into the world' (141). The belief is that infant deaths are the result of a mother carrying a spirit child in her womb, one with a foot in the land of the living and a foot in the land of the spirits, to which the child decides to return. Abikus torment their mothers by being born only to die and come back again and again from the land of the unborn. In addition, and more literally, 'Biodun spans life and death by being HIV positive, unbeknown to his mother:

> Within weeks of being told he was HIV positive, he quit his high-flying job with a software company, was kicked out of his flat (for not paying his rent. That's when he moved back in with his mother, and became the Heckler...). (274)

At first glance only, then, it appears as if 'Biodun is a well settled citizen of Brixton. Brixton, and not Lagos, from where his family originated, is his home. He won't budge from Brixton, where 'the streets of his birth' (13) are located and 'the only relocation he would ever consider would be the relocation from Brixton to six-feet-under Brixton' (13). However, this rootedness is something of a mirage; he is in denial about his health and is living recklessly on the street. He is unemployed, drinks and smokes excessively without eating properly and has lost his real, Nigerian name, becoming 'the Heckler'. The name refers to the fact that 'he was to be found wherever there was a soapbox, matching wits and trading insults' (12). The Heckler's world has spun as out of control as the list of words Bandele spews in order to describe his social circle, which consists of those Undead street lunatics: 'the Heckler locked horns with these mavens, gurus, roshis, lamas, shamans, revolutionaries, avatars, seers, illuminati, diviners, prognosticators, prophets and those who considered themselves the street clerisy' (13). They are 'kooks, nuts, schizoids and Meshuggenahs' (131). Slang, Yiddish, made-up words and standard English careen and collide off the page.

'Biodun's mother, Aunt Moni, may not know about his health, but she does know that he has lost his way and she is frustrated with his lifestyle of being 'a bum on the streets' (158). She therefore, in one of the topsy-turvy manoeuvres, so beloved of Bandele, organises him a mock 'funeral' while he is still alive in order to inaugurate his spiritual recovery. Dada, who attends this bizarre ritual, tells 'Biodun about it. The ritual itself is culturally hybrid and amounts to a kind of African styled Christian exorcism. Aunt Moni had consulted with 'Prophet Moses' of her Angelic Church of Christ and 'The Lord told him to tell me that the only way to bring back the old Abiodun is to bury the impostor that is inhabiting his soul now' (159). In a further typical reversal, the 'funeral' takes place in the section called 'The Wedding'. There may be no flesh and blood body, but ritual is fully enacted, with the extended family arriving, both 'long term UK residents' (132) as well as 'visitors from Nigeria' (133). There are pallbearers, the casket and the officiating priest, who provides the wedding overtones with his 'long white cassock with golden tassels that trailed after him like a bridal train' echoing the wedding within the funeral (137). We have a syncretised wedding funeral, which is an inverted rite of passage in which literal solid objects act as props. The weird funeral of the person, who is still alive, confronts the boundaries between life and death and between spirits and humans, born again Christians and abikus. This ritual may have spiritual purposes and goals, but it is enacted emphatically by way of lavish material manifestations. The coffin itself, for example, and its exquisite trimmings, are described in intricate, concrete detail:

> The coffin, stained a faint mahogany, was made of pinewood. It had brass fittings and golden handles. A felt-mattress, handmade and fit for a king, was spread inside ...
> A photograph of the Heckler smiled at them from the hand-quilted silk shell-shaped pillow where his head, were he in the coffin, would have rested. (140–1)

Material objects and powerful words bond together as pillars of this ritual search for the identity of the lost 'Biodun. The 'funeral' is presided over by Prophet Moses, a man of visceral odours and charismatic rhetoric. Bandele, once again, invokes these by way of a barrage of words as the Prophet Moses releases 'the pleasant but dizzying and overbearing scent of sandalwood, eucalyptus, frangipani, coconut, lemon grass, patchouli, cinnamon, mango and myrrh' (141). At the same time, 'he muttered a rapid and *inaudible swelter of words*, which Dada knew, having been dragged by Aunt Moni to church when he was a kid, as *a form of glossolalia, the gift of tongues*' (141, my emphases). This 'swelter of words' and tongues, the smells and the solidity of wood and pillow, is what constitutes the ritual. This relationship between words and solid objects in relation to migrant life is the key to the novel's explorations.

Words & things

The problem with the Heckler, Bandele suggests, is that words and things, language and material reality, have become torn apart and dislocated. This is the meaning of the Yoruba elegy, delivered by the Prophet Moses at 'Biodun's mock funeral:

> 'The hunter dies,' Prophet Moses was saying, 'and leaves his poverty to his gun. The blacksmith dies and leaves his poverty to his anvil. The farmer dies and leaves his poverty to his hoe. The bird dies and leaves its poverty to its nest. You have died, Abiodun, and left us abandoned in the dark.' (143–4)

Poverty, this dirge suggests, need not destroy individuals, as long as they are anchored to solid objects, which reflect their work. Their endeavours, are, in fact, metonyms for them – the gun, the anvil and the nest. Abiodun, however, is not centred; he has nothing to leave behind him; he is a shape shifter, not anchored to his human body or to the solidity of a house and possessions. He lacks an identity other than that of the empty rhetorician, the heckler.

The mastery that is sought over everyday material reality is imperative to the migrant stranger in a new society. The purpose of pinning down the abstract, and embedding it in the concrete realities of material culture, goes to the heart of the mode of nonsense writing, as Elizabeth Sewell indicates by reference to Lewis Carroll: 'the words which Nonsense is going to employ are those referring to normal experience, shoes and ships and sealing-wax and cabbages and kings' (1978: 99). It is for this reason that Humpty Dumpty's song includes 'little fishes, a kettle, the pump, bed, *a corkscrew*' (99, my emphasis). The ordinary corkscrew is the portal, ushering Ossie into another dimension. We will return to it. Sewell, in her *The Field of Nonsense*, goes on to illustrate how Carroll's version of 'Twinkle twinkle little star', which is rendered by the Mad Hatter, also uses imagery of the ordinary accoutrements of everyday life:

> Twinkle, twinkle, little bat!
> How I wonder what you're at!
> Up above the world you fly,
> Like a tea-tray in the sky. (100)[2]

Instead of the star of the original, which is compared to a diamond in the sky, 'a bat has been substituted for a star, a tea-tray for a diamond' and whereas 'a star is something exceedingly remote and beyond control' (100), 'a bat is something near at hand' (101). These are the things, Sewell emphasises, that constitute our daily reality and 'they characterise our familiar surroundings, clothes, food, furniture and houses' (101).

Interestingly, Bandele's version of a re-writing of the 'Twinkle! Twinkle' jingle can be found in his earlier novel, *The Man Who Came in From the Back of Beyond*. As the main character in that novel, Lakemfa, realizes that his teacher has been spinning him tall yarns, he is brought back to stark reality by seeing that 'the moon hung far away like a football in the sky' (1992: 136). This harnesses the distant planets and other dimensions of life to an everyday object, a football. Its final chapter begins with the same link between the moon and mundane objects, making it into something visceral, rather than dreamy and unattainable:

> The stars were scattered like so many pieces of *popcorn* pasted with glue to the ceiling of a room. The moon looked like a *football* that someone had kicked into the sky. (1992: 133, my emphases)

Popcorn and footballs, like cabbages and tea-trays, position the protagonist firmly on the planet and enable him to make sense of the world. Throughout *The Street* , one way of managing strange, new worlds, where things are never where they should be, or what they seem, is by transforming the abstract and the virtual into the visible, concrete and fleshy object. This object may then be touched, held or even destroyed.

We find, therefore, in Bandele the constant transformation of the figurative back into its literal mode. And so the mind is a real place to go to: 'Dada had temporarily disappeared into his own mind and re-emerged ...' (5). We saw that 'three life sentences' (49) meant literally that Johni had to live three lives. Johni's father, apparently, 'had a smile that was so bright and warm, people dried their laundry under it' (57). Dada says: "What I'm driving at" and his friend replies "Stop driving. You haven't got a driving licence" (81).

This device serves a double purpose. It exposes the figurative and reminds us of the material world on which comparisons, which have become stereo-types in their excessive usage, are based. It also gestures towards Garuba's

---

[2]   For the original, see Carroll, 1998 [1865]: 63.

'animist materialism', where the boundaries between animate and inanimate objects are porous and where the material world is re-enchanted. And so 'the traffic lights ... developed conjunctivitis' (5) And 'the light was simply mocking them' (20). A thought 'occurred to him only fleetingly, and then it disappeared, unheeded and sulking' (37). Regarding a nerve of Ossie's body, 'it died (or committed suicide)' (71) and there is 'the tetchy clock-tower that stared stolidly at the high street' (80). 'The sun was still abroad, loitering with coruscating intent' (103). Nehushta 'tripped over something which, when she opened her eyes wide and was properly awake, turned out to be a thin strip of light that had wandered into the room through the slits in the blinds from the street-lamps outside' (119). There is a door being burglar alarmed, which becomes the literally traumatised door:

> He did not notice the sign, which read: 'WARNING: THIS DOOR IS ALARMED'. When he tried to push it open, the door – which was already bruised, traumatized and suffering from low self-esteem – cowered before him and nearly flew off its hinges. (85–6)

Words themselves become solid objects and harness the writer to the street, the place and time, in which he, Bandele, is operating. The nonsense lists and made-up words in *The Street* constitute a different kind of metonymic gap from the insertion of indigenous languages into African fiction written in English. They serve the same purpose, however, and equally point to different knowledges and cultures that make up the identities of writers such as Bandele. This accounts for the wild, weird and unhinged words that scurry along *The Street* and draw attention to its paradoxically nomadic structure. Like the Undead, who ramble and rave, appearing and disappearing throughout the book, crazy words weave across its pages, dictating its style and even its purpose, for example, 'Trustafarians' and 'Afro-Saxon' (17), 'Nowheresville' (34), 'hebetude' (48), 'coruscating' (103), 'spindling' 125), 'prestidigitation' (133), 'pauciloquence' and 'underwhelmed' (136), 'lactovegetarian activist' (145), 'bizarrerie' (167), 'omphaloskepsis, or the contemplation of one's navel as an aid to meditation' (174), 'copacetic folk' (175), 'oenomaniac' (187), 'absquatulated' (195), 'exercitation' (202), 'Black Blandiloquence' and 'irrefragable claim' (203), 'parannoying' (217) and 'diseconomies' (225).

In other words, Bandele does not include Yoruba words in his novel, like Adichie includes Igbo or Aboulela uses Arabic. Instead he makes up a strange and foreign language of his own. Much of the time, Bandele's language stands, like the metonymic gap, unexplained to us readers. Occasionally, Bandele explains it, such as 'flatting' as in 'The student was flat on her back and he was flat on her stomach', i.e. beyond 'flirting' (38) or 'oneiroscopist', which is 'an interpreter of dreams' (102) or 'The call began and ended with the poignant and alliterative 'Phew! Foockin' fired,' the first word being onomatopoeic for 'you're' when uttered in 'phury' (204).

These strange words in *The Street*, point to the existence of unknown worlds, and paradoxically, in their blankness, attempt to engender a new level of communication. Nehushta, in trying to break the ice with Dada, speaks with 'each word tripping out fast on the heels of the last, as if fleeing from a house on fire, with no perceivable pauses between thoughts or sentences, no rhythm to the rhyme':

> ... if we extrapolate from Hempel's paradox that a purple crow is a confirming instance of the hypothesis that all crows are black means I think and you best know that I'm congenitally immune to Meningitis Poliomyelitis Cirrhosis Alzheimer's Anaemia Creutzfeldt-Jakob Disease pleuro-Pneumonia Parkinson's Heart diseases Yellow Fever Leukaemia Tuberculosis Repetitive Strain Disorders Restless Legs Syndrome Stiff man Syndrome and, yes, you guessed it, the common flu. (170)

The metonymic gap is to point to different worlds, cultures and knowledge bases and enables the co-existence of these different worlds, which is the framework of Deleuze's analysis of Lewis Carroll's long poem, 'The Hunting of the Snark'. This analysis is highly suggestive of Bandele's language manoeuvres. Deleuze highlights how in that poem there are the different worlds of the literal and the figurative (1990, 26). The motley crew that sets out to hunt this enigmatic Snark, use any means at hand, taken from both spiritual and concrete dimensions, placed together in a metonymy of non-sequiturs:

> They sought it with thimbles, they sought it with care;
>   They pursued it with forks and hope;
> They threatened its life with a railway-share;
>   They charmed it with smiles and soap. (Carroll, 1992 [1876]: 250)

The world of solid, mundane objects – thimbles, forks, soap – is placed together with the more abstract, imponderable world of care, hope and happiness. What Deleuze foregrounds is the existence of an organising principle in the midst of Carroll's apparent chaos, that being the made up word, 'Snark', itself (Deleuze, 1990: 26). 'Snark' is a word with no fixed meaning and yet is 'opposed to the absence of meaning' (Bogue, 1989: 75). The Deleuzian sense of structure, then, is paradoxically 'structured chaos or chaos-structure: a nomadic distribution of singular points' (Bogue, 77). That is to say, by being something blank, or gibberish or apparently meaningless, words like 'Snark' draw attention to the existence of many realities, which cannot be contained by the Law, by the Symbols and meanings of dominant discourse. In fact, 'Snark' may be one of Deleuze and Guattari's liberating 'pass-words' that operate 'beneath order-words' referred to in my introduction (1987: 110).

There is not one powerful Snark word in Bandele, but all of those strange, made-up words and lists act as portals into the multiple worlds of the novel and organise its chaos. The concrete power of words, which populate Brixton in their own right, is demonstrated by an enigmatic character called Mr Bill. He is Bandele's alter ego and is a character living on the street, one of the Undead. Mr Bill tells us, in rich, concrete detail, that he is the one writing this novel with 'a black biro on a lined notebook at my tiny desk in my home down under Waterloo Bridge' (287). Like Bandele, he lives in many worlds simultaneously – on the Brixton High Street, as well as in the cosmos – and so 'if I look deep into my heart, I may spot the Pleiades, that dazzling cluster of small stars in the constellation Taurus, seven of which are discernible by the naked eye' (287). The parallel worlds of the homeless, the black biro and the lined notebook, are interspersed with the planets and the stars in the constellation and Mr Bill, brings them all together. He 'was listening to the beats of a distant drummer, whose thoughts crashed into his, from a nearby planet visible only to those that dream on high-speed Intercity trains by the grace of Supersaver tickets' (242).

It is he who is the conduit, not only for all the other characters, but also the other paradoxical elements we have been outlining. He acts in this way through his word peddling, his buying and selling of strange words, rhymes, lists and metonymies:

> Mr Bill, a peripatetic idiot savant who was to be found every weekday during the morning rush hour standing outside the tube station, touching commuters for money by enacting one or more of his specialities, which included reciting and offering the meanings, origins, synonyms, antonyms and, where applicable, usage and abusage of every single word under the letter H in the Oxford English Dictionary. (181)

Why the letter H? Mr Bill and Bandele and, no doubt, Lewis Carroll, would reply, Why not? 'When asked … why he made all the members of the crew [in *The Hunting of the Snark*] have occupations beginning with B, [Carroll] replied, "Why not?"' (Stern, 1982: 142). In fact, Mr Bill turns words into concrete solid objects, in order to harness and lasso language itself: 'in the summer he sold words for a living' (181). The average price for a word is ten pence and one man bought a whole paragraph as a birthday gift for his wife (181). Bandele emphasises this solidness of words and Mr Bill mends words that become damaged, such as the one that had 'suffered from a fractured syllable' (182). He repairs it 'with a needle and thread' (182). He even raids rubbish bins 'for stray, homeless or discarded words' (182). One time, he bought words cheaply from a 'second-hand words seller' because they had been damaged by rain and 'he laid them out in the sun to dry' (183).

Like these solid, living words, there are also 'strange interfering objects' (Deleuze, 1990: 39) that may facilitate the crossover between cultures, worlds and dimensions. Ossie, remember, one fateful night, bumped his head on 'a sharp object (which, on investigation, turn out to be a corkscrew)' (70). This corkscrew echoes Carroll's *Through the Looking-Glass*:

> "And what are 'toves'?"
> "Well, '*toves*' are something like badgers – they're something like lizards – and they're something like corkscrews." (1998, [1872]: 187)

Toves, like Snarks and corkscrews, open up wonderland worlds existing just on the other side of the mirror. However, Ossie charts these worlds at his peril, spending fifteen years in a coma and dying soon after he comes out of it, as we saw.

There is the table, into which Dada crashes: 'a metal table whose can-nibalised ancestry included self-projecting missiles, plus various marginal and unknown quantities (such as the lightness of his soul, the simplicity of his terror and the exceptionally strong tail wind)' (187). The solid metal of the table is not a portal, but instead it is an obstacle preventing Dada's path to Nehushta, who is at the bar, and detaining him in the netherworld between reality and alcohol-induced dreams. The table incorporates many dimensions within its own life story, its 'ancestry', its social biography, as Igor Kopytoff (1986) would have it, its wind and terror, weapons and souls. These, however, may remain in chaos, without any anchoring point enabling conversations across cultures, knowledges and languages, unless Dada finds a way through the fug of alcohol and drugs.

In other words, migrants, who become unanchored from the solid daily realities of material life at home, may lose their sense of identity and place in the world, as we saw was the case with 'Biodun, who had to be re-born into the material world by way of a ritual burial. Mr Bill may be the interpreter between this world and another one, along the lines of the different, parallel universes that the novel inhabits, but potentially, this other world is a scary place, an abyss, a meaninglessness, whose threat always lurks beneath the fun and language games. Mr Bill 'gifted' words with wings 'and sent them flying into the great void beyond sound or silence, where all words uttered in the universe, and in all languages on the planet, are stored for all time, or forgotten for ever' (182). There is also the possibility, then, that the chaos is not anchored, that the organising principal, the paradoxical entity, does not enable the co-existence of multiple, different planets and universes. Migrant writers confront the threat of the abyss, even as they search for the healing words and the bridges and connections between their multiple languages, pasts, presents and futures.

Lewis Carroll also pointed to this awful, obliterating possibility, when the hunt for the Snark backfires and instead of the discovery of the enabling pass word, the Snark, there is annihilation in the form of the dreaded Boojum that may be sighted. The Boojum is the ultimate nightmare of Carroll's 'agony in eight fits', subtitle of his poem:

> "For, although common Snarks do no manner of harm,
>   Yet, I feel it my duty to say,
> Some are Boojums _____" (1992 [1876]: 239)

The terrified baker on the expedition, faints on hearing this and is 'roused' with muffins, ice and 'with jam and judicious advice' (239) along the lines of the varied dimensions that characterise this poem. He is utterly petrified that, instead of a Snark, a Boojum will indeed surface from the deeps and 'I shall softly and suddenly vanish away _____'(241).

A Boojum? Boogey man and a jumble? Peek-a-boo – a fright and a mess? Whatever it is, it is bad and the opposite of 'finding yourself', asserting an identity and re-locating in the new place. The hybridity here is no happy border space of mixed parts syncretising into something new. It is the warning that Deleuze and Guattari proffer that in the attempt to escape the death sentence of the order-word, in the hunt for the pass-word, for the strange, esoteric object, one may fall 'into a black hole' (1987: 110).

Objects, material realities, from home, from the past, from the desires of the present, are never where migrants look for them and reality shifts between what they have and what they have left behind. And so, observes Bandele in *The Street*:

> In the land of dreams, objects disappeared the moment you looked away. They travelled backwards and forwards in time and space, to part-time duties in distant planets or brief assignations in parallel universes. They reappeared just as soon as you turned round or opened your eyes to implicate them in your existence. (63)

Distant planets and parallel universes, populated by wily objects, which are animated, sums up the world of the novel. In *Anti-Oedipus*, Deleuze and Guattari refer to these strange objects having their counterparts in the imagined world of desire, a formulation, which resonates powerfully with the different universes characterising Biyi Bandele's novel. Desire, in lacking its object, 'produces an imaginary object that functions as a double of reality, as though there were a "dreamed-of object behind every real object"' (Deleuze and Guattari, 1983: 25). In other words, 'the world acquires as its double some other sort of world' a world in which the missing object of desire is imagined (1983: 26).[3] The image of doubling, twinning, such as Ossie's twin, who he eventually joins in the land of the dead, having sighted him in London, is a recurrent one in many of the novels, where more than one world exists.

The point about the missing object of desire is precisely that it is absent. This virtual object, as Deleuze puts it later in his *Difference and Repetition*, 'is where it is only on condition that it is not where it should be' (1996: 26). The elusive object of desire is always just out of reach, always somewhere else. It is Alice's Looking-Glass world in which 'the egg seems to get further away the more I walk towards it' (Carroll, 1998 [1872]: 180). So too, migrants like Bandele live in a world of partial, fragmented objects, with lives in other planets and universes, populated with objects, which disappear the moment you look away. In other words, there are these strange objects having their counterparts in the imagined world of desire, a world that migrants have departed and re-formulated through the prism of nostalgic memory.

What we have seen is that Bandele is building the connections between England and Nigeria, intellectuals and hobos, and between the languages and cultures of oral stories from West Africa and European tales, classics from Victorian England. The binaries are split apart before they hit the ground. I have been suggesting that all these lists and rhymes, narrators and languages, flying words and strange objects, constitute a politics of resistance to the hegemony of one world, or the hierarchy of one language. It is not a politics of nationalism or resistance to the particular corruptions of the Nigeria from which Bandele has migrated. Bandele, we saw, deviates from Achebe's tradition of the writer as teacher. What, then, are the politics of *The Street*?

---

3 They are quoting Clément Rosset, *Logique du pire* (Paris: Presses Universitaries de France, 1970), p.37.

'Y'ave to put your line on the head': the politics of the surface

There is a profound difference between *The Street*, on the one hand, and *The Sympathetic Undertaker And Other Dreams* (1993 [1991]) and *The Man Who Came in From the Back of Beyond* (1992 [1991]), on the other. Bandele's earlier novels, for all their nascent experimentation, were overtly political critiques of the corruption and greed, brutality and monstrousness of the new power elite of Nigeria. While this critique lurks around the edges of *The Street*, it remains at the surface, enveloped in rhymes and irreverences, in nonsense and language games.

Is it the case that Bandele has turned his back on making a serious intervention into the atrocities and need for political action and struggle? Or, is he experimenting in this novel with the potential of this metonymic site of happenstance and word play? This site is what Deleuze, in *The Logic of Sense*, refers to as the significance of the surface: 'a dismissal of depth, a display of events at the surface, and a deployment of language along this limit' (1990: 9). Parallel universes are parallel and equal, rather than hierarchical; they are the horizontal of metonymy, rather than the depth of the vertical of metaphor. Nonsense writing unravels dominant cultural metaphors. For example, 'a dark, wet setting' invariably lends itself to symbolise the Freudian womb, to say nothing of the cultural abundance of phallic symbols. A rejection of the depth of figurative associations, by way of the literal, funny meaningless surface, facilitates something new (Holquist, 1969: 154). This site of the surface is a highly suggestive one for African migrant writers, seeking to become part of the daily round of people and places and solid things in a new country, one, moreover, that had colonised them. They are weary of the tendentiousness of some of their forebears and wish to play, to blend and mingle in their new surroundings.

Even when Bandele tackles the old, serious issues regarding the betrayal of the Nigerian national dream, the portrayal is flippant and funny. The historical and political realties are disguised and masked. In attendance at the funeral is the gross and absurdly wealthy Mabogunje side of the family. Dada's uncle is satirically referred to as 'Chief Prince Bode Mabogunje M.Sc. Ph.D MLL. MQD. OFR (Order of the Federal Republic)' (133). Uncle Bode, for short, had been in the Nigerian government, 'during which time he managed, through sheer prestidigitation with public money, to acquire two houses in Hampstead, a golf course near Inverness, a holiday home in Provence and various businesses of questionable worth in North America' (133). There is no torture, rape and brutality, but rather metonymic lists of pompous, fake titles and made-up words, such as 'prestidigitation'. Uncle Bode, for obvious reasons, has been living in exile in England, on his ill begotten gains and so his son, Dapo, who lives off his father, is a horrible amalgam of Nigerian corruption, Cockney babble and American affectation. This language parodies his sentiments exhorting political involvement in Nigeria: 'Y'know y'have t'get actively involved in the oppositional struggle, so t'speak' (138).

He continues:

> 'Y'can't joost sit there and stand. *Y' 'ave to put your line on the head* ...y'know wha' am sayin'? You can't have your cake and swallow it, y'dig wha' am sayin', Dad? Y'get me though?' (139, my emphasis)

The familiar topsy-turvy of sitting and standing, the head being where the line gets put instead of the other way around, renders Dapo hilarious at best and grotesque at worst, but not very dangerous or scary. The corruption, in fact, is portrayed in the by now familiar language of word games and non-sense. For example, Uncle Dada had awarded a building contract to one of his mates, whose sub-contractor omitted to instal a lift in a twenty-two storey building. This man disappears, apparently imploding 'from the face of the earth, turning into a kite on a string, or the echo of a fart, in some place far from Earth, pausing in Lagos only long enough to collect a substantial down-payment on the contract' (133–4). This crook floats to another planet – a puff of badly smelling air. Even Brixton's 'Undead', those street wonderers, mad people and homeless seers, are described not in hell, not in the depths, but like the kite or the fart, they float just above the surface of the novel and *The Street* of its setting: 'this band of nameless vagrants that drifted like flotsam on the sporadically turbulent streets of Brixton' (183). Note flotsam – the debris that floats on the surface. Right from the start, 'the walking wounded' are described as a '*floating cast*' (11, my emphasis).

Having said all of this, what is quite perplexing is the jarring note that Bandele's deviation from the surface sounds. We saw earlier that 'Biodun is HIV positive. In an atypically emotional and serious mode for Bandele, he explains that Andre, the love of 'Biodun's life, had recently died from this disease. This explains why 'Biodun had abandoned his life and his identity, living as he was, in mourning, and on the fringes between life and death. Here the novel abandons its irony, its playfulness, its tongue in cheek, and gives us a depth, grief and loss, which, however, borders on the overblown and the sentimental. The Heckler breaks down and confesses to Dada 'I miss Andre. I miss him so much.' (277). We see a video of a real funeral – 'Andre's – with his photograph, draped with flowers, placed above his coffin lying on the alter of a chapel in North London' (277). The part ends wrenchingly: 'The Heckler was weeping. Dada held him to his chest, rubbing his neck, letting him cry' (278). This goes against the grain and structure of the novel and seems to be an add-on, right at the end. For a novel that has been skimming upon the surface, this sudden depth of feeling, in that sentimental language, appears out of place. The paradoxical seriousness of nonsense is the novel's genre and when it abandons it, it strikes a false note. Or, as Sewell puts it, rather categorically, perhaps, 'nonsense can admit of no emotion' (1978 [1952]: 29).

Perhaps Bandele felt the need to abandon his postmodern playfulness by the end of the novel and to bring some kind of postcolonial political closure on the scenario of drink and drugs and lunacy on the streets of London. By the end of the novel, the Heckler has returned to the land of the living and to his Nigerian name, 'Biodun. He has even found another partner and 'was no longer the Heckler, having come to terms with his demons, entered a new relationship, got his act together and gone back to his old job' (285). The delighted Aunt Moni, 'was convinced it was her prayers and the faux funeral that had made it all happen' (285).

For all of this perhaps simplistic closure, the lodestone of the novel rests with the attempt to juggle parallel universes and multiple, splintered and changing identities. This resonates quite powerfully with what Achille Mbembe describes as African imaginary worlds being 'simultaneous multiplicities' (2001: 145). Bandele, with his descriptions of drunken hallucinations, worlds of dreams and drink, dimensions of living beings, dead people and the Brixton 'Undead', operating in a liminal zone, is precisely charting these 'simultaneous multiplicities'. Are these distinctively African? They are certainly themselves multiple, drawing on animism, psychoanalysis, nonsense traditions of Lewis Carroll, language games of postmodernism and the literary traditions Bandele inherited from Amos Tutuola, Wole Soyinka and Ben Okri.

In other words, at its best, *The Street* is about hunting for identity in novel ways, ways that jettison the agony, incorporate the fun and games of a big, multi-lingual cosmopolitan scene, in the shifting context of a Nigerian living in Brixton, buying his soap and sitting at his computer, where he writes about his many lives. In this, Bandele aligns himself to a tradition and a style of writing about London that Sukhdev Sandhu has highlighted in relation to the fiction of both Salman Rushdie and Hanif Kureishi:

> To map the city, *The Satanic Verses* suggests, one must first dispense with real maps. Kureishi made the same point in *Sammy and Rosie Get Laid*. Could it be that palimpsests and psychogeographies, ghost-hunting, randomness, chains of association and misbegotten folklore are more effective ways of accessing 'London' than the sequential codification of the *A to Z*? (2004: 369).

The identities being sought are invariably elusive, kinetic, paradoxical and unpredictable. The term Deleuze and Guattari use is 'becoming' rather than being (1987: 232). What 'becoming' involves is 'to move and to pull in both directions at once' (Deleuze, 1990: 1). Part of this moving and pulling in more than one direction involves 'the reversal of cause and effect: to be punished before having committed a fault, to cry before having pricked oneself, to serve before having divided up the servings' (Deleuze, 1990: 3). Deleuze is referring to Alice's Wonderland, but likewise, in *The Street*, cause and effect are also bamboozled:

> 'I'm afraid, sir, but the chef has just informed me that we have in fact run out of wine.'
> 'In that case,' Dada said, 'I'll have a bottle of the house red.'
> 'Right away, Sir,' the waiter said ... (6)

The Brixton riff raff are 'paralysed with guilt for sins not yet committed' (11). This inversion characterises the dream conversation between Ossie and the demonic Apha:

'You are a vagrant,' the boy declared. Then before Ossie could respond, the boy asked the question to which he had already provided an answer: 'What are you – a vagrant?' (32)

These multiple directions and dimensions, worlds and identities are what Carroll, Deleuze and Bandele capitalise upon in their radical explorations, not only of who we are, but how we relentlessly metamorphose. The scary menacing question, however, is whether this search for those worlds in fleeting conversation through the good services of strange words and peculiar objects, are mere babble and chaos? Dada dies young and the Brixton Undead are mad, delusional and poverty stricken, up to their eyeballs in booze and drugs. There is the horror of AIDS and the awfulness of the family from Nigeria. Is the dreaded Boojum roaming Brixton High Street? The signs were ominous in Carroll's poem where his hunters found no anchoring solid material objects, 'not a button, or feather, or mark' to ground the Baker (Carroll, 1992 [1876]: 252). We are not, therefore, surprised by the sad outcome, which is that he disappears into the black hole 'For the Snark was a Boojum, you see' (252). However, the promise of personal, cultural and political regeneration, is worth the risk: 'It suffices that we dissipate ourselves a little, that we be able to be at the surface, that we stretch our skin like a drum, in order that the "great politics" begin' (Deleuze, 1990: 72).

The great politics have indeed begun, for all that *The Street* risks being sucked into the maelstrom of its excess of words and of dissolution of sanity, sense and identity. It is, however, a profoundly political novel, if different from the politics of Bandele's earlier fiction. *The Street* is original and experimental and it invites the possibilities enabled by porousness in the boundaries between continents and between histories, between magic and astronomy, between the living and the dead, the animate and inanimate. It participates in a cultural politics of language, which opens up new vistas. The last two paragraphs of the novel sum up many of its devices and deliberations:

> As Dada stepped out the front door and on to *The Street* , and headed for the Brixtonioso, an alien thought began to take shape in his mind. It assumed the form of an invisible weight pulling him down and crushing him at the same time. He decided, on a whim, to flee from his mind. He soared into the night, like a scream rising, and up to the stars.
> Then he changed his mind – into a pair of eyes. They stared dimly at him, as he walked along *The Street*. (292)

The Brixtonioso is clearly a fusion food place – perhaps Italian mixed with the particular British that is Brixton – that is to say, down to earth fare. The word, 'Brixtonioso', is a Snark, a hybrid word signifying a composite restaurant, but also the mixed, mutated identities populating an increasingly globalised world. An alien thought becomes a solid, visceral weight; his mind becomes a place from which one may, literally, rather than figuratively, flee. The stars become another dimension which is accessible to the earth. The metaphorical changing of the mind becomes transformed into the literal transformation from mind to eyes, eyes that signify the fragmented self, given that they separate from the body and scrutinise it. The dimness of the gaze upon himself is away from plumbing the depths and onto watching the surface of his walking along *The Street*, among the Undead, the shops and markets, the hecklers and preachers.

The novel's ending is indeterminate as Dada's eyes watched him dimly, but it is, I think, worth ending this chapter optimistically with one of Mr Bill's words. It had suffered a broken wrist and had 'healed into a fist unable to open'. It had to pass through another healing, rendering it less militant and didactic, more playful and less serious. Once Mr Bill had nursed it, 'it shook hands and opened doors' (183). English words and stories have imprisoned and oppressed some people, but once healed and warmed, perhaps still stuttering from the aftershock of their wounds, they may open doors and enable migrant writers and their readers to fly on their wings. These solid words, whose 'average price ... is ten pence' (181), flying between Lagos and London, the worlds of the living and the dead, are both literal and solid and also spirits on whose wings we may fly, if we listen to them carefully enough.

3 Everyday Objects & Translation
Leila Aboulela's *The Translator*
& *Coloured Lights*

'*Look Who's Talking*,' she said, 'became in Arabic, *Me and Mama and Travolta*'. (170)

The Translator by Leila Aboulela tells the tempestuous love story between a Muslim, Sudanese woman, Sammar, and a Scottish man, Rae. At the start of the book, Rae is mostly defined by his ethnicity and geographical positioning, while Sammar is marked by her ethnicity, her condition of displacement and her religion. However, Rae's religion will, as we shall see, become one of the central issues in the novel. He is 'a Middle-East historian and a lecturer in Third World Politics' (5)[1] and Sammar's job is to translate between English and Arabic for him. Sammar may translate between Arabic and English, but her novel translates Standard English into a language that has to express her own experiences, spirituality and background. In addition to this literal translation between languages, she has to find a way of translating between different cultures. One of the novel's scenarios, then, relates to the issues that arise out of the differences between a North African, Arab speaking Muslim woman and a Scottish, English speaking non-Muslim man. However, this polarisation is cut across by greater complexities and syncretisms.

Rae's intellectual life spills over into Sammar's background – he dislikes the label 'Islamic expert' (5) and is able, at times, to pass for a native, instead of an 'Orientalist'. In addition, unlike the vast majority of his countrymen: 'he knew the letters of the Arabic alphabet, he had lived in her part of the world. Rae looked like he could easily pass for a Turk or a Persian. He was dark enough' (5). He can even pass for a native in Morocco where he could walk about 'as if disguised' and 'none suspected he was Scottish as long as he did not speak and let his pronunciation give him away' (6). Likewise, Sammar's North African background is qualified by the fact that she had been born in Scotland and her parents only went back to the Sudan when she was seven (4) and she is equally fluent in English as in Arabic.

All of this echoes Aboulela's own mixed cultural wares. She was born in Cairo in 1964 to an Egyptian mother and a Sudanese father. She grew up in Khartoum where, although her family was Muslim, she attended a Catholic school and the Khartoum American School, an education which must have given her insights into other cultures and beliefs. This educational background was quite common in Khartoum. She went on to attend the University of Khartoum where she graduated with a degree in Economics and then she moved on to the London School of Economics where she read for an MSc and an MPhil in Statistics (Aboulela, 2000: 15). In other words, although her first language is Arabic, the language of her education,

---

[1] Page references to quotations in this chapter, unless indicated otherwise, are to *The Translator* (Edinburgh: Polygon, 1999).

of reading and writing, is English. She lived for some time with her family in Aberdeen, Scotland, where *The Translator*, her first novel, is partly set.

In the introduction, I referred to V.S. Naipaul's comment that 'the English language was mine; the tradition was not' (Bhabha, 1984: 95), a comment that has great relevance to a woman migrant writer such as Aboulela. I discussed how this absence of tradition could be understood in terms of Pierre Bourdieu's concept of 'cultural capital' where the deepest and unspoken cultural metaphors, symbols and meanings are imbibed in childhood – in schools and families (Bourdieu, 1984: 13). Migrant writers, steeped in their own, albeit hybrid, culture's ways of speaking and being, discover that their capital is only partly exchangeable for local currency when they find themselves in Europe or North America. This is what ensures that the migrant may mutate into the parvenu, but struggles to become a citizen. This is the context in which we understand the migrant's bewildered absence of subtle competence and confidence, of style and symbolic capital, that Leila Aboulela pinpoints when her protagonist, Sammar, walks the streets of the city, which are full of 'surprise':

> *Surprise was part of the city, the granite buildings, the buses that went down the narrowest of roads.* There were shades of surprise: surprise-sneer, surprise-embarrassed, surprise-bemused, surprise-disapproving. She had to be silent. Use her teeth and lips to keep silent. (40, my emphasis)

This queasy 'surprise' is the raised eyebrow of the citizen, who gives the stranger to understand that her behaviour is not quite appropriate. This surprise seeps into the material objects surrounding her – 'the granite buildings' and even the buses. It comes in shades and versions, which are recited in the rhythm of the language, like a demonic metonymic mantra with its 'surprise-sneer, surprise-embarrassed, surprise-bemused, surprise-disapproving' (40). In the face of all of this perplexing 'surprise', which is really something else, for which she does not have the word, all this unspoken Othering, ensures that Sammar loses her capacity for speech and has to grit her teeth to ensure that she is not tempted to speak. No translation is possible when the traveller has lost her capacity for speech.

Failed translation:
the body in pain & 'God is out playing golf'

Sammar has to find a way to familiarise and domesticate the buildings, the buses and the citizens into the concrete daily realities of her life in her new country. At first, she is unable to effect this translation between her worlds in Africa and in Britain, her English and her Arabic, her Muslim sensibility in a Christian world. This inability not only silences her, it crushes her identity, diminishes her being and renders her senseless with physical, bodily pain. This echoes with the Arabic Sudanese novel, Tayeb Salih's *Season of Migration to the North* (1969), to which I will return in the conclusion. While she does not write in Arabic as Salih does, Aboulela enacts the effort of migra-

tion by carving out an English that absorbs traces of Arabic and is infused
with Islam.

At the beginning of the novel, the pain Sammar is experiencing is overtly
the result of mourning for her dead husband, who had been killed in a car
accident, but even more deeply, we see the physical agony written onto her
body is the result of her attempts to negotiate between her worlds, which are
Khartoum and Aberdeen, a Muslim way of seeing the world and the secular
worldview all around her. The novel works hard to describe the body in pain,
something which, as Elaine Scarry (1985) has warned us, is notoriously difficult to represent. It is depicted here in terms of its shape, size, texture and its
being 'stapled' onto her – her stomach, shoulder, forehead. It is shaped like a
diamond full of liquid like oil (4). Her invisible mark of pain and mourning,
which is hidden from Rae, is 'like her hair and the skin on her arms, it could
only be imagined' (4). This pain is described in terms of Muslim codes and
is hidden, as is her hair by her headscarf, the *hijab*, as part of the framework
of Islam in this novel. When these different universes are un-reconciled and
un-translated from one to the other, Sammar's body is in pain.

For example, Sammar's doubts about whether Rae would agree to convert
to Islam, which would be the only basis on which she could have a committed relationship with him, she experiences as a 'hallucination', which results
in excruciating pain:

> She could hardly open her eyes to put the key in the lock, light was a source of suffering.
> And a headache, pain greater than childbirth. ... The silence, the absence of pain would
> not come ... She thought she must have had something between a migraine and a fit. (20)

This visceral agony, 'speaks' the gulf between un-translated worlds. Sammar
uses Christmas for fasting, 'making up for days missed in Ramadan' (28)
which separates her from Rae, whom she pictures eating turkey in Edinburgh
with his family. She realizes, sadly, that 'they lived in worlds divided by
simple facts' (29) or by simple material and ritual oppositions – Christmas
versus Ramadan, a turkey feast versus fasting. Much later in the novel, after
she has left Rae and Aberdeen and is living in Khartoum, Sammar has the
worst, most painful, dream of all:

> She was as short as a child in a room full of adults and smoke. She was in this room to
> look for him [Rae] and she was standing near a table that was large and high. On tiptoe
> she saw that the table was green, a solid rectangular green with no cutlery, no food or
> drinks. She reached with her hand and it was as if the table was a shallow box lined
> with green rough wool. ... The room was choked with people bigger than her, older than
> her. ... and, like in the other dreams, Rae came towards her and then brushed past her,
> distracted, unaware of her because she was too young and too short for him. (151–2)

This is a nightmare place, where the reduced, infantilised, miniaturised
woman has no subjectivity, voice or presence. It is Lewis Carroll's world
where the object of desire is elusive. Nothing is where it should be and she is
too short and too young. The table, emptied of food, metamorphoses as she
reaches out for it, echoing with Bandele's Wonderland, where in nightmare

moments, universes do not intersect or communicate or translate between each other. Rae does not even see her and again this dream takes its toll on her body and she is virtually unable to function for the whole of the next day when she is weak and tired and forgetful: 'only a dream and it could induce nausea in her, a dry soreness behind her eyes' (152). The crisis of the lack of communication/translation between Sammar and Rae is written on her body, through the dreams and their corporeal consequences. In other words, Sammar's regression to being a child, her lack of voice, relate to misunder-standings and mis-translations. Just thinking about the possibility that Rae will not convert is felt viscerally: 'the light in her head, blurred soapy vision. A migraine like the one she had when she and Yasmin had visited him at home' (104).

When Sammar is about to leave Aberdeen to return to Khartoum and has to say goodbye to Rae, with whom no agreement has been reached about the future, she is literally unable to translate. She is sucked into the vertigo of the computer's screen saver and through its recognisable, material reality, into the abyss:

> Windows in red and blue flew towards her. They got bigger and clearer as they came close to the surface of the computer screen and then passed away. *She had stopped changing Arabic into English*, stopped typing; and the words had flickered and disappeared into the blackness from where the flying windows now came. From infinity, specks at first and then vibrant checks and greens. (99, my emphasis)

The computer is metamorphosed from a mechanism to facilitate translation to a machine, which potentially induces a migraine with its chaotic specks of sick colour. When the relationship between Rae and Sammar reaches rock bottom, Sammar profoundly misinterprets Rae's English. He begs her to be patient and professes his great 'empathy' for her – a compliment, which she fatally mis-translates:

> She did not understand the meaning of the word 'empathy'. At times he did say words she could not understand, words she would ask him to explain. Sixties' scene, Celtic, chock-a-block. But now she did not ask him the meaning of 'empathy'. Today she could not ask. It sounded like 'sympathy', and, she thought, he feels sorry for me. To him I must have always looked helpless and forlorn. (115)

She has lost her ability to speak, to ask, to translate and she returns to Khartoum with a searing rift between them. The lack of common ground could be summed up by Rae's comment that in the secular West, 'God is out playing golf' (37). For him, this is a flippant metaphor, which describes the hedonism of Western culture, a hedonism, which amounts to a new religion. Sammar, however, takes words seriously and literally and there is genuine puzzle-ment on her part, which he, incorrectly, finds amusing: '"But why golf?" she asked. "Why *specifically* golf?" And he laughed for the first time that day' (37, my emphasis). For Sammar golf is concrete and specific and she cannot follow the idiomatic and iconoclastic inflections in Rae's use of words.

Another example of a failed translation, of incomprehension across worlds,

which Sammar experiences through the agonised body, occurs when she
hears the news from one of his students, Diane, that Rae is ill in hospital. In
Sammar's culture there are careful rituals around giving bad news, rituals
about which, Diane is, of course, ignorant. It is important to give quite a long
extract, in order to illustrate Aboulela's language and purpose in the novel:

> Sammar stared at the carpet ... If Diane had not said 'that's a fine start to his New Year',
> had not filled the room with the smell of cheese and onions, perhaps then it would
> not hurt so much or there would not be anger mixed with the hurt. She wanted to say,
> 'You have no manners, you are rude. When someone is taken ill, when there is bad
> news, there are certain things that must be said, a sympathetic word, a good wish for
> them. When that person is someone older than you, your professor, someone who helps
> you, then you should be doubly respectful. Not so callous, you are not a child to be
> so callous.' She pressed her teeth together. 'Don't speak,' she told herself, 'you are not
> allowed to speak like that.' She felt the blood gushing to her nose as if she was about to
> have a nose-bleed. She wanted it, the soft pluck noise, the sticky blood released from
> her nose. (68)

This excerpt is exemplary of Aboulela's style and also her message. It is layered with material, bodily chains and connections. The cultural difference
between the two women is underlined by what Sammar, wrongly, translates
into Diane's rudeness, which is simply her Scottish style. Without the proper
rituals of comfort from Diane, Sammar experiences rage and frustration painfully, once more, on her body, in quite dramatic terms of imagined blood
gushing from her nose. This blood is linked to her silence, her lack of voice.
Sammar will only regain her ability to translate if Aboulela finds for her a
language, in which material, daily realities, her body and words, and especially the word of Allah, are in harmony. The style that Sammar would have
appreciated is the Muslim comforting phrase that is evoked at such a time
and which provides words as bulwarks against life's hurts. These are Arabic
words, linked to the will of God, and they tide one over the moment of hearing shocking news. In other words, the verses from the Koran are metonymic
mantras to protect and shield, by repetition:

> [She] began to say silently, *All praise belongs to Allah, Lord of all the worlds, the
> Compassionate, the Merciful* ... and the certainty of the words brought unexpected
> tears, something deeper than happiness, all the splinters inside her coming together.
> (66, italics in original)

The echoed and familiar words comfort, not by way of deep meaning, but
through ritual and repetition. Sammar reminds herself that Allah dictates
everything that happens to her: 'to think otherwise was to slip down, to feel
the world narrowing, dreary and tight' (65). Without these weighty words,
Sammar slips down the hole into the terrors of the Wonderland hallucinations, which are felt on her body as fits or migraine headaches. The junk food
that Diane consumes links to a few pages earlier where we see that she is
always surrounded 'by her usual accessories of pens, Diet Coke, Yorkie bars,
a *ham* and pickle sandwich' (63, my emphasis). Their total cultural separation is signified by the ham, the bad food and the way in which these mun-

dane things contrast with Sammar's lovingly prepared, home made spicy soup, to which we will come in a moment.

Islam & the language of material culture & daily life

The language that writers such as Aboulela are crafting has to be malleable in its function of depicting multiple cultures, experiences and spiritualities. This involves capturing the rich detail of daily life for travellers like Sammar, who walk about in the strange city, here Aberdeen, whose buildings leer at them and whose supermarkets contain alien foods; it is a language designed to recover, to remember, daily life far away in another climate and landscape. Aboulela will enable Sammar to confront the innocent, vicious surprise of the citizens and their hidden metaphors and meanings, by way of realities that may be portrayed through the solidness of material culture and the straightforwardness of the literal.

For example, when Sammar first becomes attracted to Rae, the possibility of reconciling their worlds results in a wonderful day-dream, unlike the migraine inducing episodes. The dream is entirely grounded in the concrete and the everyday realities of her worlds, which are the opposite of the variations of surprise that she experiences in Aberdeen. She appears to step 'into a hallucination in which the world had swung around. Home had come here' (19):

> She saw the sky cloudless with too many stars, imagined the night warm, warmer than indoors. She smelled dust and heard the barking of stray dogs among the street's rubble and pot-holes. A bicycle bell tinkled, frogs croaked, the *muezzin* coughed into the microphone and began the *azan* for the *Isha* prayer. But this was Scotland. (19)

The smells, sounds and sights are of warm nights in Khartoum, of rubble and bicycle bells, pot-holes and barking dogs, which are transposed to Scotland. New subjectivities in strange places are forged in the realms of the concreteness of material daily realties, a site where women may find refuge from the gaze of the Symbolic Law of the Father. What we may encounter on those warm nights full of sights and sounds is what Judith Butler describes in her *Bodies that Matter* as 'not the materiality of sex, but the sex of materiality' (1993: 49). The sex of materiality, or rather, the gender of materiality, is the socially ascribed function of objects in making a safe world in which post-colonial women may find their voices.

The sex of materiality is reminiscent of Virginia Woolf's writing of Mrs Dalloway, who attends to the flowers herself (1964a [1925]: 5), and her Mrs Ramsay, who cooks an elaborate *boeuf en daube* in *To the Lighthouse*, (1964b [1927]: 92). These women and their domestic rituals are double-edged. The cooking and flower arranging are potentially oppressive, but also, and this is the key point, embody the possibility of accruing cultural capital for the parvenu, struggling to become a citizen.

A fine example of this would be the soup that Sammar lovingly prepares for Rae, to help him recuperate from his attack of asthma. This happens quite

early on in their relationship, when they are grappling to understand each
other, past the obstacles of their differences. The thick description of the
cooking of the soup has to be read as a code for the liberating possibility of
cultural translation through material culture:

> She made soup for him. She cut up courgettes, celery and onions. Her feelings were in
> the soup. The froth that rose to the surface of the water when she boiled the chicken, the
> softened, shapeless tomatoes. Pasta shaped into the smallest stars. Spice that she had to
> search for, the name unknown in English, not in any of the Arabic-English dictionaries
> that she had. *Habbahan, habbahan*. She must walk around the supermarket, frantically
> searching for something she could not ask about, and she was a translator, she should
> know. *Habbahan*. Without it, the soup would not taste right, would not be complete. At
> last, she found the *habbahan*. It existed, it had a name: whole green cardamom. (86)

The soup is an everyday item of life, apparently trivial, but of immense
importance. Its significance lies in its potential to enable Sammar to translate her feelings for Rae into material reality; it also enables her to translate
from Sudanese into English in the supermarket as she searches for the exact
ingredients, for the cardamom; it provokes her into searching for the right
word. The Arabic word, the metonymic gap, is repeated four times in this
short quotation – '*habbahan*' – a gap, which is then filled by finding the
right word, the exact translation. We see the imperativeness of the translation, given that only with the language for it, does the item exist: 'it existed,
it had a name'. By finding the English word for the key spice, by celebrating
the simple ingredients, the 'courgettes, celery and onions', and by finding
the receptacle for the feelings, Sammar begins herself to exist, having been
bodily frozen by the grief of mourning for her dead husband and the freezing
Scottish climate.

In this sense, the soup is quite classically a 'boundary' or translation object,
as defined by Bowker and Star and described in the introduction (1999: 297).
These are objects, which allow for 'naturalization' between different cultures
(297). The strangeness of tastes, ingredients and cooking styles, so critical in
everyday cultural practices, are domesticated. In other words, making the
soup with the recipe of home, but purchased in a Scottish supermarket where
the ingredients carry English names, naturalises the cultural dislocation of
living in a foreign place and enables communication with Rae, a Scottish
man, to be developed. Laura Marks points to the particular role of food in
intercultural films and videos. She refers specifically to 'African diasporic
communities', which consolidate themselves 'through memories of smell
and taste and rituals of cooking' (2000: 110). She emphasises the bodily,
material investment in taste, smell and touch that comes with intercultural
transformations. We will see the importance of perfume in this chapter or
of a smelly television in Chapter Five. Food recurs in Sammar's dreams and
hallucinations and figures prominently in her attempts at juggling different
cultures, world-views and customs.

More broadly, the lovingly detailed portrayal of the preparation of the
soup, along with the depiction of croaking frogs or the potholes in the street,
enable a new, concrete language to emerge. The novel bulges with metonyms

– a kettle, glowing coals, a bicycle lamp, a cat and smells of every kind, good and bad. Wool, socks, cushion, floorboards. There is repeated reference to body creams – glycerine, Vaseline, imported Nivea and soap. When Sammar thinks about Rae's daughter and about being good to her, this means buying her 'soap that smelt of raspberries' and ribbons for her hair (106). This soap contrasts with the bad smell of the soap in airport toilets, hostile transitory places redolent of the sterility of modern technology (118). There are Miranda bottles and 7Up and Coke and in Sammar's aunt's house constant boiling water for tea, special trays for guests, 'an elegant sugar bowl' (123). Sammar's brother's computer and printer are described in detail, given how precious they are. In fact 'everything was precious in Khartoum, even ink and paper, because it was all imported, so hard to replace' (140). Aboulela ponders the workings of the toilet in Sammar's brother's flat in Khartoum. It is at the mercy of power failures, given that the pump that lifts the water to his floor is electrical. The old toilet handle has to be yanked a few times and Sammar's niece is embarrassed and anxious until 'it finally flushed' (136). There was only one go, however, as the power had failed and later, when it comes on again, it brings with it the relief of 'the loud television, the purr of the air cooler, and from the bathroom [Sammar] could hear the toilet filling up with water' (14). This is part of daily life in Khartoum and capturing its vicissitudes contributes to forging new languages and identities.

All of this demonstrates the profound imbrication between the everyday of buses, buildings and bricks and deeper meanings, symbols and subjectivity, which is why Slavoj Žižek 'incorporates the everyday within his work' and includes in his deliberations both 'toilets and Tarantino' (Myers, 2003: 2). Solid objects, like toilets and computer screens translate, or fail to communicate, the contrasting cultures and material of different worlds. When Sammar is distant from Rae, both physically and spiritually, then these everyday realities do not translate their lives to each other.

And so, these solid objects, like soup, like soap, with their jingles, their happenstance and their echoing metonymies, acquire coded meaning. According to Spivak, women migrant writers, like Djebar (and I would add Aboulela) are world travellers, upwardly mobile and relatively empowered. Yet even they are grappling 'with various structures inherited from colonialism' and are 'necessarily *fighting to write the body* in the normative, privative, rational abstractions of a uniform civil law' (Spivak, 1993: 30, my emphasis). Writing the body is key. However, quoting from Djebar, Spivak insists that 'the body "bereft of voice" is a stone' (30). What we see is how the stone, the body and the words, and especially the word of God, of Allah, combine in Aboulela to forge her voice, to produce women's writings as what Minh-ha has referred to in another context as 'linguistic flesh' (1989: 33). As emphasised in the introduction, this is not the old, tired, woman as instinct, as body, as pre-language, as non-rational. This is to construct a new theory of language and subjectivity in which the postcolonial woman can contest the tools that paralyse her creativity and forge new ones with which she is adept and competent. This is what Minh-ha means by female writing as forging theory out the 'politics of everyday life' in which the black woman as Other is contested through the language of the ordinary (44).

In other words, this thick description of daily realities renders words themselves as material objects, reminiscent of Bandele's *The Street*. Words, fashioned, examined, recited in prayer, evoked in defence of what is special and unique in the traveller's past, are concrete and weighty objects, given that they are the solid building blocks on which to construct bridges around different cultures. The basis of the promise of Sammar's relationship with Rae is that she had found words, had found her voice with him. He had broken the rules of her silence, rules again described in visceral, material terms: 'the rules broke and burst her head in little bright pieces' (40). He is different from the smug citizens and is not 'surprised' by who she is and what she says. This means that 'what was real was that she had been given permission to think and talk, and *he would not be surprised* by anything she said' (40, my emphasis). His lack of the annihilating surprise that she normally encounters from the solid citizens enables Sammar to begin to feel at home, as if she is learning the codes. This depends on words as translation between worlds. When Rae says he feels safe with her, she 'picked up the word "safe" and put it aside to peel it later and wonder what it meant' (45). And so Rae's words were 'words that went to her head became little jewels, coloured gems, precious stones to carry around' (49). Words physically join, but also potentially separate Rae and Sammar. Eventually, when things have turned sour between them, 'she must pull his words out of her head like seaweed and throw them away' (144). What underlies their differences is the use to which words are put, such as those Sammar recites from the Qur'an, not as signifiers or symbols, but as we saw, as rhythmic, calming and comforting life supports. This contrasts with Rae's dismissal of the 'sacred' stories of his childhood – the Bible and other such fairy tales:

> 'When I was young,' he told her, 'there were books that did not impress me much. Picture books of Angels with blue eyes and wings, naive animals in pairs boarding a ship, too many fluffy clouds.'
>
> When she was young there were the words of the Qur'an, no pictures of Angels. Words to learn by heart and recite in treacherous streets where rabid dogs barked too close. 'Say: I take refuge in the Lord of daybreak ... ', 'Say: I take refuge in the Lord of humans ... ' And at night too, inside the terrifying dreams of childhood, she had said the verses to push away what was clinging and cruel. (90–1, emphasis in original)

This is the reason that the hallucinations that are most joyful are when the translation between worlds are successful, in terms of reinforcing Sammar's Muslim spirituality. For example, Sammar experiences such a harmonious hallucination when she succeeds in finding a translation of 'the Qudsi Hadiths' for Rae (36). While she is engaged in describing/translating this particular Hadith:

> she climbed the stairs into a hallucination in which the world had swung around. Home and the past had come here and balanced just for her. The stairs in a warm yellow light and sounds of a party, people talking and someone laughed. She was inside the laughter, wearing something new, carrying a tray, mindful of the children who swirled and dived around her knees. She offered glasses of something that was dark and sweet, and when

someone refused, coaxed them until they changed their minds. Someone called her name, she had to hurry, look over her shoulder, locate the voice, shout back, I'm coming now. (36, my emphases)

This is an entirely different hallucination from the nightmare visions. Here she is no longer a child; she is an adult, a nurturer, someone fully in the know in the conversation. Like the healing soup, here she is empowered to offer nourishment – something dark and sweet. She gets the jokes and is 'inside the laughter'. She is named, called, has the voice to answer and is happy, bathes in the light of the balance between home and here, the past and the present. She is able not only to speak but to shout. The literal translation becomes a symbolic moment of communication across worlds, which is possible only through Islam. All the splinters inside Sammar's bruised body, the staples, the pain, are eradicated in the certainty invested in the words, which are those of her faith.

In an interview, Aboulela stated that she wants to communicate in her fiction not merely the intellectual knowledge of Islam, 'but also the psychology, state of mind and emotions of a person who has faith'. She is 'interested in going deep, not just looking at "Muslim" as a cultural or political identity but something close to the centre' (Aboulela, 2000: 2). And so, an echo throughout *The Translator*, whispering in the ear of an ambivalent, unready Rae, is the existence of another language and a different spiritual and knowledge base. What Aboulela is attempting to achieve in her fiction is what Tymoczko refers to in her metonymic approach to translation, as 'a discourse of both/and which recognizes varying hierarchies of privilege, overlapping and partially corresponding elements, coexisting values' (1999: 283). Signalling this coexistence are the metonymic gaps, which pepper the novel and which draw attention to themselves and alter the sound of its English. Arabic sayings, meanings, word plays and names are small solid signposts pointing us to another culture and set of meanings, always invested in the minutiae of daily life. Sammar remembers her early, loving relationship with her aunt, Mahasen, mother of her dead husband. She affectionately recalls her purple hair roller, resulting in a fringe peeping under her '*tobe*' (9). This is horribly transformed in Sammar's imagination as she imagines Mahasen running to the phone to receive the worst bad news in the world – the fatal accident of her son Tarig – 'a *tobe* flung over her nightdress, one roller perched at the top of her head' (9). In Khartoum, Sammar hears 'the sunset *azan*', which she had missed in Aberdeen, and which sends her 'to make *wudu*' with '*Allah akbar. Allah akbar ...*' (130) reverberating rhythmically in her head. The inclusion of these words, these metonymic gaps, be they Arabic or Yoruba, Igbo or Pidgin enable cultural differences of experience to be 'actually *installed* in the text in various ways' (Ashcroft, 2001: 75, his emphasis). What is distinctive here, however, is that the hair roller and the sunset are material embodiments of the mantra 'all praise belongs to Allah'.

Sammar is portrayed as nearly committing the error of false worship of solid objects, of material possessions unconnected to her faith, in her love for a new coat that she picked out for herself, in a style of which her aunt would not have approved, and in the bottle of magnificent perfume that Rae buys her as a gift. The coat is described in loving detail. She revels in how clean and unfaded it is. She builds a self-image upon the coat and 'in the shop windows, she saw her reflection, the coat's *henna*-red colour, the toggles instead of buttons' (57). The coat is corporeal, like skin, and she takes off her glove, the better to feel 'the fresh silkiness of the lining' (57). Gail Ching-Liang Low considers 'how clothes might affect the body schema' (1996: 227), become an extension of our body image and libido, such that 'changes of costume may bring changes of behaviour and attitudes' (227). These changes occur in Sammar's being and her attitude to her body and to Rae, as she celebrates her new coat. The coat may be new, but it translates from her past to her present in its *henna* redness, a colour used by Muslims in body decoration; it is in the same spirit of celebration of *Eid* that she remembers from childhood. It is sensuous, pleasing and integrates and balances the different communities and cultures that Sammar brokers. It also speaks of the growth of a new self-image, an independent identity that Sammar is wresting from her powerful, influential aunt in Khartoum, an aunt, who doubled up as mother-in-law when Tarig, Sammar's husband, was alive:

> When she bought the coat, she had a choice between different styles and colours. One coat which suited her when she tried it on, had golden buttons, their colour and cool touch a reminder of her aunt.... But Sammar did not buy the coat with the golden buttons though she knew her aunt would have preferred it and her aunt's taste in clothes had always been the ideal, the guidance. (60)

The coat enhances Sammar's ability to be seen and heard, and embodies the freedom and independence that Scotland is slowly affording her. The translation, the transformation, is only partially complete. Moving closer to the skin, and after the purchase of the coat, Sammar passes the cosmetics counter of the store, where the sales lady presses on her some lotions and creams and make-up. Here the defiance, confidence and determination, exhibited in the tearing off of price tags and stuffing away of the old coat, evaporate. While the sales lady is described as 'bright' and speaks confidently, Sammar half loses her voice and her speech is laced with the uncertainty of the dots on the page that Aboulela uses to represent her hesitance. Even when the sales lady compliments her on her 'lovely skin', Sammar can hardly reply – "Oh ... thank you," (60). Likewise in response to the question of whether she wears make-up: 'No ... I used to ...' (60).

Soon afterwards, however, Sammar is again strengthened by a bottle of perfume that Rae gives her as a gift: 'a bottle of perfume, oval shaped, with a stopper not an atomiser, liquid the colour of amber' (75). Like the coat, the perfume is described in loving detail: 'the scent was neither fresh nor spicy but heavy and sweet' (75). Rae tells Sammar that the man who sold it to him was French and had said that it had 'come from Heaven via Paris' (76). This phrase tickles Sammar's fancy and it is a refrain that is metonymically repeated in the novel, precisely in the mode of the Arabic protective mantras of Islam, rendering the perfume as a kind of translation object between Rae and Sammar, investing her with new sexuality, her body released from pain. This is emphasised by way of the searching gaze into the mirror, archetypal image for the female exploration of identity:

> Downstairs, in the hospital foyer there were mirrors along one wall. Her eyes were a little pink, but their lids were as if rimmed by kohl and there was colour on her lips and cheekbones *as if she was wearing make-up.* She carried in her handbag a small bottle, sold by a man in Edinburgh who told his customers that the perfume had come all the way from Heaven via Paris. (80, my emphasis)

The perfume insulates her against the cold strangeness of the Scottish climate and provides her with inspiration for her role as translator between cultures – the scent of it 'was heavy' and able to 'soften the edge of the cold' of a Scottish winter. It enables her to think about 'all the things she would translate for him'. She would be able to translate her world to him, a world that for all his knowledge, he did not know: 'he did not know about the stream of Kawthar, the Day of Promises, or what stops the heart from rusting' (105).

The coat and the perfume recur and become powerful, magical metonymic metaphors of Rae and her new identity. Critical for Aboulela, however, is that material objects should not be worshipped in their own right, which could turn them into toxic fetishes, but should be intermediaries to God. What this means is that in Aboulela's fiction, worlds are not parallel and equal, but the material has to be the means to finding the spiritual. Sammar explains to Rae that '*Asbab* are causes, intermediaries, so *shirk al-asbab* means the polytheism of intermediaries' which is to worship material things as if they are sacred, instead of being merely portals to reach God. For example, it is problematic to love Nature such as 'to elevate Nature which is only an intermediary and set it up as a kind of partner to God' (76). This returns us for a moment to Sammar's soup. Rae feels that the soup has revived him. However, this exchange between them heralds a quite ominous difference in perception, given that 'he said it was her soup, her soup was the catalyst that made him recover' and she insists, rather, that '"Allah is the one who heals." She wanted him to look beyond the causes to the First, the Real' (90). Sammar needs Rae to understand that the soup is part of Allah's bounty, which initially he does not understand.

Everyday objects are part of Aboulela's, and by extension, her protagonist's spiritual mosaic, that adds up to the First, to Allah. This is a Muslim variation on Garuba's animist materialism described in the introduction. Objects do not embody spirits in all their different manifestations. The material world, the soup, the coat and the perfume, open up pathways to finding Allah; they are not symbolic of Allah, nor are they in a relationship of equality with the spiritual world. But they do provide the possibility for Aboulela's religious passions to translate between different places, climates and landscapes. This is not a vision that Rae, at first, shares. Sammar had been tempted by the sensual coat, the fabulous perfume and the promise of Rae, but these will only be hers if he converts to Islam: 'the balance he admired. He would not understand it until he lived it' (105). The entire structure and substance of the novel pivots on this condition. This point is worth emphasising. She will only be able to translate these worlds for him through the energy of her released sexuality if he lives the spiritual balance that accepting Islam would provide for him. When Rae refuses to convert to Islam, she leaves him, returns to Khartoum lugging these objects – the coat, the perfume – in her luggage. They are turned to stone and instead of being translation objects they are locked away in a miserable space, where dried staples such as rice and lentils are stored in sacks:

> The perfume he had given was in another room locked in a suitcase with all that she didn't need: wool and tights, her duffle coat. All the clothes he had seen her in, locked away in the storeroom with sacks of lentils and rice. (159)

The coat and the perfume appear to be turning toxic; Marks comments that 'people who are moving between cultures find that their luggage gets heavier and heavier. Their familiar objects are fossilizing' (2000: 91). The mammoth task for the migrant is 'to excavate those layers of impossible translation' (91).

The key unlocking the store, unpacking the suitcase and liberating Sammar from becoming an idolatress, a worshipper of perfume and a coat, is that she realises that she had to pray that Rae become a Muslim for his own sake and not for hers. This prayer is eventually answered and a letter arrives with the news that Rae has converted. The letter is from Fareed, a Muslim colleague of Rae's, who acts as their intermediary or interpreter, putting those precious objects back in their assigned place. She is, therefore, now able to go to the store room with its smells of dust and rice and 'the large sacks of lentils and beans' and to unpack the suitcase containing the wonderful coat and other winter clothes, and to celebrate these objects without being sinful:

> She unzipped the suitcase and looked at her winter clothes. She unfolded wool and out came the smell of winter and European clouds. She put on her gloves and then took them off, saw her tights, for a year she hadn't worn tights. Her henna-coloured duffle coat, its silky lining. She would wear it again when she went back to Aberdeen, the toggles instead of buttons. (173)

The recurrent image of the coat makes it grow into a blended metonymy as an extension of a part of her body and potentially as a new metaphor of her ability to translate between her cultures. The coat, with its silky lining, is beautiful enough for Ramadan, but warm for a British climate. The coat brings back the perfume, the body smell, the gift from Rae, aromas which overtake 'the smell of dried beans and rice' (174). Gloves, tights, scarf and coat, the smells of Aberdeen and the dust and aromas of Khartoum, with its beans and lentils, are all incorporated into the sensorium of Aboulela's multiple experiences and universes. Allah may dictate everything, but for Sammar, the translator, who travels back to Aberdeen with Rae, Islam has to be able to migrate and to mutate, taking as its baggage its weighty words, mantras and spirituality.

Postcolonial travelling writers, like Aboulela, embrace their cosmopolitanism and find a language that culturally syncretizes their experiences in Europe and in Africa. Significantly, '*here in Scotland* [Sammar] was learning more about her own religion, *the world was one cohesive place*' (96, my emphases). Scotland contributes to her ability to interpret, to translate as she comes up with a positive, instead of a demonic, meaning of *jihad* as opposing a tyrant leader. Rae asks Sammar: "What things haven't you come across before?" (96). They have the following conversation:

> 'One *hadith* that says, "The best *jihad* is when a person speaks the truth before a tyrant ruler." It is not often quoted and we never did it at school. I would have remembered it.'
>
> 'With the kind of dictatorships with which most Muslim countries are ruled,' he said, 'it is unlikely that such a *hadith* would make its way into the school curriculum.'
>
> 'But we should know ...' (96)

What Sammar learns is that the words of the Qur'an may be weightier than those of the Hadith because the Qur'an 'is Allah's wording' (37), but there is, nonetheless, more opportunity for intervention within the words of the Hadith. This is so because they 'are not forbidden to be touched or read by one who is in a state of ritual impurity' (37). This is a veiled reference to their potential for interpretation by women. George Lang emphasises this point in relation to the possibility of women as interpreters/translators within Islam. He draws attention to the Islamic concept of *ijtihad* as 'free interpretation' (1996: 2) and to the important role of the interpreter or *mujtahid*. He does so in relation to the writer, Assia Djebar, but with relevance to Aboulela as well. In other words, only in Scotland could this other interpretation have come to light enabling Sammar to reinterpret the controversial *jihad* part of her religion. What this means is that translation occurs in both directions simultaneously, as Scotland mediates Sammar's religion and simultaneously Scotsmen, like Rae, are converted to a new spirituality.

At last, by the end of the novel, then, hallucination and reality, the material and the spiritual are harmonised as Rae and Sammar play a game in which they give each other thoughts. These thoughts translate into '*tangible gifts*' (184). The thoughts, which become tangible, from Rae to Sammar are three pieces of cloth: '*I unfolded silk the colour of deserts, mahogany wool, white cotton from a cloud*' (184). Rae receives from Sammar '*the smoothest bowl, inside it a milky liquid, the scent of musk*' (184). This vision is full of solid objects, reminiscent of those that have populated the novel. The coat, the perfume, wool, cotton and silk, are all intermediaries. The translation between Sammar's and Rae's languages and feelings is so complete as to take place as thoughts and transform into the accoutrements of daily life.

This happy ending may seem too simplistic, but it signifies Aboulela's attempt to provide an antidote to the enormous pessimism surrounding the possibility of women finding a way into language and Subjectivity, against the weight of neo-colonial and patriarchal power. What she is also trying to say is that this ending is, for her, the only possible one for a love story that does not end badly, as it does in her short story, 'The Museum' to which I will turn next. This is what she means in her interview when she insists that 'I also want to write fiction that reflects Islamic logic; fictional worlds where cause and effect are governed by Muslim rather than non-Muslim rationale' (2000: 2).

At the same time, there is a tension in Aboulela's own terms, between the capacity for open interpretation and the closure of her Muslim world, which ensures that all things, both animate and inanimate, are subordinate to her faith. Ian Baucom describes Rushdie's suggestion that Islam becomes a pillar for migrating postcolonials, as it provides metaphors 'of the one: belonging to the one, confessing the one, and residing in the one' (1999: 201). In other words, 'Rushdie understands the promise of Islamic residence that Mahound makes to the people of Jahilia – the promise of inhabiting a settled and unitary space that is as much a historical locale as it is a space in the sacred imaginary – to be a promise in which the postcolonial migrant, whether Muslim or not, wishes to believe' (201). While the material world of Aboulela remains firmly grounded in daily realities, it is true that it may only do so if that world is strictly bounded by Muslim observance. This may have given rise to the somewhat too contrived and harmonious ending of the novel, as Rae embraces Islam out of genuine belief and enables the lovers to enjoy a seamless happy ending. This contrasts with Aboulela's Caine Prize winning story, 'The Museum', taken from her collection *Coloured Lights*. By looking at this story and two others from the collection – 'Souvenirs' and the title story, 'Coloured Lights' – we may deepen our understanding of the varied nature of the complex relationship between solid objects, language and faith in Aboulela's fiction.

From boundary objects to the museum's toxic displays

Initially, 'The Museum' appears to be a love story between Shadia and Bryan in the mould of that between Sammar and Rae of *The Translator*. Shadia is from Khartoum and is in Aberdeen struggling to cope with her MSc in Statistics. She desperately needs the assistance of a local boy, Bryan, but 'at first Shadia was afraid to ask him for his notes' (99).[2] It is not that Bryan is cleverer than Shadia, but he is a local, who knows the ropes, which is part of the reason that he is excelling academically and Shadia is not. The problem is that the course required 'a certain background' (100), which Shadia and her fellow Third World students lack: 'he knows all the lecturers, he knows the system' (101). He is a citizen, well versed in the cultural codes and symbolic meanings, which parvenus, like Shadia, lack. His notes enable her to translate herself into the Scottish system and to become empowered. They 'were the knowledge she needed, the gaps' (106).

The knowledge that he communicates by loaning Shadia his notes is intimate given that they provide the key to her ability to become a translated person in Scotland. Having 'spent hours and days with his handwriting, she knew him in some way' (106). This is why his writing appears in her dreams and becomes sensual as Shadia herself metamorphoses into the squiggles of

---

2   Page references to quotations in this chapter, unless indicated otherwise, are to *Coloured Lights* (Edinburgh: Polygon, 2001).

his writing that signify the profound possibilities of translation between the two of them: 'when she slept she became epsilon and gamma and she became a variable making her way through discrete space from state i to state j' (106).

By the end of the story, however, and by contrast with the ending of *The Translator*, the scale has turned against the growth of a relationship between them. Had things worked out, Shadia thinks, 'she would have patiently taught him another language, letters curved like the epsilon and gamma he knew from mathematics' (119). Note the sadness of impossibility, of the conditional tense that indicates that it will not happen. Why not? The translation does not take place between Bryan and Shadia because of the ritual of estrangement enacted during their visit to a museum of African colonial exhibits. These artefacts, instead of being portals between their cultures, like the perfume or the coat of *The Translator*, poison the space between them and make communication impossible. They are the volatile objects, which Laura Marks defined as radioactive and toxic in an intercultural context (2000: 110). For example, 'the first thing they saw' at the exhibit was

> a Scottish man from Victorian times. He sat on a chair surrounded with possessions from Africa, over-flowing trunks, an ancient map strewn on the floor of the glass cabinet.... A hero who had gone away and come back *laden*, ready to report. (114–15, my emphasis)

The emphasis is on the artefacts, the material objects with which the explorer had come back laden, trunks over-flowing with African stuff. Shadia is deeply offended by what she sees, unambiguously, as the plunder of the treasures of Africa. She is bitterly ironic about the concealment of this theft and the portrayal of the perpetrator as a hero. This is foregrounded by the italicised caption, which proudly describes how those who served the empire '*often returned home with tangible reminders of their experiences*' (115). The ironic narrator's voice mingles with the critical gaze of Shadia:

> The tangible reminders were there to see, preserved in spite of the years. Her eyes skimmed over the disconnected objects out of place and time. Iron and copper, little statues. Nothing was of her, nothing belonged to her life at home, what she missed. Here was Europe's vision, the clichés about Africa: cold and old. (115)

Shadia is critical of these explorers, who 'knew what to take to Africa: Christianity, commerce, civilization. They knew what they wanted to bring back; cotton watered by the Blue Nile, the Zambezi river' (116). She insists that they went simply 'to benefit themselves' (117); they wanted the raw materials, the cotton and also the art. She is disappointed, given that she had come looking for 'something to appease her homesickness' (116), but had found instead that 'the messages were not for her, not for anyone like her' (116). Also on display is a letter from West Africa, dated 1762, from an 'employee trading European goods for African curiosities' (116). The employee expresses incomprehension at the refusal of the natives to bring their treasured possessions for European trade (read 'plunder') and '*even ... an interpreter*' (116, italics in original) could not explain to them what was required.

This lack of translation is ominous in Aboulela and continues into the present where even an interpreter cannot span the gulf between Shadia and Bryan. Shadia feels too keenly the absence of people like herself in this account of history: 'If she could enter the cabinet, she would not make a good exhibit. She wasn't right, she was too modern, too full of mathematics' (116). The lack of comprehension between herself and Bryan is sealed when he becomes the imperialist in her view. He wants adventure, to escape, 'the imperialists who had humiliated her history were heroes in his eyes' (117).

Aboulela's depiction of the museum visit, as a rite of alienation that is historically determined, is precisely what Carol Duncan's paper entitled 'Art Museums and the Ritual of Citizenship' picks up on, with regard to museums in general. She describes the museum as a disguised form of secular, as opposed to religious, ritual (1991: 91). What museums are is 'powerful identity-defining machines' (101). The identities that they define and strengthen are usually 'the interests and self-image of certain powers within the community' (92). That is to say, museums have the power 'to define and rank people, to declare some as having a greater share than others in the community's common heritage – in its very identity' (102). The museum embodies the cultural capital, the symbolic value of shared citizenship that Pierre Bourdieu (1984) characterised as marking out the differences between classes and which Zygmunt Bauman (1997) understood as the mechanism for the exclusion of the postcolonial parvenu, as discussed in the introduction. The meaning of the objects that we see on display, or perhaps even more importantly, those which are absent, 'involves the much larger questions of who constitutes the community and who shall exercise the power to define its identity' (Duncan, 1991: 103). Aboulela's museum has defined Shadia as outside of the community of power, for all the new knowledge that her studies in Scotland, including Bryan's notes, afford her. That is why she is small in the museum and she is unable to translate for him:

> He didn't understand. Many things, years and landscapes, gulfs. If she was strong she would have explained and not tired of explaining. She would have patiently taught him another language, letters curved like the epsilon and gamma he knew from mathematics. She would have showed him that words could be read from right to left. If she was not small in the museum. (119)

This smallness, this voiceless regression, this being reduced by the dominant culture to invisibility, is Aboulela's worst nightmare. In *The Translator* it reduces Sammar in her painful migraine-inducing hallucination to a small, invisible child without language. And yet, Aboulela, who has lived in many places and experienced many cultures, finds subtle ways of contesting this polarity, even as the dominant story line reinforces it. On the one hand, there is the intricate webwork of blended metonymic metaphors around windows, shiny hard surfaces, display cases, glass, metal and guns, which recur throughout the story and reach a climax in the museum with its glass display cases, which say nothing of the reality of her world. She is the outsider, the parvenu, nose against the glass, looking in from the cold: 'she touched the glass of a cabinet showing papyrus rolls, copper pots. She pressed her forehead and nose against the cool glass' (116). There is nothing for her in Scotland, including Bryan.

But, on the other hand, in this complex, rich story of irony blended with empathy, where nothing is precisely as it seems in terms of cultural affinities and differences, the opposite is also true. She had wept over his notes until the paper becomes transparent (105) – like glass? Like a window? And 'his brain was a clear pane of glass where all the concepts were written out boldly and neatly' (107). A further example of the story's ambivalence about its own sad conclusion is the portrayal of Shadia's fiancé, Fareed. This man comes from her own cultural background, but he is depicted as a buffoon, a far less attractive person than Bryan. Fareed is overfed and greedy. He is caricatured through the solid objects, which metonymically become his presence in the story. These may not be the toxic museum relics of colonialism, but are not much better. They are the trappings of Capitalist materialism run rampant in the interests of a greedy neo-colonial ruling elite in Khartoum. There are his Mercedes, his 7Up franchise and the big house he is building for them, which requires gold bathroom fixtures (114). As alienating in their different way as the glass cabinets in the museum, are the glass bottles in Fareed's factory: 'glass bottles filling up with clear effervescent, the words 7Up written in English and Arabic' (114). The translation of 7Up is not difficult in the global world of desirable European goods, but we are left in little doubt that Shadia is selling her soul to Fareed in agreeing to marry him for his money. Fareed is 'not interested in her studies' (104), but only in the opportunity her residence in Scotland provides for her to obtain these gold sanitary ware fittings, unavailable in North Africa.

The last page may still have Bryan pronouncing her name wrongly, but this is Shadia's fault as 'she had not shown him how to say it properly' (119). And she does, finally, make a passionate, albeit somewhat futile attempt to explain it all to him, to be an interpreter, again through solid objects and material realities:

> 'They are telling you lies in this museum,' she said. 'Don't believe them. It's all wrong. It's not jungles and antelopes, it's people. We have things like computers and cars. We have 7Up in Africa and some people, a few people, have bathrooms with golden taps ... (119)

The 7Up bottle is looked at from more than one angle. It contests the stereotype of a pre-modern Africa steeped in tribal goods. For that matter, the gross bathroom fittings are also part of the interrogation of the clichés in representations of Africa. But, in relation to Fareed and Shadia's choices for her future, they are simultaneously worthless objects that make Fareed rich and make him and turn his family into complacent and unattractive people. Shadia is between a rock and a hard place. A great physical exhaustion, the equivalent of Sammar's migraine, is her dilemma written on her body, which prevents her from explaining all this properly, from finding a new language in order to interpret for Bryan and thereby to transform him, as we ultimately saw Sammar was able to do for Rae in the novel: 'it was a steep path she [Shadia] had no strength for' (119).

'The Museum' is searingly honest about the devastation wrought by impe-rialist history, about the power of attraction, which operates beneath the level of that history and about the hurdles to be overcome in relationships across the coloniser–colonised divide. Aboulela interprets this divide quite profoundly in terms of daily life and material objects, which either facilitate or block translation across that divide. We see these difficulties grow and develop in another story in the collection, where the interracial couple are now advanced in their marriage and have a child. 'Souvenirs', as the title suggests, is also structured around solid objects. The souvenir is a particular category of translation object. Whether migrants bring souvenirs from home, or collect them on their travels, souvenirs operate as conduits and portals between different places and histories. In this story, souvenirs take a particu-larly intriguing twist, given that Yassir, the protagonist, who is searching for souvenirs, is doing so ambiguously, partly as a tourist and partly as citizen. He is visiting his mother and sister in Khartoum and is taking souvenirs back to Aberdeen for his Scottish wife, Emma. These objects for which Yassir is searching, must translate his Sudanese world back to Emma, as metonymic chunks of the place her husband comes from. For Emma, as Yassir irritably puts it, the Sudan is a place, which is threatening and Other. She fears the health hazards of Africa: 'the sandfly, malaria ... Some rubbish like that' (23). Yassir is ashamed to admit this to his mother and his sister, how 'Emma wanted malleable pieces ... She desired frankincense from the Body Shop, tahina safe in a supermarket container' (23). She wanted to select palatable parts for the whole culture which she found scary; she desired a fake meto-nym in a supermarket can.

Part of the problem is Yassir's and Emma's cultural differences regarding material possessions in the first place. For example, 'what he considered luxuries, she considered necessities. Like the Bambi wallpaper in Samia's room' (15). The Bambi wallpaper, with its echoes of European stories about cute, tame animals, is not a translation object. It had to match the curtains and the pillowcase and all of these things are necessary to Emma because she had had them as a child. Yassir, who has to keep his response to himself and not speak, so as not to have an argument, thinks how far removed from the stuff of his own childhood all of this was (16).

The choice of objects to be brought back, therefore, assumes great impor-tance and Yassir and Emma discuss this in some detail before he leaves; what has to be found are objects that will carry the burden of facilitating transla-tion between their separate worlds:

'There must be something you can get,' Emma said. 'Things carved in wood, baskets ...'

'There's a shop which sells ivory things. Elephants made of ivory, and things like that.'
'No. Not ivory.'
'I could get you a handbag made of crocodile skin?'
'No, yuck.'
'Snake skin?'
'Stop it, I'm serious.'
'Ostrich feathers?'

'NO DEAD ANIMALS. Think of something else.'

'There's a bead market. Someone once told me about that. I don't know where it is though. I'll have to find out.'

'If you get me beads I can have them made here into a necklace.' (16–17)

Beneath the banter lie some serious cultural anomalies, given that Yassir may have to search for an unknown bead shop, clearly not any part of the reality of his previous life at home, in order to bring her something, supposedly, of himself. Finally, Emma suggests paintings or photographs to depict Khartoum. He buys the beads but shies away from photographs, which he finds problematic – like being a tourist in his own home – making him 'unable to click a camera at his house, his old school' (17). As Boym puts it, in describing what happens when the migrant returns home for a visit, 'the former country of origin turns into an exotic place represented through its arts and crafts usually admired by foreign tourists' (336). By the time Yassir eventually finds paintings, which appear to be just right, these objects are potentially invested with missions and codes, which puff them up beyond their material reality.

The only way these objects might fulfil their purpose in communicating between Yassir and Emma, is if they are the product of a hybrid Khartoum, one which has been transformed by colonial history, which had placed Yassir in Scotland. The paintings that might perform this task are the work of an Englishman, Ronan, who has been resident for many years in Khartoum, which has given him a genuine feel for the local light and landscape. His vision of Khartoum, however, is mediated by his English sensibility. This makes his paintings ideal as a mechanism for communicating a palatable version of Africa, and of Yassir, to Emma. Ronan is doubly able to be the mediator between them because, although he is now living in Khartoum, he knows Aberdeen well because his mother originally came from Elgin, which is nearby (27). The story takes seriously the importance of this two-way process of cultural mixture, given the genuine excellence of the artwork. The paintings depict 'village scenes, mud houses, one of children playing with a goat, one of a tree that had fallen into the river' (29). These are not the scenes of Yassir's growing up in Khartoum, and yet he feels that the purchase was a success and 'he had achieved what he came for' (29). Ronan's paintings have captured something true: 'they were clear and uncluttered, the colours light, giving an impression of sunlight' (29). They will translate Khartoum for Emma and become boundary objects. But they are not enough. While Yassir's overt quest is for Emma's objects, the sub-text, which is perhaps even more important, is what Yassir finds, in addition, for himself, to take back with him.

Yassir collects the minutiae of everyday material life as genuine metonyms of his past. What we have come to recognise in Aboulela's deceptively simple plots and stories, is the complex warp and weft against grain as she establishes scenarios and contests them simultaneously. The paintings may capture something of the light and space of Khartoum, enabling communication between Yassir and Emma through the good services of the English

artist as translator, but at the same time the story highlights just how different the couple's lives and needs actually are. The bulk of the story consists
of Yassir's journey through Khartoum with his sister. They are ostensibly
searching for the house of the artist, but the real quest is for Yassir to find
his own more meaningful relics to take back, relics that his wife would find
incomprehensible:

> Yassir drove on and gathered around him what he would take back with him, *the things
> he could not deliver.* Not the beads, not the paintings, but other things. Things devoid
> of the sense of their own worth. Manaal's silhouette against the rig's flare, against a
> sky dyed with *kerkadeh.* The scent of soap and shampoo in his car, a man picking his
> toenails, a page from a newspaper spread out as a mat. (30, my emphasis)

Their worth is in their ordinariness, the precious rich texture of everyday
life, which is lost if you do not live in a place. The metonymic gap of the
untranslated Arabic of how the sky is dyed with *kerkadeh* brings this home
to the reader. As always, there are the smells, the soap and shampoo and
even the man picking his toenails. The paintings are a compromise, which
has value. They are not entirely positive boundary objects, however, like
the benign coat with the toggles instead of buttons, or the perfume, bought
in Edinburgh, made in heaven via Paris of *The Translator.* Nor are they the
toxic displays behind the glass cabinets in the museum. They are the imperfect translations, the struggle for words that do not quite fit, but which must
suffice when languages are diverse and the lives they depict have been constituted by different religions, climates and cultures.

Finally, in her title story of the *Coloured Lights* collection, Aboulela once
again plays with the solid things of everyday life in order to explore the
complex web woven around the interface between her different cultures and
languages. This story, which is steeped in the pain of loss, suggests how
objects may successfully translate into other objects, which become their
equivalent in a different culture. These equivalent objects embed the traveller in her new home. In this story the first person protagonist is on a London
bus, looking at the Christmas sights. The objects she sees are portals, opening
up her memories of similar, but significantly not identical, objects back home
in Khartoum. They enable her to recall a family tragedy, which is otherwise
buried inside her. The bright lights she sees, which are happy and celebrating Christmas, part of a religion not her own, nonetheless echo the lights
in Khartoum which had been going to celebrate her brother's marriage but
instead electrocuted him: 'Festive December lights. Blue, red, green lights,
more elaborate than the crude strings of bulbs that we use in Khartoum to
decorate the wedding house' (3).

She is on a one-year contract with the BBC World Service to read the news
in Arabic and she is desperately homesick 'for the heat, the sweat and the
water of the Nile' (1). Even this feeling is difficult to describe, except via a
translation:

> the English word 'homesick' is a good one; we do not have exactly the same word in
> Arabic. In Arabic my state would have been described as 'yearning of the homeland' or

the 'sorrow of alienation' and there is also a truth in this. I was alienated from this place where darkness descended unnaturally at 4pm. (1)

She is on a double track – everyday solid objects in London are 'turnstiles' for their not quite equivalents in Khartoum, enabling her to recover her past, shrouded in grief:

In the shop windows dummies posed, aloof strangers in the frenzied life of Oxford Street. Wools, rich silks and satin dresses. 'Taha, shall I wear tonight the pink or the green?' I asked him on the morning of the wedding. (5)

The fine clothing in the window leads directly to her thoughts of other fancy outfits, like her choice of wedding apparel for her brother's marriage. Note the strange grammatical construction of the 'shall I wear tonight', which must be an Arabic inflection. And yet, despite the differences of language and religion, which are coded in the story in this way, 'Coloured Lights' is imbued with all the fervour of Aboulela's hopes that translations between cultures, embedded in everyday life and objects, are possible, which could be why this story provides the collection with its title. The story gives us equivalent objects, which serve similar spiritual purposes, albeit that they are radically different, arising as they do out of different places and customs. There is, for example, the *zeer*, a memorial to the dead Taha. This is the large clay pot full of water which her mother bought to refresh hot and thirsty passers-by. The twinned object is the park bench: 'In London, I came across the same idea, memorial benches placed in gardens and parks where people could rest' (8). The idea is the same, but the objects are radically different: 'My mother would never believe that anyone would voluntarily sit in the sun but then she had never seen cold, dark evenings like these' (8). The young woman on the London bus, translator into Arabic for the BBC, is the hope for the postcolonial migrant future. Her mother may not understand the purpose of the outdoors bench, but her daughter has experienced both the scalding sun of Khartoum and the freezing cold of London. The bench and the pot are the same and also radically different and the translation here does not compromise the difference.

Look who's talking?

Solid objects in Aboulela's fiction speak a coded and concrete language. She depicts material culture as fundamental to the texture of life and the loss suffered by those who have to negotiate between diverse identities, religions and tongues. The language that emerges in her fiction may be English but it is the English of migrant writers living in the West, an English, which, according to Chambers, is 'appropriated, taken apart, and then put back together with a new inflection, an unexpected accent, a further twist in the tale' (1994: 23).

Right near the end of *The Translator*, at the moment when Sammar receives the wonderful news that Rae has converted, she had been having a mental conversation with him, in which their understanding is perfect and described by way of a successful translation. She had seen the poster in the local video shop advertising the latest John Travolta movie, in which '*Look Who's Talking*', had become in Arabic '*Me and Mama and Travolta*' (170), which is, of course, the Arabic translated back into English. In this imaginary conversation, this nurturing hallucination, by contrast with the ones that induce pain in the body, becomes a shared joke, a deep understanding, beyond the surprise of insiders against outsiders. Rae laughs and suggests that the Arabic version is a much better title (170). What is undeniably the case is that Aboulela, through her protagonist Sammar, is announcing that it is, in fact, *she* who is talking, loudly, clearly and through translations back and forth between Arabic and English, and between Khartoum and Aberdeen.

The final lines of *The Translator* see Sammar's niece, Dalia, after some struggle, smoothly negotiating her bicycle between the cacti and bougainvillea, between the indigenous plants and those brought in by the coloniser. Dalia battles to lift up the bicycle, but eventually 'she succeeded and they watched her cycle between the pots of cacti and bougainvillea, wheels smooth on the tiles of the porch' (183). The landscape bears the marks of cultural transformation and there is the hope that a new generation will successfully translate between these worlds.

4 Possessions, Science & Power
Jamal Mahjoub's *The Carrier*

In *The Carrier*, Jamal Mahjoub examines the nature of scientific knowledge and technological discovery within the context of the power struggles of history. That is to say, the novel exposes the ways in which science, far from being objective, is implicated in the power politics relating to issues of wealth, trade and colonialism.

The novel works through two protagonists, who live in different historical periods. The first is Rashid al-Kenzy, who we first encounter in the early seventeenth century in Algiers. The second is the twentieth-century man, Hassan, who is a geologist. The connection between the two men will emerge on an archaeological dig, to which Hassan has been sent by the museum in Copenhagen to solve a mystery in a remote corner of the Danish peninsula, called Jutland. The remains of a body have been dug up, and along with them, a 'collection of odd items' (42)[1] including a brass case engraved in Arabic and which contains a device, whose purpose it is to enable the devout Muslim traveller to find the direction of Mecca in his prayers.

The body is not Rashid's, as we will find out, but the case is engraved with his name and a narrative thread throughout the novel is provided by Hassan's increasingly obsessive pondering over what could have happened in the past, with 'the apparent arrival of a visitor from the Middle East at the beginning of the seventeenth century' (251). We discover in the novel that this had come about when a greedy sea captain, in return for a rich reward, passed onto the rulers in Algiers a story he had heard of a wondrous invention, a Dutch optical device, which would ensure mastery over sea routes and trade riches to whichever nation owned it. At that time, Rashid was a prisoner of the qadi of Algiers, unjustly accused of a crime. The qadi realized that Rashid, a strangely scholarly man, would be the perfect agent to enable them to acquire this wonder. He is hauled out of his imprisonment and sent on the voyage in search of this grail 'to ensure that the matter is dealt with appropriately' (54).

Hassan is deeply frustrated by how his knowledge of Rashid remains partial, given the limited tools of investigation he has. For example, he surmises that 'by the time al-Kenzy arrived in Europe the telescope was becoming widespread. It would make little sense to come all this way for something like that, surely? Hassan dismissed the idea' (225). It was a mistake to do so. The knowledge of the past is partial. Accidents and unpredictable currents merge with the forces of history. The reader knows that Rashid was precisely sent on this mission, on a quest to find a telescope, but what happened was that he had been shipwrecked off the coast of Denmark before being able to accomplish it.

---

[1] Page references to quotations in this chapter, unless indicated otherwise, are to *The Carrier* (London: Phoenix House, 1998).

How could a mere abject former slave have been deemed worthy to be the carrier of this rare scientific wonder? What makes the qadi, in his discussion with the Dey of Algiers, so sure that Rashid is just the man who would be inspired by the idea of attaining such a technological invention? Rashid is an enigma: 'the dark hue of his skin suggests a man of lowly origins, a Slave even.' However, 'the refined manner in which he speaks the language of the Prophet tells us that he is, or once was, a man of some standing' (14). A slave scholar, Rashid is a liminal man, the in-between traveller so beloved of migrant postcolonial novelists in general, and of Mahjoub, whose own cultural wares are so mixed, in particular.

Rashid had indeed been born the son of a slave woman, but then, through a twist of fate, received the finest education of the time in the following way. His father was a merchant who owned his mother as his slave and who he had impregnated. Rashid was born on the same day as the merchant's wife gave birth to his legitimate son, Ismail. The slave son was as clever and sharp as his half brother was sluggish and slow. When the time came for schooling, the only way Ismail could cope 'under the rigorous demands of the madrasa' (32) would be if Rashid joined him there, not, of course, as brother and equal, but 'as his personal slave' (33) to assist him with his studies. This was how 'Rashid came to pass through the gates of the prestigious school which thus marked the start of the curious and convoluted path of his education' (33). This education, well above his station, renders him an in-between man. He is neither one of the ruling elite, but nor is he any longer one of the underclass. Mahjoub has him perched in the social interstices. His identity thus remained disjunctural and bizarre. He occupies that small dark space between his knowledge and the power that others have over him to dispossess him of his tenuous social standing as a learned man.

This interstitial site, where travellers metamorphose, is where objects translate between cultures. Mahjoub himself occupies a liminal position as a trained geologist and an Anglo-Sudanese writer who is compelled to interrogate the objectivity of 'scientific' evidence when considered within the history of Western Imperialism and racism. Mahjoub describes how his own aspirations as a geologist began:

> One day, while I was still a boy in the Sudan, a geologist turned up in a landrover. I was completely awe-struck by him. That decided me: I wanted to become a geologist when I grew up. It was a life that seemed to promise extraordinary adventures and discoveries. (Versi, 1993: 36)

Mahjoub, with his skills in the geological sciences, no doubt, found himself dissatisfied with the material landscape he was expected to investigate, devoid of history, power struggle and racial identities. This echoes with his protagonist, Hassan, a scientist, who is attempting to make sense of his world of the twentieth century. Mahjoub wears the mask of Hassan, a bewildered Asian geologist in Denmark, who is searching for more stratified, complex and multi-dimensional knowledge than his training had qualified him.

In other words, Mahjoub, in the best tradition of Bruno Latour's science studies, integrates questions of scientific knowledge into the latticework of all of life's multiple dimensions – political, personal, cultural, social and historical. Latour's book, *Pandora's Hope: Essays on the Reality of Science Studies*, is highly illuminating of Mahjoub's novel. Both Latour and Mahjoub, in their different genres, emphasise that science cannot be divorced from history and that knowledge is implicated in power and power is buttressed by scholarship. They both would reject what Latour calls the 'science warriors', who want science to be 'like an Idea floating in Heaven freed from the pollution of this base world' (108).

Latour offers us some concrete and useful tools of analysis through which we may examine Mahjoub's vision, which grounds sciences, like geology or archaeology, in the contaminated, messy world of politics and history. Latour defines his science studies in terms of five types of activities: 'instruments, colleagues, allies, public, and finally, what I will call *links* or *knots* so as to avoid the historical baggage that comes with the phrase "conceptual content"' (99, emphasis in original). The last refers to the substance of the knowledge and theoretical language to describe it, available to scientists. The relationship between all five is, of course, crucial: 'each of these five activities is as important as the others, and each feeds back into itself and into the other four' (99).

In *The Carrier* the interaction between these dimensions involves conflict, dislocation and contradiction. In other words, we will see humans interact with solid objects, which are puzzling and elusive and with instruments, which are mysterious, nurturing or inaccurate. This they do in the context of communities of scholars, who are threatened and destroyed, or else absent. We will see how, in Mahjoub's dystopic vision, the allies, the State, the Law, are zealots, destroying rather than facilitating, the advance of science. The public, equally sadly, in Mahjoub's hostile world is the howling mob, baying for blood. All of this ensures the fundamental aloneness of Mahjoub's protagonists, be they the scholarly Muslim, Rashid, forever a slave, or the Scandinavian Heinesen, whose hopes and aspirations come to nothing, as we will see, or the alienated, diasporic twentieth-century, Hassan. And the knots, the 'conceptual content', is skewed in Rashid's life and times by the wishful thinking about an earth at the centre, of a humanity, around which all the light revolves.

What both Mahjoub and Latour do is to construct a chain of connections between objects, such as the brass case, and history, bodies and power. Or, as Bruno Latour puts it: 'Science and technology are what *socialize* non-humans to bear upon human relations' (1999: 194, emphasis in original). There is, in other words, 'a social history of things and a "thingy" history of humans' (18). Or, as the words of Donna Haraway, another advocate of the connectedness between science and society and between humans and non-humans, suggest: 'science has been a travel discourse' which is implicated in the colonial and decolonising ventures, which have profoundly constituted 'the marked bodies of race, sex, and class' (1991: 221). In this way, the innocence of science is interrogated and the neutrality of its findings is exposed as posture. Science impacts on history and becomes intimate as bodies are colonised, enslaved or raped.

In this complex network of science, technology and history, objects mediate between people and society. Mahjoub explores the role played by telescopes and boxes as the ritual props in the social dramas that people play out every day. And so, 'real artefacts are always parts of institutions, trembling in their mixed status as mediators, mobilizing faraway lands and people' (Latour, 1999: 193). The brass case is one of these mediators mobilising Rashid and Hassan, who are from different times and places, but who share a history of being strangers, nomads and outsiders, albeit of somewhat different kinds. There are other mediating nonhumans that interact with the protagonists in *The Carrier*. There are the brass orb models of the planets, the gift of a wooden trunk and slabs of building stone. There is the telescope, which eventually surfaces, anti-climactically and too late. And finally, there is a demonic, furry toy monkey. These are solid objects, markers for social interactions, power plays and human endeavours.

The brass case across the layers of time & space

Hassan wonders about the instrument in the case 'and how it came to be buried here' (112). What interests him is 'what could not be proved in any scientific manner. The dark spaces between the evidence' (114). And so, rather ominously, Hassan 'slowly, carefully, raised the lid of the brass case' (44). The overtones are of the curiosity of Pandora. Hassan may be unleashing the messiness of war and hatred, bloodshed and pain, betrayals and murder into the supposedly neutral cleanliness of the scientific dig. Or, as Latour puts it: 'In opening the black box of scientific facts, we knew we would be opening Pandora's box' (1999: 23).

Hassan scrutinises the once-buried brass case, in the partial light afforded to him over the fractures and discontinuities of time, and desperately attempts to understand the life of its original owner, and thereby his own life. In other words, the brass case is a transcultural object, a metonym for Rashid, and through its mediation Hassan is attempting to translate himself into his own time and place with more ease and certainty. Mahjoub's vision, however, unlike Latour's, is quite bleak and what the narrative catalyst of the case reveals, as we scratch about in the past with Hassan, is violence, cruelty, loneliness and failed endeavours, all the ills. We have yet to see whether the hope that Pandora finally discovered at the bottom of the box, follows on their heel.

If Hassan is obsessive about Rashid, this is because he is at a crisis point in his own life. It becomes clear that his marriage is breaking down and he is searching for answers to big questions about his future. Rashid is a mask for Hassan, who is a mask for Mahjoub. And so, 'a man's fate is tightly bound in a thousand layers of sheer muslin which can take a lifetime to unravel' (2). Mahjoub's narrative structure is itself a stratigraphy of layers, palimpsests and Chinese boxes. Thus Rashid ponders that 'as in Aristotle's scheme for the movement of the celestial bodies, so it seemed that his life was a series of firm shells placed one inside the other' (58). Layers and fragments are scattered through the centuries, and are sometimes partially uncovered by scientists in archaeological digs:

> Whatever might have been recorded about the man known as Rashid al-Kenzy has been scattered down the passage of centuries like a fine trail; difficult, if not impossible to follow. A thin and fragile course indeed, leaving only disparate fragments in the way of clues to be pieced together; a task only to be undertaken by the mentally unsound or by the most stubbornly persistent of scholars. (2)

The novel echoes with the tenacity of scholars throughout the ages and across cultures. We encounter them in Africa, in Jutland, in Copenhagen, and always they work within the compromised spaces that the forces of power, the stern Law, make available. They work within accepted traditions of knowledge, sometimes shared across cultures and sometimes behind great walls of ignorance and prejudice. These layers of generations of intellectuals, who build on each other's knowledge, are conceptualised as an ascension up the great hill of learning: 'Azimuths, ecliptics, precession; all of these things he passed through like layers of warmth falling away as one ascends a mountain ... ' (70). Rashid's thirst for knowledge is couched in this same extended metaphor: 'he wanted to dig his way through page by page, line by line until all the knowledge hidden there in signs and ciphers was his' (220). Hassan, who is the recipient of whatever knowledge previous generations dug up, wonders how much 'things changed in four hundred years?' (9) The answer that Mahjoub plays with in the novel resonates with Michel Foucault's *The Archaeology of Knowledge*.

Foucault suggests that when science is viewed through the prism of power, it splinters into many different paths of knowledge. For him, research reveals 'several pasts, several forms of connexion, several hierarchies of importance, several networks of determination ... for one and the same science, as its present undergoes change' (1972 [1969]: 5). Change takes the form of rupture and discontinuity and uncovering the layers of these several pasts, constantly under review in the light of the present, decentres the sovereign role of an all-seeing subject. It is only in the partial light thrown by the angle to which one has access that one may examine the past. This Hassan himself understands as he scrutinises the perplexing brass case by way of the light from a table lamp, which 'only partly illuminated' it (44). Hassan recognises that 'he was peering into the past and yet ... he was seeing only a portion of what had once existed' (44).

What makes Hassan's task more difficult is the gulf between his and Rashid's time, with regard to the knowledge of the universe. Rashid lived in the interregnum brought about by the Copernican revolution, which radically altered how people viewed themselves in relation to the cosmos, given that 'man' was no longer at the centre. This discovery had particularly searing consequences for a devout Muslim, like Rashid. The Copernican rupture consolidates the novel's narrative discontinuities and explains its astronomical focus, out of which flows the recurrent images of the sun and the stars, light and darkness.

Hassan tries hard to piece it all together: 'What was happening in astronomy at the start of the seventeenth century?' (223). Hassan identifies that 'there was a huge gap' in the knowledge of Rashid's time: 'there was no mention, for example, of Copernicus' theory of heliocentricity until the end of the seventeenth century, and then only in passing' (224). Or, as Foucault puts it, regarding this period, 'the affirmation that the earth is round ... does not constitute the same statement before and after Copernicus' (1972: 103). Hassan realises that 'to defer the centre of the universe to the sun, away from the world and away from man would have been considered a dangerous area' (224). He sums up that 'sixteen-ten was a strange time; ideas about the way the universe worked were going through radical reform' (224). The imperfection of knowledge at this time is embodied in its technology, in the big brass orbs. For us to encounter them, in this ruptured narrative, which moves back and forth between, and also within, the centuries, without regard for linear order, we have to go back to Rashid's biography and the period before he sets out in search of the telescope.

The huge brass orbs & the valley of dreamers

We left the strange passage of Rashid's education at the point at which he entered the madrasa with his half brother. When the latter dies of a fever, the young Rashid's life is endangered by the jealous rage of the merchant's wife, and with the assistance of one of his teachers, at age fifteen, Rashid fled to 'the outcast colony of scholars which was known as the Valley of Dreamers' (34). These outcasts and nomads operate as a community of intellectuals. The emphasis at this secret place of learning is on science and technology, on the ways in which the bodies of scientists fold into technology, in this case, the giant brass orbs. The knowledge that 'the outcast colony of scholars' (34) are dappling with is explosive, given its potential to threaten entrenched power. These giant orbs are a model of the universe, as conceptualised in the seventeenth century: 'each globe represents one of the celestial planets. They circle through the air suspended on hollow brass rods in perfect synchronism' (68).

They are models into which Rashid's body merges as he 'feels the pull in his stomach and wishes that he could be the motion itself' (68). The description is visceral, with the orbs compared to giant hawks breathing into Rashid's ears, making him want to fly. He feels the splendour of them, not in his mind, but in his stomach. Humans, nonhumans and scientific tools merge into the fug of an embrace and the 'air is warm and thick, caressed by the passing of these spheres' (68). These are Latour's instruments, which are 'all the means by which nonhumans are progressively loaded into discourse' (1999: 99), they are 'Big Science', including 'the *instruments* and major *equipment*' (100, emphasis in original).

In this way, Mahjoub underlines the link between flesh, bodies, science and instruments. The anatomist at the Valley of Dreamers uses a sharp knife that slices away 'layers of the face of the dead man' (67). Organically, literally, metonymically, these steel and brass instruments are Rashid's parents, his family: 'his hands caress their polished smoothness with the tenderness only an orphan can know' (70). In this way, 'learning became his life, his family, his home' (68). Ink becomes thicker than blood, is the blood flowing in Rashid's body. He recalls the 'great stone arches' on which the motto is inscribed: '*The ink of the scholars is worth more than the blood of the martyrs*' (58).

Like the possessions that insulate you from the world of harm (Scarry, 1985: 262), books and scientific instruments provide Rashid the protection of home and family. His mother had no such protection of solid possessions – she was simply 'a slave woman with nothing but a few pots and a bundle of clothes to her name' (58). However, like his mother, Rashid belongs to the disembodied, the colonised and enslaved. Theirs are bodies 'that do not matter in the same way' (Butler, 1993: xi). Rashid is dark skinned, advertising his slave origins (14). Furthermore, 'he had a back which was so curved as to draw comment in whatever circles he happened to show his face' (16). This lowly, hump-backed, homeless and parentless former slave boy strives to re-constitute himself as scholar-subject, by way of merging bodily with the giant model of the universe. This he may only accomplish by integrating into communities of scholars, both in his present and also through knowledge handed down over the generations. Communities of scholars bring to mind the category of Latour's *colleagues* who dictate 'the way in which a discipline, a profession, a clique, or an "invisible college" becomes independent and forms its own criteria of evaluation and relevance' (1999: 102). The point is that working within such a community of scholars is essential for the growth of knowledge. This is not the everyday life with which Bandele or Aboulela's fiction teems, but it is the commonplace reality of academic daily practice, which cannot function without these collegial networks.

Findings through the ages are passed on to Rashid and contribute to shared human knowledge, comprising the image of stratigraphies of narratives, of science, of the generations. And so, Rashid dreams 'of visiting the great libraries of Cairo, of travelling through the world and living in an observatory, devoting himself to the science of the celestial spheres' (58). What Mahjoub brings to light is the wealth of scholarship of the East, buried under the hegemony of Western traditions. The weight of names counters the arrogance of these Western assumptions about its own monopoly on knowledge production and I must reproduce this list quite fully, in order to make Mahjoub's point:

> The mysteries of the heavens could not be unravelled by one simple man. But the torch was passed on, from the Babylonians and the Pharaohs to the Greeks and Persians, then to the Indians and the Chinese. The walls of the academy rang with their names, so many that it would take a lifetime of devotion simply to learn who they were and what they had done: Imhotep; Akhenaten; Ammizaduga; Thales; Anaximander; Pythagoras; Eudoxus; Aristotle; Aristarchus who invented the scaphe to measure time; Apollonius and his epicycles; Hipparchus who gave us precession; Ptolemy's *al-Majisty* which later gave Abdelrahman al-Sufi his start in plotting the heavens; Abu Mashaar and Mash'allah the Jew who illuminated the Sassanian theory that all major political events coincided

with the conjunction of Saturn and Jupiter.
> Al-Biruni; Abu'l Wafa; Ibn Yunus; Ibn al-Haytham; Nasr al-din al-Tusi and Ibn Shatir.
> (71. See also 89–90)

This wealth of knowledge production, outside of the West, has been underlined by scholars such as Mudimbe (1988) and Diop (1991) in their critique, as Mahjoub puts it, quite bluntly, of 'the shameless arrogance of the Christian mind' (219). The long list of names of Arab scholars is a metonymic gap to counter the weight of Western assumptions about its own monopoly on knowledge production. These listed names, foreign to Western ears, act like untranslated Igbo or Arab words, to draw attention to the existence of other knowledge traditions, here quite literally so. This is why Mahjoub recounts the legend of the growth of Arabic scholarship and its relationship to the Greek: 'al Mamun, was visited one night in his sleep by Aristotle the Greek' from whom he gained learning, but the Greeks themselves 'learned from the knowledge of the Ancient Egyptians' (97). In repeatedly setting up these lists of scholars, across the borders of time and space, Mahjoub is making a powerful and concrete political commentary about the ways in which the much-vaunted partnership between knowledge and power actually works.

For Rashid, science and technology are a way of soaring like the giant hawk, freed from his hump-back and slave origins. And so 'his real interest lay in the Revealed Sciences, that is to say, science as described in the holy texts' (34). Here is the rub: his religion will not happily accept the rupture in knowledge brought about by the Copernican revolution, which would remove the earth from the centre. Mahjoub does not romanticise the East and, even as he brings Western arrogance down to size, he demonstrates that the giant magnificent brass orb model of the cosmos is fatally flawed, in that it is scientifically incorrect:

> Standing at the centre of his memory was this model of the universe: the shiny edges gleam in the fragile pillar of light that filters through the circular hole in the roof high above, *one orb is located at the centre and marks the earth, for all things turn about this world.* How fast they move and how beautiful it is to behold such firm precision in motion. (68–9, my emphasis)

The threat to the wondrous orbs however, comes not only from their fatal conceptual error, but also from the forces of the Law. Mahjoub shows us what happens to communities of scholars in the context of prejudice and power. These dreamers are social outcasts and constantly in danger of extermination, along with their orbs and observatories; their secret Valley could go the same way as the Observatory at Tabriz, which 'was built and torn down' in the ten years it took to build the giant orbs (68).

This relationship between science and the Law is what Latour calls his 'third loop' after instruments and colleagues and refers to the 'alliances' between scientists and outside groups. And so 'the military must be made interested in physics, industrialists in chemistry, kings in cartography' (1999:

103). What Mahjoub demonstrates is the terrible consequences of outside groups being hostile to the scholar. Knowledge production, which welcomes the son of a slave is too democratic for 'the zealots', in that: 'is it not written that the lowliest of men is equal to the noblest, that each man's faith is between him and his Creator? But such arguments are frail protection against the swords and spears of the zealots' (72). These zealots do inevitably come and destroy the Valley of the Dreamers. Rashid escapes and we must skip the years and complex narrative plot structure leading to his imprisonment in Algiers and then his selection for the quest for a telescope and return to Jutland, where Rashid was shipwrecked on the ill-fated voyage.

The wooden trunk, the great stone slabs
& the metamorphosing human lizard

Scavengers scurry amidst the wreck, without regard for Rashid, the battered, surviving sailor, until nothing is left: 'everything around him has been stripped. Lanterns, fittings, nails, wood' (171); they care nothing for this human wreck and 'brush him aside with their sacks and awkward loads' (172–3). We saw that one of Latour's science studies activities was the 'public' (1999: 99), which Mahjoub, quite problematically, depicts as the mob, the howling, ignorant, threatening masses, whether they are Algerians, who were instrumental in Rashid's wrongful arrest, or Danes, who are looting and scavenging. They are termites, greedy vermin. They are without redeeming features, for all their own poverty; they are 'tiny insects, people, scurrying like rats, falling over one another in their haste to secure the best of that which is left' (171). Throughout his life, Rashid is as much oppressed by the powerful as tormented by the powerless. The qadi of Algiers may have imprisoned Rashid at the opening of the novel, but it is 'the jeering crowd', 'the common people', who had 'spat upon his dusty, soiled form' (3) and who had 'slashed at him with palm fronds and pelted him with pebbles and stones' (3). This new unruly crowd, far from Algiers, thinks that the dark skinned, hump-backed Rashid is the devil, arrived from 'his palace of sin' at the ends of the universe, possessed of the evil eye, which could 'bring them out in a rash of boils and inflict such pain as they had never known upon their bowels' (150). Rashid is denuded of clothing, possessions and dignity, by the poor, but also by the rich.

What possessions? Rashid had acquired a beautiful wooden trunk and the brass case already referred to, as gifts from a rich merchant in Cyprus, in whose employ he had found himself after fleeing from the Valley of Dreamers. I do not wish to digress here, regarding the nature of his employment and the complex reasons for his resigning from it, but rather to focus on the 'fine wooden trunk filled with gifts and gold' (95) that the merchant had given him. The brass case, with its instrument enabling Muslim prayer to be properly conducted anywhere in the world, is part of the treasures contained in this trunk full of precious possessions that Rashid had taken away with him to Algiers, where the novel opens and where the quest for a telescope had begun. The trunk 'contained the sum total of his worldly possessions' (56). Rashid has only these gifts to comfort him on his perilous journey and he will be dispossessed of them.

A demonic 'scientist' is summoned by the town's authorities to examine the strange specimen washed up on their shores – a surgeon, who 'studied in Bologna and Basel' and whose 'knowledge of the human corpus is unrivalled' (147), according to the priest, who stands for the power of the Church, aligned to that of the State. The description of the surgeon's practices is grotesque and visceral. We see Rashid not only dispossessed of his things, but stripped of his very flesh and body. This so-called surgeon poured scalding, hot water over Rashid's nakedness, 'tied a cloth around his mouth and nose and approached the dark creature across the room' and:

> For the next two hours he prodded and poked at every corner of the creature's anatomy. He rubbed its skin with alum and its fingertips in gunpowder. He stuck wooden rods up its rectum and copper pipes down its throat. (149)

Rashid is an animal, a creature, treated like an object, which feels no pain. 'It' is an unnatural animal and the surgeon searches for 'its' gills and webbing:

> He kneaded it and stretched every muscle and ligament, bent the joints this way and that, looking for gills, valves, ventricles, features that should not be there. He examined the spaces between the fingers and toes for signs of webbing. (149)

There is more, including the insertion of long needles into 'its' belly, the draining of much blood from 'its' armpits and the weighing and measuring of 'every available inch of its body, including the penis' (149). Knowledge is betrayed by prejudice and the horror of this is narrated omnisciently by a bitter, angry Mahjoub. As for Rashid, 'they do not realize that he has already died and come back to the world as an animal' (170). This is the only moment in the novel that reads in the style of an epic African tale, with a repeated chorus and a story of creation, of moon and sun, lizard and drum:

> The moon's bones are made of white silver. They gleam with an audacious voracity. Their keen edges protrude sharply, cutting through the taut drum of this world. This lizard's eye finds the bars of the cage where our hero lies rotting. And if the bones of the moon are silver then the sun's heart is made of stone. (170)

No longer objects of astronomical scientific knowledge, the sun and moon become punishing parents, bodies procreating and bringing forth, not a human being, but an animal, a lizard. The chapter ends with the same lines, but with a crucial metamorphosising sting in its tail:

> The moon's bones are made of white silver. They gleam with audacious voracity. Their keen edges protrude sharply, cutting through the taut drum of the world. This lizard's eye finds the bars of the cage where Rashid al-Kenzy lies rotting. *He has died and come back to the world as an animal.* (177, my emphasis)

Whereas the orbs and the community of scholars were parents to the orphaned Rashid, he is now reincarnated by way of a cruel cosmos into a slithering creature, without language. Rashid, the scholar, the linguist, has been reduced, divested of his humanity and unable to be constituted as a subject within language. Therefore the sounds round about him are for him like those uttered by 'forest creatures' (174). Their language remains 'obscure and unfathomable' (180). The point that Mahjoub is underlining is the impossibility of being a scientist and a flesh-and-blood human being, outside of the context of politics, power and history. Rashid enters Scandinavia as a de-territorialized nomad; he is, in Deleuze and Guattari's parlance 'becomings-animal' (1987: 232); he is, again in their terms, experiencing 'the violence of these animal sequences, which uproot one from humanity' (Deleuze and Guattari: 240); he joins the band of sorcerers, werewolves and vampires, all hybrids with no family (Deleuze and Guattari: 241).

What of Rashid's treasures, his trunk and his brass case? The Law, Latour's so-called 'allies', are in this historical context a powerful enemy. The town authority, the provost, has seized 'a small wooden trunk' from 'those peasants and simpletons out there, who no doubt would have chopped it up into firewood' (135). He has recognised its value and Mahjoub takes care to describe its intricate magnificence in concrete detail:

> It was made of some fine-quality hardwood, mahogany most likely. The ornamented brass corners and reinforcements made it a very solid and very handsome cabinet indeed. The top had been carefully inlaid with sandalwood and mother of pearl in a complex pattern of intriguing geometry. (136)

Inside the trunk is 'a flat brass case' containing a mysterious instrument which depicted points of cities and towns in the world in Arabic script (136). Here is the brass case that Hassan will puzzle over hundreds of years later, when it surfaces from beneath the ground and forges links between humans and objects. At this point in time, the local provost is at a loss as to what to do with this creature and his things, given that he would be torn apart by the mob if he set him free. He manages to find a solution through an eccentric scholar/landowner called Heinesen, who he persuades to take Rashid back with him to his estate. Heinesen is engaged in dreams and scientific projects of his own. Rashid, at this stage, is an animal, an object of exchange, even less valuable than his possessions. The trunk is part of the trade deal and Rashid, again a slave, is referred to as 'the purchase', part of which is the precious trunk which Heinesen negotiates in the deal (156).

Rashid is set to work on Heinesen's estate as a labourer, lugging massive slabs of stone on a building site, designed to become an Observatory, where Heinesen hopes to witness the astrological secrets of the planets. Hassan, centuries later, puzzling over the landscape, in which 'massive blocks of stone' have been dug up, along with 'the remains of the body' (4), is aware that these finds are on the site of the land of a man called Verner Heinesen and that this man's strange endeavours, so many hundreds of years ago had 'something to do with the stars' (189). Slowly Mahjoub will reveal to us the extraordinary relationship that develops between Heinesen and Rashid, catalysed by the stone slabs.

These slabs of stone have their own biography entwined with the lives of humans. While Rashid is working there, a terrible accident occurs on the site and a boy is buried alive by one of these stone slabs falling on him. The sheer weight of the slabs, the terrible weather, the mud and slippery terrain, all contribute to the accident. But, most horribly, the final cause of the tragedy rests with the distrust on the part of the locals for Rashid, the Stranger, the Other. In attempting to balance the heavy stone against the wind, Rashid had inadvertently brushed against one of the other labourers, who recoils from his touch and the stone tips, 'veering slowly earthwards, twisting out of his hands, his fingers, downwards, into the core of the hill' (185). Flesh and stone are hybridised in the crucible of prejudice:

> The shovels and mallets, heavy iron hammers and chisels for splitting stone lay scattered around. Discarded, dismembered limbs, lifeless notes that trickled away down the tarry gash in the raven's back. (186)

This tragedy, ironically, and in a roundabout way, sets in motion the next stage in the story of Rashid's life and that of his wooden trunk, in that it eventually leads to Heinesen's discovery of the true nature of Rashid's abilities. Like the zealots that destroyed the Valley of Dreamers, this terrible accident is linked to the presence of the devil stranger and gives the good City Fathers an opportunity to descend on Heinesen's estate. Again, they are Latour's so-called 'allies', turned demonic foes, who are metonymically described as 'a delegation of black hats' (194) of church, trade and commerce and state. They are 'sombre men' (194) and 'like so many crows, the three black hats settled themselves around the big fire, noses wrinkling at the chaos of books' (195). Mahjoub loathes these arrogant, prejudiced pillars of power and his under-statement: 'The town fathers were worried' (199) curdles with his dislike of their class. They are worried about the human animal in their midst and the bad luck he might bring.

Heinesen summons Rashid into their presence, in order to demonstrate to the zealots his 'simpleness of mind as one might expect in a harmless creature' (203). He gives Rashid a piece of paper to scribble on, only to have to conceal his own amazement when the 'meaningless scribble' (205) turns out to be 'the constellation of Pleiades' (205). There is a marvellous turning point moment, after the Law has retreated, when Rashid and Heinesen gaze at each other, see each other, as it were, for the first time, across the gulf of language, culture and power. Heinesen now understands from Rashid's 'scribbles' that he knows Greek and has been observing the stars (208–9). If, centuries later, Hassan is separated from the mystery of Rashid's life by time, then Heinesen is perplexed by the differences between their worlds in space, for all their shared learning: 'What are you, Moor? A magician? A sorcerer?' (211).

Now that he has been recognised as a scholar, Rashid may begin the journey of returning to his human form, through, in the first instance, having his possessions back again: 'Heinesen reappeared, pulling Rashid's wooden trunk behind him' (211). But his special trunk, his insulation against the world, has had its own life experiences, has been damaged and is only partly the object it had been: 'the trunk was bruised and battered. A large crack had appeared in the side' (211). The trunk, albeit harmed by its ordeal, comes with other stuff, other solid, material things that make us clean, warm, fed, and most importantly, human:

> He was given hot water with which to wash and scissors to trim his hair and beard; new clothes – thick, warm breeches of wool and a shirt of fine linen. Over this a thick jacket of woven horsehair and on his feet stockings and then shoes made of wood. They fed him warm milk, into which he broke hard stumps of dark bread. (216)

Thick, warm, hard, hot – all visceral, protecting, comforting things – consequent on his scholarly knowledge. These are measures of his value as a potential colleague. But it is not enough. Heinesen may have understood the implications of the Copernican revolution and gone further than his teacher. But he has not sufficiently understood the workings of power and how scientific knowledge, when it threatens deeply entrenched privilege, will be suppressed, burnt and destroyed by the good citizens.

Before this happens, however, *The Carrier* toys with a love affair between Rashid and Sigrid, Heinesen's sister, an attraction that will complete the process by which the human lizard, Rashid, is restored to his humanity. She too is a scholar and appears to span his world and this European one, in that she wears a 'plain black scarf' (228) like a Muslim woman, a scarf from which her fine hair escapes and dances 'like spun silver on the sun's beams' (229). She is described in terms of the play of light and dark, white and black, a crossover, fair Scandinavian woman becoming Muslim in the eyes of the beholding enamoured Sudanese man. Mahjoub, himself the product of a marriage between an English woman and a Sudanese man, returns repeatedly to the hazards and promises of these relationships in his fiction. He touches on it somewhat opaquely in this novel where we assume that Hassan's estranged wife is Danish – she is called Lisa and is staying with her sister while Hassan is on the site (162). He deals with it centrally in his next novel, *Travelling with Djinns* (2003). In seventeenth-century Jutland, however, a relationship between Sigrid and Rashid is beyond the boundary of the imaginable, which Rashid realises. Nonetheless, it is Sigrid who enables Rashid to regain his manhood, from the degrading metamorphosis that we saw occur when he first arrived in Jutland. He had become a lizard, a creature devoid of humanity. Then the 'remarkable thing' happens (246). Like so much in this novel, it is expressed in terms of light passing into him from her gaze and enabling him to be re-born: 'it was as though in that instant in which she looked up, that he came into being. A part of him that had been dead to the world was suddenly located' (248).

In gender terms, however, what are the implications of her disembodiment, her transformation from metonymic flesh into metaphorical light, into being 'the flame' to which he is also fatally stretching out? (250). Sigrid metamorphoses into a chimera, as the means by which Rashid returns to his male body. Sigrid becomes a mere reflection of Rashid's desires, through the deception of the mirror, a phase, which Mahjoub is depicting as infantile and delusionary: 'Narcissus knows that the beauty which gazes back at him from the brook is not his own. His folly is that he wishes to make it so' (250). She must remain a lack, an object of desire, which is, as always, elsewhere. She is the opposite of the material, which elsewhere embeds the novel and provides the launching pad for its newly formed meanings. And so 'he knows that in the moment in which he reaches out to touch the *shimmering chimera*, it will fall apart in his hands' (250, my emphasis). In other words, 'in the instant in which he traverses the boundary between the hand and the eye, he will destroy the very object of his desire' (250). Woman must remain abstract, holy grail and flash of light. Sigrid becomes a variant of the goddess trope, which paradoxically elevates her and thereby simultaneously diminishes her active participation in the world of political and social reality.

However, it is the demonic power of prejudice that concerns Mahjoub here and what he depicts is that two men and one woman, from worlds apart, cannot stem the tide of hostility from the masses and from the black hats of the European Law. Heinesen and his household are blamed for a fire that burns the town's cathedral. Rashid, Heinesen and his sister, like the scholars in the Valley of Dreamers, are hounded and persecuted by the Law and the mob in cahoots. Heinesen's observatory does not get built. He is broken, disillusioned and dies. It is left only to Rashid and Sigrid to bury him in a 'rough' (not thick, strong, protecting) coffin (268). The coffin does not fit the hole in the ground and Rashid, who is exhausted and alone, has to damage the body of the man who had made human contact with him across the gulf that separated them. Bodies are implicated in objects and Rashid smashes the coffin and the corpse, using a shovel:

> Then he lifted the shovel high into the air and with a cry plunged it into the chest. There was a splintering sound. He raised it again and there was a crack. The end of the chest burst into two and out of this Heinesen's blue face thrust itself into the rain. (269–70)

Again flesh and matter merge, as Rashid cradles the head of the white man, but it has already metamorphosed from flesh to stone object 'like a kind of wood or stone, but harder' (270). Like moulding an instrument to fit a task, Rashid has to bend this rock-hard head to fit its burial place. Amidst splintering wood, he tries 'to bend the body forwards and finally, with great difficulty, managed to force it further into the hole, bowing the neck forwards' (270). This explains the damage to the human remains, which Hassan and the team of archaeologists dig up, centuries later, and for which they will never be able to find an explanation.

The situation deteriorates after Heinesen's death. The house is set on fire when the avenging and ignorant multitude, out of their prejudice and fear, come to seek revenge, for the dead boy, for the harboured stranger. Again the body of Sigrid is described in symbolic terms. When tropes take over from reality, political consequences may be dire, as when Sigrid's demise in the fire is portrayed, not in terms of the horror of her charred flesh and this violence wrought upon her body, but as the magnificence of the light coming from her off the fire. Sigrid is light refracted through desire, insubstantial and eventually sacrificed to the mob. For Rashid, she was 'finally becoming that which she had always been at last' (274). She is revealed in the fire 'as incandescence, as light itself' (274). This is so strange, given the novel's political sensitivities. Instead of grief, it seems that Rashid experiences the joy of the light coming off her. This is to re-enact symbolic male stories and mythical imaginings, which give them power over women, at the very moment that Mahjoub is rejecting the racist and vicious revenge on the enslaved stranger and the eccentric scholar. And then, after all of this death and burning and horror, the forgotten telescope surfaces. What possible significance might it now hold?

The anti-quest, the Copernican rupture & the bathos of the telescope at last

The telescope had been Rashid's holy grail. He had imagined it to be a wondrous scientific tool, a new technology from which great discoveries would follow. However, desire for the telescope recedes as Rashid has had a whiff of more fundamental miracles and wonders. In Heinesen's library, he had encountered Copernicus and was amazed and receptive to the implications and consequences of the fact that man is no longer 'at the centre of all creation' (227). Rashid may be confused and frightened by the existential implications, by the impact of this knowledge on his religion, but his new journey is towards knowledge and 'onwards towards Copernicus' (238) at the same time as being daily filled with terror 'at the fear of losing ... his religious faith' (242).

Rashid battles with absorbing all this new knowledge, such as the shocking realisation that Aristotle was wrong about the stars being 'fixed in a crystal latticework' and 'what had previously been believed to be fixed and unchanging was not actually so' (237). Even this radical new knowledge could only come from the generations of scholars across cultures, which is not of the East or the West, but Copernicus 'must surely have known of the ideas of Nasr al din al-Tusi' (239). In other words, the task Rashid sets himself is no less than to 'establish the line of thought connecting the two apparently separate spheres of East and West' (246). This is Rashid's re-defined quest. Rashid's epiphany is that perhaps his altered destiny is to return home carrying this radical knowledge instead the telescope:

> The ideas of this Copernicus would have been laughed away by his peers, by his teachers. To break the firm hold of the Almighty's seven heavens? What was left was a void. *But he was becoming convinced now that this was the mission of his lifetime: to reveal.* To return home bearing this knowledge was surely a greater feat than any mechanical instrument, no matter how strategically useful. In this way the course of his life signified *not gradual progression but a tool of change.* (243–4, my emphases)

Change, discontinuity, transformation. This is the point of Rashid's life, or as Mahjoub himself puts it in an interview: 'I think he is trying to understand something which involves a complete break with what he has believed in up until this point' (Sévry, 2001: 87). He is riding on the cusp of the moment of rupture in Foucault's archaeology of knowledge. He is transformed: 'he had learned that the sun was the source of the world's life and that the earth was a simple singing orb' (274). This is a more revolutionary quest than for the instrument in search of which his journey had begun. And then, long after he has ceased to look for it, after Heinesen has literally and spiritually been broken and buried, the telescope arrives, out of the blue as it were. Heinesen must have ordered it:

> A telescope, then.
> Life swells, funnels through the brass casing. He clutches the sacred instrument in his numb fingers. (277)

It is a sensual, visceral object of beauty, as much as a functional piece of apparatus, wrapped in 'soft velvet' and comprising the 'smooth, gleaming, round softness of brass' (265). Like the big orbs, which Rashid caressed and tended with his body, the telescope exudes sexuality: 'a brass casing open at either end into which hard droplets of glass are squeezed' (276). However, having it, holding it, destroys it as an object of desire. It had been 'like a chimera, shimmering in the distant future ahead of him. A form of magic' (59). It had been his dream of accomplishing something that would secure his position in the world, in which he shifts, slips and slithers: 'Was this the mission which he had been waiting for all of this life? If he managed to survive, to bring back this Dutch optical device, would he find the solace and content he sought?' (59–60).

The telescope, however, like Sigrid, is a 'chimera', like the shifting, elusive objects in Bandele's land of dreams in Chapter Two: 'the Dutch optical instrument is not real' (102). Bandele, too, portrayed precious sought after things as not to be found where these migrant writers and their protagonists search for them. These slippery objects exist in the imaginary world of desire (Deleuze and Guattari, 1983: 25–6) and as Deleuze puts it later in his *Difference and Repetition*, the sought after object 'is where it is only on condition that it is not where it should be' (1996: 26). These shiny, virtual objects torment migrants, who try to reconcile their many worlds through elusive, material objects, like tables, sacks, vials of perfume and now, in *The Carrier*, a telescope. By definition, the telescope plays havoc with reality and 'light enters and is transformed' such that 'What seems at first far thus becomes near' (276). However, what use is the telescope to him now?

Rashid knows that the mob, incited by the Law, will be coming back for him and this it does; he knows there is no place for him in 'this world of theirs' (272). He tries to pack manuscripts and books, but 'weighed down with books and sodden parchments, useless, cumbersome instruments that might be mistaken for weapons' (277), he abandons them. The telescope too will burden him and hamper his escape. Technology is useless in the face of the hostile Law and the ignorant masses and so 'he gets to his feet and tosses the brass casing aside, hearing it strike a hollow note against the frozen surface of the world. It vanishes in the descending darkness' (278) as Rashid begins his homeward journey, whose outcome the novel leaves unknown:

> In the quickening distance there is a nameless ship waiting for him and a passage to work his way south, back to the world he left behind, away from the dark climates. With each step, he tells himself, it will get easier. (278)

Meanwhile, and centuries later, what is happening to the quest of Hassan, who is searching for knowledge of Rashid, and fighting demons of his own?

A horrible furry toy monkey but is there any hope?

Hassan is on his own quest for understanding and happiness. He has come to this small and isolated place at a moment of crisis in his marriage. He is full of discomfort and painfully aware of the growing racism in Denmark (107). He is particularly nervous in rural areas, like this one where he has found himself, and where 'he stood out like the proverbial sore thumb' (108). Martin, the only local person who genuinely wishes to know him, is a young man who says 'they know nothing about who you are or what you are doing here' (222). Hassan himself refers to 'their ignorance and fear' (223), echoing the response of the populace to Rashid's Otherness, hundreds of years earlier.

What of Hassan's colleagues, those crucial collaborators, who Latour rightly insists are part of the whole enterprise of science studies? Hassan's relationship with them is cold and tenuous. Okking, an archaeologist on the site, finally invites him to dinner only right at the end of the job (251). They have remained strangers all this time and know nothing about each other. The dinner is stiff, formal and awful. It is described in great detail, including the minutiae of the Okkings' home, dress and the menu for the dinner. All is neat, tidy, tasteless and contained. Mrs Okking is slim, with her hair in a neat bob and a 'thin string of pearls around her neck' (252). The food is 'conventional' albeit 'excellently prepared' and consists of 'fluffy pastry shells with a mushroom filling followed by roast beef, very rare, with potatoes and sautéd carrots and then a small gâteau smothered in whipped, low-calorie cream' (256). All of this material culture embodies the non-communication across cultures. The cream is thin and the meal is the opposite of the healing soul food soup that we sampled in the previous chapter. This meal is toxic and does not operate as furthering translation between the scientists.

There is an awkward, frozen moment at the dinner when Okking's wife asks Hassan about his personal life and, having commented on his excellent Danish, makes the following comment: 'I didn't mean to pry, but you know how it is. We are all curious to know where people come from' (254). Hassan is deeply offended: 'He would have forgiven her, except for the "but"' (254). Hassan's taking offence has to be understood again in terms of cultural capital, where subtle forms of inherited behaviour, language and style, translate into acceptance, or its opposite. We also saw how Bourdieu and also Bauman, who referred more specifically to migrants, understood the dilemmas of what they term parvenus, who remain newcomers, given that they do not quite exude the right style and breeding (Bourdieu, 1984: 95, and Bauman, 1997: 72). It is, moreover, the bane of those dark skinned citizens, born and bred in England or Norway, that they are always supposed to be from somewhere else and to have a mother tongue, which is not the language which they speak 'so well'; they are always asked from where they actually, originally, essentially come. This is why Mrs Okking, with her assumption that he knows he is not one of them, and that, moreover, he never will be, is so offensive. The Okkings worry about their daughter, who lives in the city, and Hassan wonders whether 'this was leading towards an oblique comment about immigrants', about a world 'inhabited by people like him' (256).

Hassan had attempted to interest Okking in his own fascination with the life of Rashid. However, he loses Okking's attention and Hassan realises that he 'did not wish to inform them of the hours he had spent letting his imagination guide his path, trying to get into the mind of an elusive figure, a four-hundred-year-old-shadow' (256). We are, therefore, not surprised that Hassan cannot interest Okking in his quest for the life of Rashid. We are reminded at this moment of subtle and patronising discrimination, of the moment when Hassan had first arrived at the site, when the prejudice and ignorance were momentarily visible. Okking had introduced Hassan to a colleague on the site as 'this is the man they sent to read *that gobbledygook* we found' (42, my emphasis[2]). He has no scruples in referring to the Arabic on the brass case in these insulting, ignorant terms. This is the 'gobbledygook' that migrants turn into an alternative metonymic language that thrusts the existence of other cultures into the fluffy mushroom filled pastry shells.

All of this prepares us for the shock awaiting Hassan at home, on his return from this awkward dinner. The racism that was just beneath the surface in the Okkings' home has risen into horrible, material view. Hassan's house had been vandalized, all the windows smeared and a furry toy monkey hammered to the door: 'a children's stuffed toy had been hammered to the door with a large nail. He pulled it off and held it in his hand for a moment, turning it over: a small, furry monkey' (257). A monkey is an animal with an inauspicious history of being linked to racial insult, as we will see in Chapter Five when Moses Isegawa's white, racist priest, in *Abyssinian Chronicles*, insults his black pupils by calling them monkeys, with dire consequences. This object has been unleashed by racial hatred and yet it seems to spur Hassan on to action and to help him decide to make some constructive decisions about his life. It seems to tell him to stop thinking about the past and to begin to live in his own present. In other words, demonic and 'radioactive' as this object is, it appears to carry a modicum of hope in Hassan's response to it:

> He had been away too long, he decided. *It was time to leave the past alone* and come back to the real world. It was time to go home. Placing the monkey on the table in front of him he sat down. (257, my emphasis)

---

[2] I am indebted to Tina Steiner for pointing out this moment in the novel to me.

Hassan may or may not patch up his marriage, but he will begin to act and 'after a time he reached for the telephone and called his wife' (257). Albeit that there are no clear cut answers from the past, what is unambiguous is that, along with the furry monkey, Rashid al-Kenzy's life, or what Hassan had been able to deduce about it, had acted as a spur to his own decisions: 'he had begun to think of Rashid al-Kenzy as a kind of catalyst. His Rashid, that is. An outside element that, once introduced, tended to accentuate the light in some way' (252). 'His Rashid' is the one he imagines, the object of his own frustrated desire, rather than the flesh and blood man, whose complex realities Hassan never successfully excavates. Like the furry monkey, he is an outside element, reminiscent of the strange interfering objects of Bandele's *The Street*. The monkey and Rashid's imagined life act together to force the passive, secretive Hassan to begin to make concrete decisions. This is hopeful in a quite pessimistic novel, albeit that, like the outcome of Rashid's journey home, *The Carrier* leaves open the outcome of Hassan's phone call. Closure is antipathetic to Foucault's understanding of history, Latour's conceptualisation of science and Mahjoub's narrative stratigraphy.

We have seen the alienation deeply embedded in the vision of the migrant scientist Anglo-Sudanese writer, Jamal Mahjoub. His protagonists – both in the seventeenth and the twentieth centuries – are perched between the demonic Law of the power holders and the howling mob. Mahjoub, perhaps as much as Hassan, is a privileged, mobile traveller, but one who finds himself a misfit, exposed to racism, deeply insecure about his identity and battling in his personal relationships. The folding of humans into nonhumans and back is a collision of objects and wills, instruments and failed experiments. The brass orbs were fatally flawed, the wooden trunk is battered and bruised, the brass case is buried, the slabs of stone kill a small boy and sink into the earth, the telescope comes too late and is hurled into the abyss and the furry toy monkey is toxic. Is there any hope to be recovered from shipwrecks and a lizard, which had once been human?

> Now that it has been opened, with plagues and curses, sins and ills whirling around, there is only one thing to do, and that is to go even deeper, all the way down into the almost-empty box, in order to retrieve what, according to the venerable legend, has been left at the bottom – yes, *hope*. (Latour, 1999: 23)

In order to excavate Mahjoub's hope, we need to return to Rashid's brass case, with which we began. We need to understand how it had come to be buried in the grave with Heinesen and unearthed hundreds of years later. We saw how Rashid had found it necessary to break Heinesen's body, to fit it in his grave. Thereafter, however, he transforms that demonic ritual burial of splintering flesh and smashed bones into a moment of hope, humanity and affirmation. In a reverse move from the plunder of the wooden trunk, Rashid gives the dead man one of his most treasured possessions as a gift. Rashid buries his precious brass case in the mangled coffin, with the dead man (27). He thereby insulates this broken body with a solid object, in order to send him on his way safely to the other world. Bodies and objects are implicated in social structures; two intellectual men from different cultures may not have formed a new community of scholars able to build an Observatory to look at the spheres, but in their brotherhood, they stand against the venom and power of the black hats. This buried brass case is a translation object across time and space, cultures and languages. It is a pact of hope, however, between Mahjoub and his readers, given that the perplexed Hassan will never be able to decipher its meaning through the scientific evidence he had at hand and he had not himself been able to forge this connection with his own colleague.

We do not ultimately know the destiny of Rashid; perhaps Hassan does not make it back into a life of love and sociality. *Travelling with Djinns*, Mahjoub's next novel, charts the breakdown of the marriage of its protagonist, who seems to be another version of Hassan and in which he remains profoundly alienated from other people:

> I belong to that nomad tribe, the great unwashed, those people born in the joins between continental shelves in the unclaimed interstices between time zones, strung across latitudes. A tribe of no fixed locus, the homeless, the stateless. I have two passports and quite a variety of other documents to identify me, all of which tell the world where I have been, but not who I am, nor where I am going to. (2003: 5)

Writers like Mahjoub struggle to translate their flimsy words into visceral, material realities in order to anchor themselves against the vicissitudes of their nomadic lives:

> My language is a bastard tongue of necessity, improvisation, bad grammar and continual misunderstandings. I am a stranger wherever I go. My history is not given, but has to be taken, reclaimed, piece by solitary piece, snatched from among the pillars of centuries, the shelves of ivory scholarship. My flimsy words set against those lumbering tomes bound in leather and written in blood. (2003: 5)

The centuries of scholarship, of discovery, of knowledge ruptures, are the ivory, the solid, saving framework for the words. This ivory scholarship, however, is steeped in trade, in poaching, in the violence of history and its struggles over wealth and power. Leather and blood capture the words as they flee and, paradoxically for all their violent past, create the fleeting possibility that strangers, like Mahjoub, will find their still point of belonging, if only for a moment. Alienation is deeply embedded in Mahjoub's vision. His fiction echoes with some of the horrors of migration and the impossibility of relationships across cultures of his literary forebear, the Sudanese writer, Tayeb Salih, and his path breaking novel, *Season of Migration to the North* (1969), to which I will refer again in the conclusion. The only harmonious community that Mahjoub can envisage, and that only sometimes, is an elite one, between communities of scholars. Perched between the ordinary people with whom he has lost touch, the warring rulers in a Sudanese maelstrom and the arrogance of the racist West, the space Mahjoub occupies is an unstable and uneasy one. His protagonists – both in the seventeenth and the twentieth centuries – are similarly perched between the demonic Law of the power holders and the howling mob. Is Rashid, ultimately, a carrier of new knowledge or is he rather a black scapegoat carrier of the transgressions of the oppressor, Frantz Fanon's 'Negro' bearing the burdens of original sin?

> ... without thinking, the Negro selects himself as an object capable of carrying the burden of original sin. The white man chooses the black man for this function, and the black man who is white also chooses the black man. ... After having been the slave of the white man, he enslaves himself. (Fanon, 1970 [1952]: 136)

Perhaps he is another kind of carrier, a bearer of something wondrous and new. Rashid threw away the telescope, ostensible object of his quest, and yet the novel ends with the possibility of his bringing his discoveries about the universe back to Africa. Mahjoub says in an interview that he left the outcome of Rashid's life 'ambiguous' because he 'wanted to keep him from being dead. I don't think he's dead. He is almost dead. But to my mind, he survives' (Sévry, 2001: 88). Although most of Mahjoub's solid objects were virtual, unattainable, flawed or demonic, here is another bit of hope. It is that Rashid survived his ordeals and that the knowledge that he brought home to Africa had an impact on the generations that followed him, who were thus able to understand the configuration of the cosmos a bit better.

5 Words, Things, & Subjectivity Moses Isegawa's *Abyssinian Chronicles*

Abyssinian Chronicles explores the nature of the relationship between words, solid objects and postcolonial subjectivity. Fragile and distorted subjectivities emerge out of the allure of solid objects, of possessions, which beckon and tease and glitter in societies of great scarcity and poverty. The thread throughout the novel is the pivotal question of what is the nature of subject formation, within the particular power relationships that arise in this context of extreme material scarcity. It is a context within which despotism flourishes as the scarcity of goods drives ordinary people to feats of both extraordinary courage and violence, looting and questing. Or, as Achille Mbembe puts it in relation to the postcolony more broadly, there is a relationship 'between subjection, the distribution of wealth and tribute, and the more general problem of the constitution of the postcolonial subject' (2001: 24). As corruption, desire and struggle for power filters down, asserts Mbembe: 'the masses join in the madness and clothe themselves in cheap imitations of power to reproduce its epistemology' (133). Isegawa traces the life of Mugezi as he joins in the madness and then withdraws from it, over and over again, in a dizzying display of instability, hovering above the abyss, which gives the novel its title.

Mugezi is born in a Ugandan village, grows up in Kampala, is sent to boarding school at a seminary and eventually flies off to Holland. Mugezi's parents, strangely named Serenity and Padlock, raise their family and run their home as a dictatorship, one which mimics the military rule of Idi Amin. In *Abyssinian Chronicles*, dictatorship operates simultaneously on every level of life and seeps into the psyche of the individual. The 'Family', the 'Church' and the 'State' act in unity as multiple parts of one big system, such that 'the public and the private become interchangeable' and 'Padlock's despotism echoes that of Idi Amin' (Jones, 2000: 96). The family is part of the society, which has become dictatorial and 'in *Abyssinian Chronicles* the personal *is* the political' (98). This is what Isegawa means when he suggests in his interview with Jones that he was seeing how to insert politics into the family in the novel (Jones, 91). The family is the state and the state functions through the family as part of the network of dictatorship itself. Mother and Amin are choreographed together in the ritual birth of Mugezi's distorted identity.

And so when his mother, Padlock, violently beats him, 'as more and more strings of bloody saliva dripped through her fingers onto the front of my shirt', Mugezi finds a new, sinister language, blending with his body fluids: 'Amin's words dripped through the filters of my brain into my consciousness' (*Abyssinian Chronicles,* 131).[1] Dictators beget dictators and Padlock's beating

---

[1] Page references to quotations in this chapter, unless indicated otherwise, are to *Abyssinian Chronicles* (London: Picador, 2000).

becomes a ritual of the birth of Idi Amin in Mugezi's pubescent growth of consciousness. Or, as Achille Mbembe puts it, the relationship between the powerful and the apparently powerless in the postcolony is 'convivial', bred out of 'familiarity and domesticity' (2001: 104).

Mugezi's growing up in Kampala, then, is immersed in the grotesque family intimacy of domination. Serenity exacts total obedience and subservience from his children: 'Serenity espoused benevolent dictator tactics to the nth degree' (95). Padlock, their mother, is his enforcer and Serenity 'never interfered with the work of his enforcer, except in the most dire of circumstances' (96). Mugezi, therefore, experiences his parents as 'the dull harmony of the dictators' (103). Because Padlock is his enforcer, Serenity 'let reports of individual misdemeanours hover round him like flies on a slumbering crocodile' (95–6). The sinister buzzing of flies around the vicious Father, metamorphosed into crocodile, hints at the unnatural, demonic nature of Mugezi's nurturing.

The father and the crocodile are linked at the very outset of the novel, which begins with a time warp, a leap into the future as Mugezi foresees his father's death, which is to be devoured by the crocodile. Mugezi tells us that 'three final images flashed across Serenity's mind as he disappeared into the jaws of the colossal crocodile' (3). Mugezi leaps across the boundaries of focalisation as he is simultaneously acrobatic first person and also omniscient narrator. In his first person persona, he could have had no such knowledge of his father's morbid imaginaries, but in this novel of porous boundaries and far-fetched exploits, this hardly matters. What is significant is that the first final image that Mugezi describes his dying father as imagining in a flash, is 'a rotting buffalo with rivers of maggots and armies of flies emanating from its cavities' (3). The visceral invocation of the decaying monstrous buffalo, the maggots, flies and malevolent crocodile, into whose enormous abyss the Father, the Law giver, disappears before the novel has even had a moment to get underway, sets its scene. This scene, of course, could be the product of Mugezi's demonic desire, given his hatred of his parents. We will see him imagine similar horrors for his mother in a moment.

This unnatural hatred means that what Moses Isegawa charts so shockingly in *Abyssinian Chronicles* is how monstrous subjectivies are produced, as the culture of everyday life becomes distorted by the entwined dictatorships of civil society, such as Church, School and Family, and the State. Isegawa is asking what it means for the nature of the subject, the citizen of the postcolony, if the sign of his coming into being is that of the human metamorphosing into snake, crocodile and chameleon? He may be Mbembe's autocrat, who 'is not only a vampire. He also appears as a reptile. He is a boa' (2001: 160–2). He could be a priest, teacher, a father. Perhaps she is a mother. What we observe in *Abyssinian Chronicles* is Mugezi's identity forged in the hatred for his family, particularly his mother and her cruelty, her withholding of love, her 'Padlocked' heart. As a result, Mugezi's sense of self is profoundly twisted, blurred and negotiable.

To survive the tyranny of his parents, Mugezi 'had to strike with the padded stealth of a leopard, hiding my tracks as well as my claws'. He 'had to act with the stubborn mischief of a pig' (109). Isegawa is aware that this toxin, with which the novel is so preoccupied, contaminates its protagonist, even as he fights against it. What we have to wonder is whether Isegawa's own endeavours are undermined as the novel potentially becomes mired in the distortions of human pigs and leopards, crocodiles and rotting buffalos, maggots and flies. All of these participate in strange versions of ritualised subject formation, within the depravities of subjugation. And so 'ours was a family trapped in decay' (315). In this world, violence, beating, blood-letting and torture, both physical and psychological, rule the everyday. Here the ritual death of the patriarch, the dictator, passes through the gateway of the malevolent crocodile.

Serenity had always been threatened by the abyss, by the terror of the stinking hole of the crocodile's gut, by becoming nothing but food for the maggots and flies. This danger of being sucked into the black hole of non-existence was touched upon by Biyi Bandele in his *The Street*, as discussed in Chapter Two. But here, the abyss is the organising image providing the novel with its title. It is Serenity who had conceptualised Uganda in terms of it, and then was himself sucked into it:

> He said that Uganda was a land of false bottoms where under every abyss there was another one waiting to ensnare people, and that the historians had made a mistake: Abyssinia was not the ancient land of Ethiopia, but modern Uganda. (440)

The threat is that of being swallowed by the crocodile, instead of being consti-tuted in language. The abyss is the space between concrete anchoring reality and the words, the use of language which could capture, contain and embed it. In this gap between solid objects and words, lies 'the big howling lacuna' (6). Like 'Biodun, who is unanchored by material realities, as intoned by the Prophet Moses in his mock funeral, so Serenity is unhinged by his morbid relationship to everyday objects. Serenity is far from serene and his insecu-rities render his name ironic – a piece of wit on Isegawa's part. Serenity is tormented by solid, everyday objects, which appear to contribute to the chaos of his life. They induce in him panic and emptiness and loss of self:

> Who would believe that sacks of sugar, salt and beans, packets of sweets, matches and exercise books, released the worst fears in him? The fact was that the sight of all those things opened wells of insecurity, canyons of instability and craters of panic in him. (27)

Wells, canyons and craters open up before Serenity inside shops full of objects. They do so because those objects, with their solid indifference, make Serenity 'shrivel with insignificance' and even induce envy in him because they 'exuded an air of preciousness, desirability and indispensabil-ity so profound that he could not bear to look at the way they were cared for and secured' (27). Serenity's own lack of substance is flaunted by these everyday, concrete and secure objects. Given that language and subjectivity are mutually dependent, a consequence of this lack is that Serenity's ability to speak is impoverished. His own father, who had been a chief and who is self-confident and articulate is able to destroy his insecure son with words:

Overcome by his father's avalanche of saliva and words, Serenity could hardly feel his feet. He seemed to be sinking in mud. His father's green-roofed brick house seemed to be moving, disintegrating, turning into liquid mud, sweeping forward to swallow them. (22)

The supposedly solid house disintegrates in the face of the saliva and mud of words, words that threaten to swallow Serenity, much like the slimy crocodile later does. Here in the slime is the interstitial zone between being and nothingness, between subjectivity and the black hole that is induced by an avalanche of words. This is the site of teetering on the edge of the abyss, a slippery in-between space, which is neither solid nor liquid.

In this way, Isegawa forges the relationship between subjectivity and solid objects, a relationship which structures the novel. Objects in *Abyssinian Chronicles* lose their solidity and are invested with struggles for ascendancy, revenge, expropriation, expulsion, theft and vandalism. They are defiled and evil smelling, reeking as they do of domination and bad blood, until they may be restored to their literal ordinariness by way of language. This is so of the relationships of power in a dictatorship, which affect every aspect of existence and permeate 'even the remotest, tiniest corners of everyday life' (Mbembe, 2001: 107). Even ordinary solid objects become implicated in the performance of demonic dictatorship. Serenity had hoped that his frantic scrounging of possessions from the expropriated Asians would lift him out of the avalanche of slime and combat his terror of things. The objects around which the novel revolves are the Asian television and headboard, the mother's bobbin from her sewing machine, a blue car and a boat belonging to priests in the seminary. They become fetishised and invested with illegitimate, symbolic power, representing the entwined dictatorships of State, Family and Religion. These things will need to be returned from their increasingly symbolic functions to their literal realities, as Mugezi finds the language and a volatile, eccentric sense of self with which to combat their unnatural power. Let us now enter with the father into the Abyss of these Chronicles and their fishy, poisonous objects.

Fishy goods: the expropriated television & a headboard

Rumour was rife of Indians taking their own lives, selling all they had, pouring salt in car engines, giving things away. There were moving sales everywhere. (122)

The goods, obtained cheaply from the departing Asians, who have no choice but to sell, are metonymic in that they stand for, and are also part of, those Africans, who lost their citizenship. The objects that those who were expelled left behind are concrete reminders of dispossession. In the context of the violence, excess and plunder after independence, these metonymies begin to metamorphose into metaphors of expropriation. These are exemplified by the newly acquired television set, the 'black-and-white Toshiba', which 'had the peculiar habit of stinking like a mixture of burned leather and rotten fish after only two hours of service' (122). It is as if rebelling spirits live in the television and protest their relocation, such that 'the stench diminished when the set was switched off, but returned fifteen minutes after it was turned back on' (122). Later, Mugezi imagines that there could be 'Indian curses invested in all their forcibly relinquished goods' (133). These goods are the stubborn relics of bad deeds, from which ordinary people are prepared to benefit. This is another example of the collusion between the big dictators, like Amin, and the little demagogues, like Serenity, who rushes to avail himself of these tainted objects.

Among the objects that Serenity brings home from the stock of Asian possessions, there is a particular item, 'which greatly fascinated' Mugezi. It was 'two-legged like a billboard, had a rectangular shining face and was so burnished and smooth that one could see one's face in it' (126). It stands for the power of the parental dictators, mingled with Idi Amin's despotic decree of expulsion and the exoticism of Asian cultural aesthetics. This object, a fetish, whose mysterious, hidden identity adds to its allure, is a magnificence that Mugezi is expressly forbidden to touch. 'A fetish is, among other things', says Mbembe, 'an object that aspires to be made sacred; it demands power' (2001: 111). The headboard, snatched from the Asians, shines, beckons and ignites Mugezi's developing sexuality:

> I was going to open their [his parent's] drawers and boxes, and examine their clothes and jewelry, and see if they had dirty little books filled with smudged secrets. *The magnet at the heart of this putsch was the glittering object.* It had razored the darkness at the center of my fear with its lightning swords, and the concomitant blood of courage had birthed this coup, this rebirth of my old days of power. (127, my emphasis)

The 'putsch' echoes Amin's coup and evokes the bloody beatings to which both Padlock and Serenity subject their son. Note the mélange of politics, putsches, both familial and country, blood, power, sex and the glittering object. Notwithstanding that Mugezi does not even know the purpose of this shiny, lovely object, he intuitively invests it with the power of Amin's dictatorship and the possibility that he may dispossess his parents of it, even as they had opportunistically acquired it from the desperate departing Asians. Its fetishistic power fuels his adolescent lustful fantasies, mired as they are in struggles over ascendancy. He masturbates with it and enacts the visceral link between solid objects and the body. These objects, puffed up with symbolic and toxic power, open the portals into the abyss of what Deleuze and Guattori (1987: 151) refer to as unnatural 'becomings':

> I closed my eyes and explored the very cool, very smooth surface, my fingers going deeper and deeper into imaginary orifices.... The sensation of swimming in a dark pool, warm and slick with swine sperm was intoxicating.... I turned to the glittering board, the pressure in my loins more palpable. What was beneath this glittering magnificence, this slick dryness? (129)

The sperm of the swine will spawn unnatural progeny; the dark, slimy intoxicating pool signals the danger of the abyss. There is but one route that will save him and that is his drive for knowledge, his wish to know what exactly, literally and materially, the headboard is made of:

Using my thumbnail, I attacked the edge of the board. I worked slowly, trying to attain a good rhythm, but got nowhere.... I wedged my thumbnail beneath the veneer and the glue and the frame. A piece of veneer as big as a man's fingernail broke off. Beneath the veneer was mere wood! Dull brown, long-grained wood! (129)

The glamour is dismantled; this object is mere surface. Its pretension is part of the desire for display, for goods, for show and status. Mugezi is brought back to the sanity of his grandparents in the village, where 'Grandma or Grandpa would have told me straight away that the glittering thing was just a bloody headboard for a bloody bed, wooden, veneered, period' (130). Ultimately a fetish is an impostor, 'endowed with more power than it actually has' (Low, 1996: 223). What happens is that it '*accrues metaphorical energy in its function*' (Low: 223, my emphasis). It is precisely this metaphorical energy that Isegawa attacks, exposes and reduces. The politics available to ordinary people in the postcolony, who contest the power of dictatorship, lie in the capacity to drain the excess and to strip the metaphor back down to the everyday solid object that it is. It is a liberating process, capable of contesting dictatorship in the postcolony: 'the fetish, seen for the sham it is, is made to lose its might and becomes a mere artefact' (Mbembe, 2001: 108). In a similar way, Isegawa has neutralised the 'disturbing power' of objects such as the fake, glittering, ordinary wooden headboard. This is a device that we saw Biyi Bandele put to good use when the figurative was repeatedly returned to the literal in *The Street*'s insistence on operating within the material realities of daily life in London. Laura Marks has also identified the radical potential of this device in intercultural cinema (2000: 78) where 'the dissolution of the fetish is accomplished by its re-embodiment' (Marks: 122), its return to material solidity.

Mugezi pays a painful price on his body for his transgressions in damaging the headboard. He receives a vicious beating from Padlock and an even more terrible whipping by Serenity, unnatural animal father, who 'struck with the bare-clawed fury of a leopard at the end of a long antelope-stalking session' (134). He is beaten to a pulp, nearly to death. However, in the topsy-turvy of dictatorship, Mugezi ominously revels in the pain, as a ritual of growth and purification: 'Every blow drained off the chaff, leaving me pure' (134). What manner of purity is this, other than the reinforcement of naked power that Mugezi is apparently resisting? He survives through evoking none other than the biggest dictator, Amin himself: 'Amin's spiritual help was the ointment which oiled the wounds of defeat and stopped them from festering into gangrenous ulcers of despair' (135). This battle of wills, this potential to evoke dictatorship in order to fight the dictator, will take Mugezi to the edge of the precipice, to that dangerous site where collusion mingles with resistance to corruption. He is 'falling, falling, falling' and the beating takes him back to a childhood incident, 'to the slopes of Mpande Hill, where I almost lost a foot in the spokes of a bicycle gone wild' (134). Back on this imagined hill, he now has to fight 'to keep the bicycle on course, away from the ravine' (134). To fall into the ravine is to be sucked into the slime, the swamps, in which he is drowning 'going up and down, up and down, swallowing green water' (134). This image of a slimy threat will recur.

Notwithstanding his discovery of the mundane ordinariness of the glitz of the headboard, Mugezi will remain vulnerable to the dictatorial power of the object turned fetish. Much later, towards the end of the novel, and as a young man in Holland, Mugezi is drawn to the red-light district, where he joins 'the stream of pilgrims to the shrine of the sex industry' (437). Here, like the allure of the glittering object, Mugezi is attracted by the whores, who are displayed in cages. He pays out the monumental sum of forty dollars and is bitterly disappointed: 'the buy turned out to be bad', which it always will, given that '*the whore reminded me of the despots' hypnotizing headboard*' (437–8, my emphasis). Beneath the glamour is the stark, loveless reality. This seems to be a lesson that Mugezi has to learn over and over again. He puts it to good use against his mother, whose sewing machine is the source of her economic independence and identity. He will attack this machine by stealing its heart – the bobbin. This time, he will begin to buttress his victory with wit, with words.

Family dictatorship & the theft of a bobbin

Padlock's domain is the sewing room, otherwise known as 'her Command Post', from which she runs her dress-making business. This room 'was fitted with a Singer sewing machine, and Padlock spent her day there pedalling away and receiving her customers' (92). Like the headboard, her sewing machine is vested with unnatural power as embodying the military might of the Mother. Mugezi imagines the machine as a possible instrument of her torture: 'in my imagination her foot got stuck underneath the treadle, her finger trapped under the furious needle' (92). He fantasises about his mother's pain and suffering, fantasies in which he listens with glee to her cries for help, futile cries, which are eaten up by the din (92). Mugezi decides, as a form of 'guerrilla warfare', to stick pins 'into a despot's backside' by raiding her Command Post and incapacitating her sewing machine (154). The image of stabbing her backside with pins also ridicules, and reduces her physical power. This is a demonic version of the rite of separation between mother and son, via a distorted alternative to Oedipus, by way of a unique ritual destruction of the mother.

Crucial to Padlock's sewing machine is the tiny, but indispensable, little solid object – the bobbin. A bobbin in a developing country, which is short on supplies, is more valuable than a little nugget of gold. Mugezi knew, moreover, that 'the Singer agent had already gone back to Bombay, Nairobi or London' (154). The precious bobbin is 'made even more valuable by the scarcities created by ... General Idi Amin' (166). The theft of the bobbin is a ritual slaying of the power of the mother enacted by the boy protagonist whose subjectivity is forged in violence, rebellion and deceit. The bobbin is the part for the whole of the mother, a metonymy acting as a metaphor of transgressive power. Like the headboard, the bobbin too is autoerotic for Mugezi – 'I stuck my finger in a small cavern, slippery with lubricant. Polished steel felt perversely smooth in the darkness. I extracted the bobbin' (155).

Padlock is driven demented and to further acts of violence against her family by the loss of this bobbin and her deep suspicion that Mugezi is the culprit, but her inability to prove it. Mugezi's power is increased by his growth into language. He has the edge over his mother, given that she only understands and appreciates 'brute force and raw power' and therefore what she utterly fails to comprehend is the 'sneaky *wit*' of the theft of the bobbin (164, my emphasis). 'Wit' is an intriguing word here. It signifies a form of rhetorical cleverness, a wiliness that is more about strategy than about crime. Mugezi surmises that 'if Padlock had been a woman of words, she would have cursed holes into the roof' (164). Her inability to find the right words, at a crucial moment when Mugezi is contemplating returning the bobbin, is her undoing:

> Suddenly she was towering over me, blocking my view ... 'You, you, you, you,' she puffed, bending over, her breath hot on my forehead. 'You, you, you, you, and I said you.' For emphasis, she cracked me hard on the top of my head with her knuckles.... I reversed all my plans. I would never return her bobbin.... Now she could rant, rave or go on a rampage and break my nose or arm.... (166)

Padlock is incoherent, rambling and raving. The pubescent thirteen-year-old Mugezi, on the other hand, is developing words, along with his growing pains and sexuality. Language and mental prowess will be his weapons: 'this was obviously a mind game, and I was cleverer than she' (169). But the Law, the Father, has not been obliterated; he is not the ineffectual and equally unloved Serenity, but rather the Dictator, Idi Amin, still the hero of the growing boy's aspirations – 'I would never let [General Idi Amin] down again by allowing this woman to beat me for nothing or for anything I could get away with' (169).

Economic and sexual perversion, dictatorship, monetary gain and the stench of toilets and insects are part of the whole Ugandan scene. If Mugezi 'failed to find a buyer for it [the bobbin], I would enjoy the perverse joy of seeing it swallowed by latrine shit and maggots' (167). This joy is perverse for more reasons than one, including the desire to see the mother's body reduced to the stench and rot of the market: 'I would have advised her to veer into a less sedentary line of business, say, selling fish in the filthy Owino Market, where she would imbibe the stench of rotting offal and garbage' (167). This echoes the fishy smell of the illegitimate television, a fug that envelopes the family. All of this visceral disgust becomes part of the language of wit that Mugezi will fine tune, in order to survive. As Mary Douglas points out, the structure of the symbolism of bodily pollution 'uses comparison and double meaning like the structure of a joke' (1996: 122). This anticipates the strategies that Mugezi will devise as he grows to maturity and eventually leaves Uganda behind. We will first have to endure his defecation over sacred objects in the seminary.

At this stage, however, Mugezi does not easily win the war against the rampaging mother. Padlock becomes 'very dangerous', a wicked witch 'pumping the house full of poison' (167) as she impotently sits at her throne, threading the paralysed Singer and 'driving the thick steel needle in and out' with 'cold fury' (167). It is not surprising that Mugezi begins to have bad dreams, 'odd nightmares with Padlock bearing down on me, the bobbin in one hand, a hammer in the other' (168). Again we have the melange of sex, shit, stories and language, crystallising around the solid, everyday material objects – a bobbin or a hammer. Mugezi's development of language and subjectivity is beset by European fairy stories of wicked witches casting spells linked to vicious, stabbing sewing machines and embroiled in the excrement and violence of postcolonial dictatorship in Uganda. Mugezi's resistance is wily, witty and subversive, but it is also contaminated by bad smells, bad dreams, crime and hatred. This hatred of the mother in particular, raises the question of whether *Abyssinian Chronicles* is itself tainted by the horrors it depicts. Isegawa could be retaining the stereotype of Mother Africa, merely inverting its content from positive to negative. Instead of the nurturing mother, this bad mother Africa has turned bully and once again flesh and blood women are potentially sacrificed at the alter of symbols and tropes. Padlock, and by extension Uganda, is unnatural mother, reeking of cursing, apple poisoning, needle contaminating wicked witches. This echoes Mahjoub's incandescent Sigrid, who is disembodied as she becomes pure light, as we saw in the previous chapter. The one may be light and the other darkness, but both women are objects of Rashid's and Mugezi's respective figurative imaginings. Mugezi may bring the bobbin down to size, but in the process the mother metamorphoses into metaphorical witch. In other words, the vehemence of *Abyssinian Chronicles*'s portrayal of the vicious mother threatens to overwhelm the narrative with a degree of unappetising misogyny.[2] The war with the Mother is just about to the death.

The adult male, who emerges from this rite of passage, could be himself the monstrous progeny of dictatorship. For him, '[Amin] was indomitable, indefatigable and as indispensable as air' (176). Eventually, the bobbin is replaced in the particular way that things are in Africa: 'Serenity bought black-market dollars and asked a friend to import a bobbin for him from neighboring Kenya' (172). Padlock may not have had the power of language, but she did have access to the word of God. In the midst of the search for the bobbin-stealing culprit, 'Padlock stepped up her campaign of terror by reading frightening passages from the Old Testament and praying for maladies like leprosy to afflict the thief' (169). Elaine Scarry has mapped the relationship between the scriptures, solid objects, the power of God and the body. She describes how God's 'invisible presence' is 'made visible' in the transformations he renders on the material world and the human body (1985: 181 &183). As regards the human body, Scarry emphasises the worrying recurrence in the scriptures of 'scenes of wounding' (183). That is to say, what makes God's 'realness' most visible is 'the wounded human body' (200). In *Abyssinian Chronicles* Padlock refers manically to her Old Testament scriptures with their scenes of bodily mutilation and torturous punishments, like leprosy, as part of her sleuthing campaign. She 'lingered on the three thousand people who died' as punishment for 'the sinfulness of the Israelites in making the Golden Calf' and she emphasises 'the disease among the survivors which God meted out for good measure' (169). This biblical tirade again

---

2   I am indebted to Lyndall Gordon for this important insight: personal correspondence, December 2005.

demonstrates the combined forces of Family and Church to oppress and torture the young boy's body and mind. This leads to the next part of Mugezi's
life. Along with his sexual coming of age, the theft of the bobbin results in his
expulsion, not from the Edenic paradise, but from the dystopian wilderness
of home. Although not discovered, Mugezi remained the prime suspect in
the bobbin case. Serenity and Padlock decide to send him away to the seminary to continue his schooling. From the frying pan into the hellish flames
as family and the clergy buttress each other with their dictatorships and their
tortures: 'in the darkness, the sewing machine resembled a medieval instrument of torture on which sinners were punished by sadistic clergymen' (155).
It is to the sadistic, dictatorial clergymen and their fetishes that we now turn
in order to see Mugezi's lessons of resistance put to further use.

Catholic dictatorship: the blue Peugeot
& *Agatha*, the boat

> The hydra at the heart of the autocracy commonly known as the seminary system
> bore three venom-laden heads: brainwashing, schizophrenia and good old-fashioned
> dictatorship. (185)

Mugezi finds that the seminary is just like 'the dictatorship I had left behind'
(186). Fr. Mindi, a priest, is a 'dictator' who is 'blinded by his own sense of
unquestionable power' (208). Here, food, or its absence, is a scarcity around
which the dictatorship operates. This scarcity is shaped by imperial traces
and shot through with racial, gendered and generational hierarchies of power,
with the European Fathers at the helm: 'White, nuclear-warhead-privileged
priest above the black, shit-scared peasant priest, who was above the shitty-
assed peasant nun, who lorded over the wormy peasant faithful – man,
woman, child' (253). Bluntly, the pupils are black, hungry and at the bottom
of the pile. The most powerful teachers are white, affluent, well-fed and the
proud owners of amazing possessions like cars and boats. These vehicles
become metonyms, standing for their owners. Like the headboard and the
bobbin they slowly grow and metamorphose into fetishes. They become symbols of colonial might and oppression in cahoots with the church. We will see
them also reduced to size. But first, the basis of all that transpires is hunger,
basic bodily deprivation: 'food was the most important element' and 'we went
to bed with food on our minds and awoke the same way' (216). It rankles
Mugezi that the 'gaping mouths' of these priests 'would soon be gobbling
a rich breakfast' while 'we lapped thin, worm-infested porridge' (252–3).
      The two white priests, on whom the novel focuses, are Fr. Mindi, who
is simply a prelude to the more exotic and handsome, Fr. Gilles Lageau.
Fr. Mindi, master in charge of discipline, beats up hungry boys desperately
seeking contraband outlets for their terrible hunger, given that 'boys fed on
bad *posho* (corn bread) and weevilled beans … had to supplement their defi-
cient diet' (199). The priest enjoyed inflicting pain on boys caught searching
for food beyond the confines of the starvation belt of the seminary. He was
thus 'the most hated man in the seminary' (199).

This hatred was expressed by way of boyish prayers for the destruction of Fr. Mindi's body, for God's wounding punishment. Boys 'prayed for him to get into a car accident and live the rest of his life in a wheelchair. They prayed for him to become blind, to get cancer and to be afflicted with every purulent disease on earth' (199). This echoes Mugezi's fervent desire for pins in his mother's backside. The onslaught on Fr. Mindi's body is eventually accomplished, in the first instance, by way of a violation of the solid object that stands for him, his precious blue Peugeot. Mugezi spreads his excrement all over this car in a description of unparalleled grossness:

> I had eaten a few pawpaws, bought from a truant, and combined with our weevilled beans, the stench they gave my excrement was overpowering. I held my nose as I opened the plastic bag ... I used a trowel to smear the seats, the roof, the floor, the steering wheel, the gear shift, the dashboard and all the carpets. (202)

This time, Mugezi has not just scratched the surface of the headboard, or stolen, bobbin-like, a crucial part of the engine of the car. He defecates on it, using forbidden bodily excretions to fight the power of the colonial-style priest. In the process he reduces the fabulous car to a toilet. Predictably, this act of obscene damage does not lead to the priest reforming himself and Fr. Mindi subsequently, therefore, finds himself more directly shat upon with a shower of shit: 'a soggy mass covered his face, then dripped down his throat, the front of his shirt and on to his trousers' (208). He is saturated with the horrible slime, which permeates his body – 'the stench would not go away. He tried to vomit, but only strings of bile dropped from his mouth' (208). Fr. Mindi is destroyed and he leaves the seminary.

However, Mugezi's victory is not certain. The slime and stench are dangerous weapons, ones that could backfire. As Mary Douglas has pointed out, bodily refuse signals both power and danger (1966: 12). Excretions from the orifices – 'spittle, blood, milk, urine, faeces or tears by simply issuing forth have traversed the boundary of the body' (Douglas: 121) and boundaries, margins 'are dangerous'. This is so, because 'if they are pulled this way or that the shape of fundamental experience is altered' (Douglas: 121). Mugezi, as we have seen, is himself vulnerable to the abyss – that slimy site in-between, into which he could also disappear, along with his victims. He will have to refine his tactics when Fr. Mindi is replaced by Fr. Lageau, the French Canadian missionary from Quebec.

Lageau is ruddy and golden, his suntan matching 'his reddish hair and the golden fluff on his thick, meaty arms' (215). This 'well-tended body' announced his 'naked power', which combined 'American power and French arrogance' (215). He is an ideal film star embodiment of perfection and he walked with 'the swagger of American silver-screen heroes' (215). In fact, he 'looked very much like Sean Connery portraying James Bond' (217). Mugezi is at first captivated by the man and his aura. Like the headboard, '[Fr. Lageau's] power ... glittered with the sharpness of silver and the richness of gold. It frightened me and held me hostage in its glare' (220). This sharp, glistening power in the context of scarcity, the appearance of 'this flamboyant man in the midst of poverty-stricken souls', resulted in 'a finely tuned idealization' of the rich (218). In other words, at first Mugezi is alienated from the evidence of his own senses and experience within his family, and is magnetically drawn to the power of this golden priest and his magical objects. These he fantasises as able to liberate him from the poverty, scarcity and ugliness of his life: 'This was the ideal power which shielded one from the ghastly sight of dying babies, emaciated adults and stinking geriatrics' (250). Gold pens and watches and, most of all, *Agatha*, are the embodiment of Lageau's allure. The bedazzled boys go so far as to imagine that he is their Messiah, come to save them from their terrible hunger. Mugezi, therefore, makes this appeal to him in relation to 'the deplorable food we eat every day':

> The beans are weevilled, tasteless and far from nourishing. The maggots in the maize flour have become very fat and look fatter on our plates. We would like to have better, more nourishing meals. We would like to have a more balanced diet. We would like the nuns to take more care with our food, especially on Sundays, when the rice is usually half-cooked and has pebbles in it. (220–1)

Unsurprisingly, Lageau's response is more than unsympathetic; it is self-righteous and enraged. And with the dismantling of Lageau's messianic persona, Mugezi has a revelation about Lageau's true character as 'an empty braggadocio who did not even have the decency to make good his boasts by at least rewarding us with good meals' (221). He is the headboard stripped of its veneer all over again. Rebellion is set in motion, but nothing happens until the arrival of *Agatha*, Lageau's splendid boat: 'a glossy twelve-footer, she sat on her dolly, awash with fluorescent light, and glowed like a new alabaster Virgin' (245). Given the punishment meted out to Fr. Mindi's Peugot, we are full of foreboding. *Agatha* could have been the mechanism to assuage the boys' gnawing hunger, given that Lageau nets boatloads of fish in her. No Christ-like figures, whose fishes fed the multitude, these priests eat their full of juicy fish and then fill up their freezers, while 'rotten beans continued to be part of our daily diet' (245).

Beside its practical function as a fishing vessel, however, *Agatha*'s allure rests with her symbolic power, which, again like the headboard and the bobbin, is invested with fetishised sexual fantasy. She is the celibate Lageau's substitute for the arrival of his glamorous European wife. Prior to her coming, the boys ogle a photograph of the boat, a picture, which 'changed hands faster than porno magazines in a military barracks' (244). *Agatha* is also the pinnacle of all the wondrous possessions that the priest flaunts, and which bathe him in a golden aura of power, wealth and status. Fr. Lageau, insulated by his wealth, which is made visible by his stuff, embodies the might of the Church linked to Empire and to international Capitalism:

> In Fr. Lageau I saw the might of the Catholic Empire, advancing, conquering, subjugating, manipulating, dictating, ruling. ... This man also gave off intimations of the World Bank and International Monetary Fund hegemony. He personified cast-iron rules forged in golden rooms, immortalized in gold-edged books with thick golden pens in faraway gold-sprinkled cities. (250)

This puffed up emperor, this 'empty braggadocio', wears the ceremonial clothes of international European and American wealth and clout, with his books, pens and boat. Mbembe's 'postcolonial African subject' resists this be-dazzling display and potentially finds a voice by claiming a concrete, material world through 'his/her eyes, ears, mouth – in short, his/her flesh, his/her body' (Mbembe, 2001: 17). This is what Mugezi attempts to do, but ambivalently. What Isegawa repeatedly depicts is Mugezi's collusion with the power for which he lusts, alongside his resistance to it, a condition, which Homi Bhabha has documented as characterising a trend in the nature of the resistance to colonial power (1994: 107). Mugezi 'was on my knees.... I was worshipping power in its glorious isolation' (250). But this is being sucked into that black hole and out of control and he is once again 'juggernauting down the hill like the winds that had devastated Mbale's village' (250). This is the engulfing slime – 'Snot was creeping ticklishly down my nostrils' (250). He must retreat from this power, from Lageau, and he must do so through his mind, through his wit, by logic and language: 'I slowly regained my wits. Exorcised by my increasing consciousness, the demons of power retreated. I started asking questions' (251). Mugezi remembers that the reason he hated Padlock was that, exactly like Lageau, she arbitrarily used her power against the weak (251).

Once again the solution is to expose the emperor as sham and his boat as the commonplace solid object that it is. Again, the strategy is to take the Dictator's trimmings and trappings and to violate them, defecate upon them, vomit all over them. This reduces their power, and their owner's, by exposing their shallowness and hypocrisy. Mugezi knows what to do:

> Not too long ago, Serenity had beaten me nearly to death just hours after Padlock had tortured me and bled my mouth for tearing a strip off a banal secondhand headboard cast away and accursed by departing Indians. I had, from then on, become a non-respecter of property. Now *Agatha* no longer awed me. (252)

Or, as Mbembe puts it: 'is the subject aware of being taken over by the demonic thing? How to escape? By breaking the demon? By coating it with excrement?' (168). The blue Peugeot had been subjected to this coating, but while Mugezi reduces the priest and his possessions to 'money-awed turds' (252) in his mind, he will find more sophisticated methods of attack.

However, while Mugezi is agonising about the precise nature that his revenge on Lageau should take, someone else gets in first and gouges a 'two-inch scratch on *Agatha*'s second rib' (246). We will return to this mysterious ally shortly. In the meanwhile, the horrified priest is no longer a bronzed and golden hero: 'a tomato-red Lageau, Elvis hair standing on end, concluded that *Agatha* had been assaulted' (247). This attack provokes Lageau into a frenzy of rage: 'Who did not know that Agatha happened to be the name of his mother, his first girlfriend and his ideal woman?' (247). Lageau merges metonymically with his boat, which is a part of him; he suffers this nasty scratch on his own body where 'excruciating pain seared him, making him afraid that he was going to have an improbable heart attack' (247). Lageau's body, *Agatha*'s and his mother's are one: 'He felt the approaching pounding devastation of a migraine, his mother's staple affliction' (247). In fact, the unknown attacker provokes Lageau into coming out from beneath his shiny veneer and to express his brute power and crass racism without gleaming trappings. In a shocking sermon delivered after the scratch on his boat, Fr. Lageau, stripped of all his urbane sophistication, calls his black students monkeys, the ultimate racist insult:

> 'Monkeys, black monkeys. Monkeys with no regard for aesthetics or property. How could anyone desecrate *Agatha*? What had she done to them? Why would anyone cut her rib? You know why? Because they are monkeys. During this mass, join me to pray for these monkeys to gain a modicum of respect for other people's property.' (248)

Mugezi, who now has wit and irony as weapons at his disposal, inverts this insult by turning the monkey into trickster rebel. Lageau's 'disdain' for the monkey originated with the 'missionary-colonial era' (251). By contrast, within indigenous knowledge and oral tales, 'to us, the monkey represented cleverness' (251). This wily monkey is not frozen as idealised symbol of a pre-colonial African past. It is a weapon, fashioned for resistance appropriate to more recent times. The monkey insult intensifies Mugezi's war against Lageau. He devises a military strategy consisting of two prongs. There are, firstly, words, book learning and the library. Secondly, this strategy finds itself a more sinister ally when once again Mugezi summons General Idi Amin for assistance. So, simultaneously with going 'deeper into the library' (221), Mugezi also finds that 'General Amin, whom I had neglected for a long time, suddenly surfaced like a leviathan.' This is so especially in relation to his preaching on 'self-empowerment' (222). There are obvious dangers in resorting to a dictatorship to fight the dictator.

Taking Amin first, Isegawa provides us with a complex portrait of a dictator, who was also a tower of strength to ordinary people, who saw him as a weapon against their weakness and their vulnerability. He always surfaces for Mugezi, when he is threatened. For all its dangers, the interesting point that Isegawa is making is that if one does not appreciate the nature of the empowerment Amin promised, one cannot understand Ugandan history, or that of the postcolony in general, with all its survivals, newness and struggles. This is precisely the point that emerges in a fascinating conversation between Isegawa and Mahmood Mamdani, himself a Ugandan Asian, who suffered under Amin's expulsions. Mamdani sees Isegawa as portraying Amin as 'an empowering force' (in Vazquez, 2000: 133). Isegawa expresses his debt to Mamdani for this portrayal and refers to the influence of Mamdani's (1973) book, *From Citizen to Refugee*, where, according to Isegawa, Mamdani was 'the first person to take Idi Amin seriously'. He was

> the first person to analyze him in an intelligent way. Everybody else was saying, 'Idi Amin was an idiot, he was nothing.' And you said, 'No, Amin knew exactly what he had to do in his *own* situation'. (in Vazquez, 2000: 134)

Later in the novel, in the midst of the scandal that erupts from Lageau's monkey remarks, Mugezi reflects again on General Amin, asking himself whether Amin had not 'time and again, charged that the Catholic Church was built on murder, terror, senseless war, genocide and robbery?' (252). Mugezi may become disillusioned with Amin later, but in his formative years he was his inspiration. Isegawa is insisting that the reality of what Amin stood for, in the daily lives of ordinary people, who had been psychologically devastated by colonial racism, was quite complex and, perplexingly, not totally rotten.

Mugezi will also struggle against the Catholic Church and the powerful, white, racist Fathers, by way of their own libraries and books; he will turn their treasuries against them, but in his ambiguous longing for their power, with the stain of Amin on his armoury, he will also be partly defeated by them. This was a path along which the young Mugezi had begun to travel prior to coming to the seminary, and we saw his superior use of language and of wit against the raving and inarticulate Padlock.

From early on in his stay there, Mugezi had found solace in books in the seminary: 'books took over' (204). He recognises that these books are political weapons: 'As others caved in to total submission or to sporadic fits of bravado, I turned to books' (204). Nonetheless, it does not immediately occur to Mugezi as to how to realise this weaponry. If anything, in the face of their ill treatment and hunger, words seem ineffectual: 'it was at table that one realized how words were divorced from reality' (217). That is to say, 'there was a lot of talk around the theme of equality, but those sweet words disappeared in a miasma of pig food' (217). Mugezi ponders how to unite words and the material realities, like the disgusting food on the table. Like wit, he realizes that: 'Irony was the best ship home across the swirling waves of frustration and outrage' (254). Armed with words, Mugezi searches for just the right irony with which to defile *Agatha*. He invokes the forked tongue so beloved of postcolonial resistance and scratches the blasphemous, but also archetypal exclamation words 'OH GOD!' on *Agatha's* belly (255).

Again, this desecration is etched onto Lageau's body when, on discovery of this graffiti, he 'had his first real migraine that morning. One half of his head, neck and side felt paralyzed' (255). The direct inscription onto his body of the insult to *Agatha* is emphasised: 'he felt like vomiting, diarrhea grated in his rectum, light hurt his eyes' (255). To add the proverbial insult to this injury, Mugezi returns to the scene of his crime at a later date and 'I etched the words RED INDIAN under OH GOD!' (257). 'Red Indian' has become the irreverent slang name for Fr. Lageau, whose body has become red with rage. Mugezi's verbal weapons are carved concretely on wood, reducing the symbolic Imperial power of the fetish of the boat.

At face value it could appear that the onslaught on Fr. Lageau's boat is less awful than the shit inside Fr. Mindi's car, but this is not the case. The blasphemy and insult by reference to Lageau's changed body– from James Bond and Jesus to a Red Indian – is devastating. From the moment of his anger and anguish, Lageau's blood pressure seems permanently up. He is referred to as an ugly red on many occasions – even his ears 'glowed!' (248). No longer the ruddy, suntanned god, he is demoted to being parodied as 'Father Red Indian' (254). The skin colour of whites has itself been de-fetishised. No longer snowy white and pure, it is red, blotchy, pink like the pig food dished up by the greedy, silly priests. And, of course, here is the rub. The fact that Mugezi stoops to ridiculing skin colour and uses native Americans as an insult to the red faced priest, is further evidence of his own only partial liberation from the stereotypes of colonial thinking, and his ambiguous collusion with it.

The important point is that *Agatha* has now been rendered ordinary and vulnerable, along with her silly, red-faced owner. She joins the fetish junk heap, along with the headboard and the sewing machine. She may have been repainted and a 'German-made monster of an alarm installed on her', the cost of which could have fed them for a whole year, but she has been exposed and boys 'now made jokes' about her and referred to her as 'a little yellow-haired Canadian whore' (260). Sadly, again we have the attack on women, here white women, entwined with the Red Indian mixed message in order to make the postcolonial critique of the racist Priest and his white body. And again, we wonder whether Isegawa himself, in the creation of his slippery protagonist, does not sometimes fall into the cracks as his narrative excesses potentially overwhelm him.

A solid character and role model does stand out in this novel of dictators, human leopards and duplicitous priests masquerading as men of god. It is Dorobo, the seminary watchman. Mugezi wants to use his irony against the priest and likens it to the weapons of the night watchman: 'I wanted to stab Lageau and his ego, but which word could I sharpen like Dorobo's monstrous arrows?' (254). It turns out that Dorobo had been the first perpetrator against *Agatha*, the one who made the initial scratch with his giant bow and arrow, which literally are his defensive weapons for his job (201). Dorobo was, moreover, aware of Mugezi's nocturnal crimes against *Agatha*. Instead of reporting him, he thanks him, significantly, in one of the very few examples of non-standard English in the book "Sank you fa *Agasa* job, he-he-heeee" (259). With more irony than he may realize he tells Mugezi that "Faza Lago ask about boat and I say I watch fa thief not fa writer, ha haa ..." (259). It is indeed his skill with words that lifts Mugezi's strategy out of the mire of common crime and physical violence. But without the protection and support of Dorobo, he would have been caught and expelled. Dorobo, the uneducated and poor watchman, rather than Lageau, is the true Jesus figure and in realizing this, Mugezi makes progress in decolonising his mind: 'I kept thinking that he [Dorobo] was Fisherman, the power saboteur. A real fisher of men' (260). Out of the ruins of theft and vandalism, something positive seems to be emerging. Dorobo's language is the less than powerful, albeit expressive, English of the ordinary people. Mugezi will take Dorobo's strength and transform his language into the figurative arrows of educated English, sharpened into a weapon of resistance. Dorobo is 'very tall, very strong, soot-black' (201). He is the salt of the earth. He is not the library-seeking postcolonial subject, like Isegawa, like Mugezi, his creation. He is part of the masses and he too is fed up with dictatorship.

The solid arrows, which had literally defiled the boat in an act of resistance, become metaphors for Mugezi's combative words. In this way, Isegawa gestures towards the possibility of creating new metaphors, outside of the arsenal of colonialist discursive stereotype. This is only possible once the toxic imperialist tropes have been defiled and reduced to their material ordinariness. In this way, there is the hope that the educated elite, for all its scars and defects, finds a language and a mode of identity that incorporates the grassroots. Ultimately, Mugezi uses his way with words to escape from the seminary and expels himself on his own terms: 'I forged my own expulsion letter, signed and stamped it with the seminary stamp we kept for library purposes. I also recommended myself to the best schools I knew' (263). The words and the wit, however, of which Mugezi is so fond, need to anchor him to the material realities of life, so that he does not continue to be threatened by his bicycle careering downhill without any brakes.

Negotiating subjectivity & the abyss: words & things

This anchoring offered by solid objects and by language Serenity had tried hard to achieve, but we saw that he was doomed to failure from the very outset. Along with the television and the headboard, Serenity had acquired heaps of other stuff on the backs of the expropriated Asians, things that are 'spilled forth' from a 'puke-yellow Uganda Postal Service truck' including 'a fridge-cum-oven, a mighty spring bed, a box of black tea cozies which were in fact Afro wigs, a few other bits and pieces' (126). These are the accoutrements of everyday life, the bric-a-brac with which Serenity vainly hopes to barricade his tenuous existence. What is visceral in Isegawa's novel is the pain of changing identities, which solidify, only to turn into slush and jelly as they are threatened with extinction. We have seen how it is only language, and its tools of words, wit and irony, that can forestall the descent. This Serenity also appears to intuit and in the melange of his purloined stuff, there are also the books, perhaps most powerful of all in their potential to buttress him and stave off the inevitable annihilation:

> Serenity discovered Oliver Twist, Madame Defarge, the Artful Dodger and many more ghosts in the Dickensian jungle, but it was the American jungle that stole his heart. American writers, with their migrant's fascination and obsession with money, success and power, spirited him off into a world of dreams where likeable rogues had it all. Ensconced in their penthouses, they cut deals, sipped champagne, participated in orgies with perfect-bodied nymphos and indulged in excesses just this side of madness. (123–4)

These books are doubly defiled, by colonialism as well as by postcolonial expropriation on the part of the new African ruling dictatorship. Like Mugezi's bedazzlement by Lageau's fancy possessions, Serenity is mesmerised by the promise of sex orgies, by imagining the perfect, white bodies and an excess of riches linked to power. The gulf between concrete reality and the world of these books, for which Serenity yearns, is cataclysmic. By contrast with this golden, bubbly world, the atmosphere in Serenity's home is one of distrust, theft and punishment. The network of Isegawa's imagery is thick with multiple associations. Take the old, red covered copy of *Waiting for Godot*. Serenity sits reading it, in the atmosphere of terror created by the fact that Mugezi's younger siblings, known only as 'the shitters', are suspected of stealing the 'rat money' (150) (known in gentler homes as the tooth fairy money, paid out in return for a lost milk tooth). Links are forged between books, money, rats and the deformed, shitting body, all united by red, the colour of blood:

> We ate our food inches away from the condemned shitters, their foreheads gleaming with the beads of guilty sweat, their eyes red with fear. We washed our dirty fingers with water poured and trapped by the two criminals in small bidet-like plastic basins such as I would, years later, find in a foreign brothel, and which I would always associate with smut, soap, fish smells and poisoned meals. Serenity, high in his chair like Pontius Pilate, washed his fingers absentmindedly, looking neither at the block of blue soap proffered nor at the trembling shitter making the offering. *Godot, encased in red, tired-looking hard covers, was the only being on his mind.* (151, my emphasis)

There is an excess of elements: blocks of blue soap, the book, betrayal, fish smells linked to Asian property, the body, the brothel, the shitters and warfare, red eyed children, turned into frightened rats, along with the book of Godot also metamorphosed into red eyed rodent. The book, metonym of the departed Asians, turns metaphor of the blood of Christ and the futility of waiting for God/ot's salvation. Bathed in the sweat and excrement of the terrified shitters, the victims of the dictator, their betrayer, their father, becomes the treacherous Pontius Pilate. And there, in the midst, is the triumphant, defeated Mugezi, whose sexuality is born in the mire of poison and fishy theft, and who will play out his desires demonically in Dutch brothels, which reek of tired old family filth and depravity. As for Serenity, having established the terms of the dangers lurking in the abyss, where he saw that Abyssinia was Uganda, with himself in it on a freefall, he is unable to negotiate the terror of words and things, which remain unconnected.

To avoid his father's fate of being sucked into the black hole of non-existence Mugezi realised that he had to harness words, in order to negotiate his material world. To begin with, Mugezi, like his father, was also overwhelmed by words: 'a mangled mass of words boiled inside me, clogging my mouth' (81) and 'I had to kill those words' (98–9). A turning point is reached for him 'as the words whistled and the air vibrated' when he hears his parents fight (104). His parents' wild words at first send him to the edge 'on the rim of this seething crater' (104), just as Serenity's father's words had sunk the supposedly solid house into the mud. Mugezi is a man in transition perched in the nether-space between abyss and safe landing. Neither body nor symbol, this is slime, what Kaufman calls that 'in-between register', that 'middle term used to illustrate the solid and liquid in relation' (2002: 124). It is also Mugezi's snot that 'was creeping ticklishly down my nostrils' (250) when he experiences his confused love–hatred for the power and trappings of authority enjoyed by Fr Lageau. It is also his experience of vertigo when 'everything seemed topsy-turvy' (250). Eventually, his project becomes that of sharpening his language, so that his words may be weapons, like Dorobo's arrows, in his struggle against the fetishised power of *Agatha*. And so, when a more mature Mugezi finally leaves Uganda for Amsterdam, he 'attacked the Dutch language course like a madman. ... I was not a journalist, but I was near where words were beaten into weapons, and I was gradually forging mine' (461). Mugezi's identity hovers and metamorphoses above the crater. The danger is of disappearing into the grasping for power, without the knowledge of its corruption. As Isegawa puts it in the mouth of his unstable protagonist, who may himself go either way: 'The seventies were dominated by self-made men who, defying their limited backgrounds, rose to vertiginous heights of power *before dashing their chariots into the abyss*' (265, my emphasis). Drawn to the luminescent flame, those who aspire after power burn their bodies and are destroyed, like the yellow moths dancing 'round Grandpa's hurricane lamp' (265). Mugezi is himself one of those vulnerable moths, hovering on the edges of extinction. He engages in illicit practices – 'seduction of piracy was like a lantern to a suicidal moth' (369). Power games are motivated by his desire to be 'on top' and Mugezi turns his talents to underworld smuggling prior to his emigration to Holland. He 'craved being on top' and questions himself regarding 'how far was I ready to go?' (369). He is aware that 'the urge to test our omnipotence was irresistible' (369).

Mugezi is hero and anti-hero, protagonist and omniscient narrator, vicious son, oppressed brother and loving grandson; he is teacher, lawyer, pirate, aid worker and gigolo; he is victim and perpetrator; he is a street-wise Ugandan and ultimately a cosmopolitan migrant living in Amsterdam. He is 'an "excessive" figure who resists any attempt (by the reader) to foreclose on his alterity' (Jones, 2000: 100). His subjectivities are transient and multiple as he wades through the clutter and muck all around him:

> Just as in the [parental] dictatorship I had left behind, at the seminary I found myself in acting school, because survival here depended on how well you adapted to your new role and how wonderfully you performed it. (186)

The whole purpose of this performance of identity is to be able to be the one with power, the one at the top, and here we see Mugezi's confusion. This lust for power veers between resistance to the system of autocracy and metamorphosis into the autocrat himself, so that the time would come 'when the faithful would grovel at your feet for blessings, exorcism and deliverance from sin' (186). These excesses of subject positioning are what Mbembe refers to as 'simultaneous multiplicities', which characterise identity in the postcolony (2001: 146). The autocrat himself indulges in 'an intertwining of multiple identities'; in him we have a 'proliferation of allegiances' in that 'one minute, the Christian he used to be is transformed into a Muslim. Next minute, prostrated on the ground, he will recite his suras' (2001: 155).

In like manner, Mugezi continues to metamorphose and constantly to shape-shift. Mbembe's metaphor for these transformations within the postcolony is that the subject emerges under 'the sign of the chameleon'. This is a subject, who says, 'I can change depending on where I am' (Mbembe, 2001: 165). However, unlike the ease of the colour kaleidoscope of the chameleon, each shifting shape exacts a price and poses a threat of obliteration for Mugezi: 'this peeling away of old skin hurt. I felt sore, lost, trapped' and 'shuddered to think about the task of re-defining myself' (266). Mugezi will shed his skin, painfully, yet again, as he flies off to Amsterdam and enters a zone of plenty. His flight felt 'like purgatory', separating his soul from his wounded body: 'I felt like a soul hovering above its bleeding corpse, caught between the shreds of the man I had been and the vague outline of the man I wanted to become' (418).

Excess, scarcity & the postcolonial subject

The survival strategy, then, for the wily citizen of the new African state, is to de-mystify the trappings of power and domination by vandalising, appropriating and defecating on these fetishes. The most powerful weapon for so doing is not to deface them or to shit on them, but to play with language in order to be able to expose their magical potency as showy sham. The outcome, however, is not always predictable or palatable as the dictator finds new ways of entering through the back door of the postcolonial subject's psyche, even as his fetishes and symbols are exposed and apparently abandoned. Even Mugezi's grandfather, a strong, moral centre in the novel, unlike his son, is vulnerable to the opportunity of acquiring goods, offered by Amin's deportation of Asians:

> Grandpa partook of the bonanza of cheap sales by going up Mpande Hill to the shops. He got himself a fifty-kilo sack of sugar, a ten-liter tin of cooking oil, a twenty-liter tin of paraffin, and cement for repairing cracked graves in the family burial ground near my favorite tree. (119)

This Grandpa did, albeit that he 'could see that Amin was a robber baron, a corporate raider, a mafia boss' (119) and yet he could not afford to lose out on the material bonanza, given the scarcity of these goods and their necessity for survival. Likewise, albeit that Lageau is a braggart and a racist, his gold watch and the fact that he wore only French clothes carry weight with the starving poor kids of the seminary and 'much was made of the expensive belts, checked socks and genuine leather open-toes sandals he wore in class' (218). Isegawa's tone here is considered and serious, along with its ironic edge. In the gross deprivation out of which these youths are growing into manhood, the gleam of these goods offers the promise of an alternative kind of life. The lure of the gleam mingling with the stench of pawpaw and bean shit, echoes the world of Ghanaian novelist, Ayi Kwei Armah's *The Beautyful Ones Are Not Yet Born* (1969). Armah too, in this much earlier novel, while criticising the materialist longing for the corrupt Capitalist goods introduced by Colonialism, emphasises the logical nature of their magnetism, given their cleanliness, comfort and sparkle, in a society of deprivation and scarcity. This is the phenomenon that Mugezi's grandfather wryly observes when he describes how young people desperately smuggle coffee for American dollars so as to obtain 'bell-bottom trousers, radios, Oris watches' (282).

This scarcity in postcolonial Africa gives rise to a paradox that Mbembe identifies, which is that the postcolony, in spite of, or perhaps because of, being characterised by scarcity and poverty, brimmed with what he referred to as 'excess' or 'overloading' – 'everything leads to excess here' (2001: 147). Mbembe portrays the piles of goods along the side of the road, the 'vegetables, fruit, bread, fresh drinks, small pets, doughnuts, sugar (by the cube), toiletries, palm oil, cigarettes, matches' (147). This overloading, then, occurs in a context 'of extreme material scarcity' (24). What Isegawa explores in the Ugandan context, which has been emphasised by Mbembe as well, are the consequences of 'where authoritarianism is coupled with shortage and scarcity' (Mbembe, 2001: 165). This is the world of *Abyssinian Chronicles* under Amin, where Isegawa describes how people became 'more and more materialistic', given that everything became scarce. Books, regarded as non-essential, basically disappeared and 'you thought about food and household goods which you felt were necessary for life' (Jones, 2000: 90). Mugezi roams the city and encounters hawkers in the taxi park displaying 'baby wear, shoes, plastic basins, cheap jewelry, anything' (408).

In conclusion, the chameleon Mugezi evokes Ben Okri's monster of the greedy road. In *The Famished Road* (1992), Azaro, Okri's protagonist, meandered through the maze of Lagos's markets, bars and bush. Azaro is an *abiku*, a spirit child, who occupies the interstice between the land of the living, the dead and the unborn and he travels back and forth between these worlds. The shape-shifting Mugezi also wanders about the city, here Kampala, looking at the mountains of stuff, stripped of their shiny veneer, and which Isegawa lists in concrete metonymies of excess:

> I opened my eyes and thought I was dreaming. The *majestic greedy road ...* was clogged with people bearing the weight of fridges, squeaky beds, greasy motor parts, new and used tires, rusty and new iron sheets, slabs of clear and stained glass, hissing sofas, bales of cloth, boxes of medicines, cartons of laboratory mercury, gigantic office typewriters, hairy sacks of rice, sugar and salt, greasy tins of cooking and motor oil and more.... Full-scale looting was on. (305, my emphasis)

The monster, the crocodile, whose insatiable belly is the gateway, not to the Law, but to an alternative, demonic subjectivity constituted through the lust for possessions, is the African dictator, Idi Amin, and his potential progeny, such as Mugezi. Dictatorship permeates the porous boundary between dimensions, as Isegawa simultaneously integrates the politics of the day into African belief structures, and also pays homage to Okri, as fellow writer, who attempted to portray the violence of transition in Nigeria, through an understanding of the worlds of the body and the spirit. The links between their worlds of corruption, greed and the desperate search for a secure humanity is captured by Isegawa's description of the bloody violence of Ugandan politics, in the style and terms of Okri's *Famished Road*:

> The sky was alive with ghosts of people killed in the coup, killed before the coup, killed during the state of emergency, killed at the dawn of independence as politics wore hideous masks and became bloodier all the time. The night was full of ghosts redolent with earthly smells ... (103)

If Mugezi's damnation occurred in the scarcity that bred an excess of violence and pain in Africa, then it is a vain hope that he will find the salvation he seeks among the overload of glitzy European goods in the airport's duty-free shops. Once again, Isegawa underscores the link between subjectivity and material goods, in dizzying display at the airport on Mugezi's arrival:

> Dazzled by the light, I groggily walked about the grotto to see if there were any gifts dangling from the Christmas trees, *tokens of the salvation I was seeking.* I went to the duty-free shops to look at the watches, the cameras, the jewelry.... To buy one such article on my former teacher's salary, I would have had to work for five years. (418, my emphasis)

In this liminal airport space, in this newly arrived interregnum, Mugezi looks for a safe landing, in the magical cave of powerful, fetishised objects, which he will in all likelihood have to deflate again if he is to survive the journey. The airport, the taxi park and finally, at the novel's ending, the Central Station in Amsterdam, are in-between topsy-turvy spaces that fall between departure and arrival, echoing Kampala as much as Lagos:

> People seemed to be walking upside down, the dead rising from their graves, the living diving into fresh graves. There was motion and inversion everywhere: the invaders were being invaded, the partitioners being partitioned, the penetrators getting penetrated. The mixing and juxtaposition of peoples became mind-blowing, the destinations and points of departure mythic. I held on to the cement bank in order to stop myself from spewing or getting spewed. (462)

The power balance is interrogated and even overturned. The boundaries are porous and traversed. In this maelstrom, the gravitational pull of the abyss is resisted by holding fast onto the cement bank and by the end of the novel, Mugezi has found a solid object to protect and sustain him: 'I had found myself a stone to lay my head on, an enchanted hilltop made of boulders from all the corners of the globe' (462). Nonetheless, this solid object is enchanted, reminiscent of Garuba's materialist animism that re-enchants the world (2003: 265). It is African and global, with its rocks magically drawn from the world at large. The rock of concrete support is constructed by the wily migrant, the foxy trickster, who 'was back in my element: watching, planning, waiting for the right time to strike' (462). He will strike with his acquisition of the Dutch language to overlay his English and to meld with his father's fleetingly witty moment of finding the right word: 'Abyssinia was on my mind; so was my new foothold on this precipitous hilltop. It has always been a Herculean task for Abyssinians to get their foot in the door, but once in, they never budge. I was in' (462).

And so Mugezi has charted a path across, found the entry, into the magic mountain, and assumed a new name, a new language, new words to anchor, protect and harness his identity. This language is forged in the knowledge and words of more than one world, both Ugandan and European: 'my new surname was a common name for the second male twin back home in Uganda' (453). He can negotiate his multiple identities if he can imagine himself as occupying parallel universes:

It felt wonderful to lie awake at night and imagine the world in slumber. It gave you the feeling that you were living in a different time zone, in a different universe, in a place where people awoke as you went to bed and put on their nighties as you slipped on your school uniform. (103)

Intertexts, and parallel universes resound with the worlds of Biyi Bandele, which we charted in Chapter Two. Mugezi literally takes on a new name and identity by buying a forged European passport. He becomes a British citizen named John Kato, a name taken from a real person living in Britain. Isegawa could well have been gesturing towards Bandele, his fellow writer in London, struggling with many of the same issues, when he has Mugezi ponder that his new name is twinned with someone in Britain, someone who has shape-shifted in familiar ways into an insect: 'somewhere in Britain there was an ant going by the same name, unaware of the existence of a twin brother negotiating the wetness of the Dutch polders' (453). Isegawa, in fact, doubly twins Mugezi, in that Kato also 'was a common name for the second male twin back home in Uganda' (453). Again twinning refers suggestively to split worlds and more than one dimension as Mugezi thinks about Uganda, about the abyss, about Amsterdam and even about Britain where another foxy ant like him is slowly but surely finding a way through the city's fortifications.

6 Breaking Gods & Petals of Purple
Chimamanda Ngozi Adichie's *Purple Hibiscus*

Chimamanda Ngozi Adichie strives for a holistic vision in her novel, *Purple Hibiscus*,[1] one that integrates Igbo customs and language with Catholic ritual. It is a vision which incorporates men into her gender politics and embraces the literary traditions of her elders – Chinua Achebe, Ngũgĩ wa Thiong'o and Alice Walker. Adichie represents this syncretised world through the material culture and everyday realities of life in modern Nigeria. Tables and chairs, grains of rice and ceramic ornaments are syncretised with bodies and infused with spirituality. They create multiple universes, where the boundaries between the living and the dead, the animate and the inanimate are breached.

In the Igbo world that Adichie is depicting, constructing and transforming, the spirits live inside the mundane objects of everyday life. If Moses Isegawa's *Abyssinian Chronicles* took ordinary, solid objects that had become toxic fetishes and reduced them to size in order to expose the workings of dictators, the Chimamanda Ngozi Adichie takes similar, everyday things and 're-enchants' them, in order to heal the society which has abandoned its past. We saw in the introduction what Harry Garuba called 'a *continual re-enchantment of the world*' (2003: 265, his emphasis), which relates to animist thought in which the spiritual is manifested in material, everyday things (267). This is nowhere better illustrated than in *Purple Hibiscus* where Adichie is, as she puts it in an interview, 'interested in colonized religion, how people like me can profess and preach a respect of their indigenous culture and yet cling so tenaciously to a religion that considers most of indigenous culture evil' (in Anya, 2003: 15). I will be tracing precisely how Adichie juggles the pieces that make up the kaleidoscope of her varied vision. I will also demonstrate that these pieces sometimes slip away from her reach, and I will be suggesting possible reasons for this.

Purple Hibiscus is the story of Kambili, who is the fifteen-year-old first person protagonist. She lives in the violent and repressive atmosphere of her father, who physically abuses her meek mother and also herself and brother, Jaja, by beating them into submission. Yet he is a pillar of the community. Not only is he an avid Catholic Churchman, he is also a very successful businessman who owns many factories. Most perplexingly, he is also an incorruptible defender of democracy in Nigeria.

Purple Hibiscus works around a complex time-space axis. The novel's time line is divided into four parts. The first part begins on Palm Sunday with a family row when Papa smashes Mama's precious ceramic dancing figurines, displayed on their showcase, or what Adichie calls the étagère,

---

[1] Page references to quotations in this chapter, unless indicated otherwise, are to *Purple Hibiscus* (London: Fourth Estate, 2004).

which we will be discussing in some detail. Papa's rage is provoked by Jaja, who refuses to go to communion. The bulk of the novel takes place in the second part, which is a flashback to before that fateful Palm Sunday and describes events leading up to Jaja's previously unheard of rebelliousness and thus to the smashing of the ballerina ornaments. The third part takes us to the time after Palm Sunday. It reaches its climax with Papa's violent death. The final part is situated in the present and describes life after Papa. The repeated physical abuse and domestic violent crimes provide the thread joining up all of the parts. Alongside this domestic realm, still in the temporal zone, is the growing crisis in the public political arena of the Nigerian State and its own increasing violence.

Alongside this temporal flashback and forth, are journeys to and from Enugu where the family lives. These spatial translations from one place to another map the transformations in Kambili and Jaja's circumstances and perceptions. The family travels from Enugu to their village house in Abba for Christmas. Here the children interact with their father's sister, Aunty Ifeoma and her children, all of whom will play a definitive role in the unfolding events. In Abba, the children are allowed a strictly circumscribed visit to the compound of their grandfather, Papa-Nnukwu. They may stay for only fifteen minutes and eat and drink nothing, given that their father has condemned and rejected his father for being what he calls a heathen. Although the visit is short, Papa-Nnukwu's compound and his shrine will play their own powerful part in the unfolding dramas.

Also in Abba, Aunty Ifeoma puts pressure on Papa to allow the children to come and visit her and their cousins in Nsukka, which they eventually do, and where they participate in an entirely different kind of family life. They stay in Aunty Ifeoma's flat and encounter her tiny, fabulous garden, including the purple hibiscuses. During their visit, Papa-Nnukwu becomes gravely ill and their Aunt brings him to the flat, where he eventually dies.

Jaja and Kambili return to Enugu, armed respectively with stalks of purple hibiscus from Aunty Ifeoma's garden and an unfinished painting of Papa-Nnukwu, given to Kambili by her cousin. Papa punishes them horrendously for tolerating living under a roof with his unconverted father by burning the soles of their feet in scalding water. Later, he discovers the painting of his father, which he rips up into fragments, echoing the smashing of the figurines. The punishment for harbouring this painting is so fierce that the beating Papa gives Kambili nearly kills her and she lands up in hospital. When she has sufficiently recovered, the children go back to their Aunt in Nsukka, for Kambili to recuperate further. The family continues to cover up the father's violence with stories of accidents. Mama arrives in Nsukka at one point in a dishevelled state and we learn that she, too, has again been beaten, and lost another pregnancy as a result. Nonetheless, she insists on going back to Enugu with the children.

All of this takes the flashback up to Palm Sunday and to the point where the novel began. Jaja's revolt against his authoritarian, disturbed father continues after the smashing of the figurines and he decides that he and Kambili are going to spend Easter with their Aunt and Cousins in Nsukka, not least of all to say goodbye to them as they are emigrating to America. They return to Nsukka, go on a pilgrimage to Aokpe and learn about their Papa's sudden death from poison, seated at his desk in his office. The suspicion is that the State has murdered him for his resistance to its corruption. The family returns at once to Enugu, where, in a quite shocking climax to the novel's violent tensions, Mama confesses to having poisoned Papa. Jaja insists on taking the rap and is imprisoned, as everyone believes Mama to be attempting to confess in order to protect her son, rather than the other way around. *Purple Hibiscus* ends with Kambili and Mama visiting Jaja in prison, the final space of the novel, with the good news of his impending release, given that the Head of State had died a few months earlier and suspicion had, not improbably but incorrectly, fallen on 'the old regime' as responsible for Papa's murder. All of these places and their furnishings and the gardens and their plants – the houses in Enugu and Abba, Papa-Nnukwu's compound and shrine in Abba, the flat and garden in Nsukka, the sacred shrine at Aokpe and finally the stinking prison – become significant spaces, which are richly, thickly and intricately described in all their material detail.

Throughout the novel, we see Kambili's inability to cope emotionally with the mixed feelings of love and terror for her father, and adoration and disdain for her passive, abused mother, all of which she is unable either to acknowledge or understand. She cannot make friends, or enjoy any peace of mind or happiness. She never laughs and she represses all knowledge of the violence being wrought on herself and her family. The woman's silenced voice is again the central issue, reminiscent of Aboulela's protagonists. Kambili stutters, chokes on her words, stammers and whispers. The novel traces how she finds her voice and provides an intriguing role in the process for objects like the beige figurines, with whose demise the novel begins, and the purple hibiscus of its title. We will see how these figurines and flowers exist in that potent and porous boundary space of blending in which metonyms become metaphoric and hesitant new tropes begin to flower. All of this takes place in the context of a belief in Catholicism, which has to be 'colonised' within the material culture and spirituality of African life.

Resurgent spirits: mmuo, solid objects & bodies

During the family's visit to their home village, Abba, Aunty Ifeoma takes Kambili and Jaja to Abagana for the Aro festival to look at the procession of *mmuo* spirits (73). She also sneaks in contact between them and their forbidden grandfather, who she brings along on the expedition. On the way, Papa-Nnukwu and Aunty Ifeoma have a bantering conversation in the car, but one which introduces the reader to the nature of the 'High God, the *Chukwu*' and the chi, which is a person's own spirit. Papa-Nnukwu promises that his spirit will intercede 'so that *Chukwu*, will send a good man to take care of you and the children' (83). Aunty Ifeoma quips that his spirit should rather 'ask Chukwu to hasten my promotion to senior lecturer' (83). For all its lightheartedness, this exchange establishes the significance of the spirits and their role in a changed world, where women pray for promotion, rather than for a man to earn the money to care for them. This new world is exemplified by the traditional procession of *mmuo*, which is integrated into modern, everyday life in a Nigerian city, like Nsukka, with cars 'bumper to bumper' and people dressed in every which style – 'wrappers blended into T-shirts, trousers into skirts, dresses into shirts' (85). Kambili had first heard of the *mmuo* from Papa, some years ago, where he had explained, dismissively, that 'the stories about *mmuo*, that they were spirits who had climbed out of ant holes, that they could make chairs run and baskets hold water, were all devilish folklore' (85).

The novel distances itself from Papa's rejection of Igbo beliefs and customs as 'devilish folklore' on many occasions and not least of all here. The *mmuo* are spirits, which integrate into solid objects, and inhabit these baskets and chairs and animate them, thereby contesting the boundaries between dimensions and worlds. With minimal explanation, Papa-Nnukwu points to 'our *agwonatumbe*', which is 'the most powerful *mmuo* in our parts, and all the neighboring villages fear Abba because of it' (86). As Kambili watches a huge *mmuo* float past she thinks that 'it was eerie, watching it, and I thought then of chairs running, their four legs knocking together, of water being held in a basket, of human forms climbing out of ant holes' (87). These *mmuo* silently and unspokenly pervade the novel and are an example of the metonymic gap, to which I have often referred in this book. Although they are cursorily explained here, it is clear that the looming, living everyday objects that both haunt and comfort Kambili, and appear in visceral shape and form in all the moments of stress or emotion in her life, are linked to these *mmuo*. This the novel never directly states, given that it does not abandon its Christian base. What it does is to demonstrate how African traditional beliefs and practices continue to permeate daily life and in so doing are not in contradiction with modernity, with cars, European fashions and, most importantly, with Catholicism.

From the beginning, ordinary, solid objects are animated through these resurgent spirits that occupy them and which inscribe cultural difference. At the opening of the novel, with the smashing of the figurines, Kambili's emotions are expressed in terms of the walls narrowing and bearing down on her and 'even the glass dining table was moving toward me' (7). A few pages later, when she is filled with the terror induced by her father, she becomes convinced that 'the compound walls would crumble' and 'squash the frangipani trees' and that 'the Persian rugs on the stretches of gleaming marble floor would shrink' (14). She becomes ill with the stress and in a feverish dream 'thousands of monsters played a painful game of catch, but instead of a ball, it was a brown leatherbound missile that they threw to each other' (14). These monsters we will later identify as the crafty spirits, the *mmuo*, who play havoc with the family. This they do in response to Papa's onslaught on their sacredness, when he throws his leatherbound church records book at Jaja, which smashes the figurines that they inhabit.

As a further example of the vitality embodied in objects, Kambili gets stuck to a bench in Papa-Nnukwu's yard and is unable to get up: 'the bench held me back, sucked me in' (66). Although this is partly the result of Kambili's conflict and discomfort consequent on Papa's prohibitions regarding contact with her grandfather, it is also implied that spirits are at work within the solid objects they inhabit. Kambili seems particularly sensitive to their power and on the way to see the *mmuo*, when they pass Kambili's family house in the car 'the sight of the looming black gates and white wall stiffened my [Kambili's] lips' (83). Flesh and objects meld as spirits contest boundaries between animate and inanimate dimensions. Kambili's body dissolves into the furniture in terror when Papa arrives, unexpectedly, at the flat in Nsukka, just after Papa-Nnukwu has died. Like the wall, which stiffened her lips, Kambili 'froze on my seat, felt the skin of my arms melding and becoming one with the cane arms of the chair' (187). Her flesh literally freezes and merges with the chair, as boundaries between living and dead matter are once again contested.

The alienated and abused Kambili may experience the mischievous, metamorphosing spirits inside these chairs and benches as terrifying, but she also begins to grow and develop spiritually in the flat in Nsukka, where she perceives that the furniture is alive. Again, her body, her hand, engages with the furniture and 'shook as I tried to straighten a piece of the table surface that had cracked and curled tightly around itself. A line of tiny ginger-colored ants marched near it' (142). These ants are deeply suggestive of the *mmuo*, which climb out of ant holes. The significance of the material culture, which is alive in Aunt Ifeoma's home, accounts for the wealth of detail, the thick description, covering page after page, of the flat, its furniture, the neighborhood and then also the garden, with its purple flowers and many other wonderful plants. Without an understanding of Adichie's emphasis on the nature of daily life for ordinary people, a life which is imbued with spiritual significance, this amount of apparently mundane detail could appear digressive and excessive.

For example, Aunty Ifeoma's flat is in 'a tall, bland building with peeling blue paint and with television aerials sticking out from the verandahs. It had three flats on each side, and Aunty Ifeoma's was on the ground floor on the left, fenced around with barbed wire' (112). The blandness of the peeling paint and barbed wire mingles with the 'pungent fumes of kerosene smoke mixed with the aroma of curry and nutmeg from the kitchen' (113). All the stuff in the flat is portrayed – furniture, wood, books – filling up most of the next two pages of the novel. There is the kitchen – chipped, but clean tiles, pots, stove and 'the walls near the window and the threadbare curtains had turned black-gray from the kerosene smoke' (115). This flows onto the next page where the rough cement floors contrast with 'the smooth marble floors back home' (116). The shy Kambili focuses on the desk, rather than meet the eye of her cousin, a desk 'which was full of things – books, a cracked mirror, felt-tipped pens' (117). The following two pages continue with the inventory of the house and its contents, including dining room table and chairs, the food, the mismatched plates (119–20). The following page describes the house, the narrow room in which 'there were no soft rugs, no furry cover for the toilet seat and lid like we had back home. An empty plastic bucket was near the toilet' (121). There is no water in the cistern as water only runs in the morning.

The inventory moves on to the tiny backyard full of 'old car tires and bicycle parts and broken trunks' (126). Poking in amongst these multiple objects, are the many plants and flowers and, note, also bushes of purple hibiscus among them (128). The following page takes us back to the house and life buzzing around material scarcity: bathing with limited water and instead of a mat, there is just an 'old towel placed on the floor' (127). Food and its preparation play their part. A meal here is just a snack at home and there is always the question of whether there is enough fuel in the car to drive it (128). A jaunt in the car, on the precious, limited fuel, gives us a tour of the neighbourhood, also in solid detail. Through the gaps in the hedges of sunflowers, we see into backyards of houses with their 'metal water tanks balanced on unpainted cement blocks, the old tire swings hanging from guava trees, the clothes spread out on lines tied tree to tree' (129).

For all the privation in Nsukka, the children are insulated there by their family and by these solid, yet living, material possessions and gardens. When they return to the brutalities of their father in their affluent home in Enugu, the luxurious objects do not protect them in the same way. The dead glass of the table contrasts with the live wood in the Nsukka flat: 'our furniture was lifeless: the glass tables did not shed twisted skin in the harmattan' (192) In addition, 'the leather sofas' greeting was a clammy coldness, the Persian rugs were too lush to have any feeling' (192). However, there are solid objects, which were also alive at home in Enugu. These are precious belongings of the mother – the étagère, which displayed ceramic dancing ballerina figurines, before they were smashed. We must look at them more closely to see how objects are animated through the resurgent spirits that occupy them and what happens when they are abused and how this relates to the Catholicism that the author unambiguously professes.

Breaking gods: the revenge of the figurines

Purple Hibiscus begins with a mystery. The opening part is entitled 'BREAKING GODS' (1). It refers to Papa smashing the figurines, foregrounding their significance: 'Papa flung his heavy missal across the room and broke the figurines on the étagère' (3). How can the breakage of these ornaments constitute the destruction of gods? The étagère, or display unit, is the stage, the miniature set, for the events that follow. The incident is repeated on the following page, which gives the impression of a re-play in slow motion of a major and catastrophic occurrence, which it is:

> He picked up the missal and flung it across the room, toward Jaja. It missed Jaja completely, but it hit the glass étagère, which Mama polished often. It cracked the top shelf, swept the beige, finger-size ceramic figurines of ballet dancers in various contorted postures to the hard floor and then landed after them. Or rather it landed on their many pieces. It lay there, a huge leatherbound missal that contained the readings for all three cycles of the church year. (7)

It is significant that the weighty object that is the weapon in the destruction of the figurines is a book of planned biblical readings. Given that gods are being destroyed, it appears to be the Christian church that has a hand in the destruction. The figurines may be ceramic, but their demise is visceral and their pain indicated by their 'contorted postures'. Sad Mama does not rant and rave and merely 'stared at the figurine pieces on the floor and then knelt and started to pick them up with her bare hands' (7). It is impossible for the still oppressed Kambili to find the words to criticise her father: 'I meant to say I am sorry Papa broke your figurines, but the words that came out were, "I'm sorry your figurines broke, Mama"' (10). Words 'come out' involuntarily, do not say what Kambili means and are instruments of concealment of the reality of Papa's crimes. These figurines had played a crucial role in Mama's life as her coping mechanism for the physical violence to which Papa subjects her. After a beating, instead of crying, she had washed the little ballerinas in soapy water. This she had done in a loving ritual: 'she spent at least a quarter of an hour on each ballet-dancing figurine' (10). Again, after she had lost the child she was expecting, as a result of one of Papa's beatings, Mama repeated the ritual starting 'at the lowest layer, polishing both the shelf and the figurines' (35).

Given that we are in the flashback time zone, we have to read right up to the third part of the novel, 222 pages later, which brings us back to the moment in time with which the novel had begun, immediately after Papa smashed the figurines. This third part is entitled 'THE PIECES OF GODS', substantiating the need to understand that the shards are more than inanimate objects. Adichie is breaking down the boundaries between old and new gods. She re-fetishises objects linked to pre-colonial rituals, but, as we will see, these are transformed and syncretised with the Church and with European culture and integrated into a global modernity. The figurines, in other words, are Mama's protecting spirits, albeit hybridised in the African Catholic home. The étagère was Mama's shrine; the spirits of old have resurged. Papa has desecrated the sacred space and he will be punished. Immediately we see the change in Mama on the destruction of her ballerinas and the end of her coping ritual:

> When Mama asked Sisi to wipe the floor of the living room, to make sure no dangerous pieces of figurines were left lying somewhere, *she did not lower her voice* to a whisper. *She did not hide the tiny smile* that drew lines at the edge of her mouth. *She did not sneak* Jaja's food to his room, wrapped in cloth so it would appear that she had simply brought his laundry in. (257–8, my emphases)

Mama's new, tiny smile is not a great belly laugh, but it is a beginning. This is rather creepy and wonderful. Mama too is about to rebel; she is beginning to find her voice after a fashion, ceases to whisper, ceases to cover up her actions and no longer 'sneaks' around in a concealed and subversive manner. At the same time, these figurines are redolent of the material culture of women more generally, and echo the soup so lovingly prepared by Sammar, Aboulela's protagonist in Chapter Three. Susan Stewart in her *On Longing*, which is a study of *Narratives of the Miniature, the Gigantic, the Souvenir, the Collection* suggests that miniatures occupy a 'privatized and domesticated world' (1993: 172). It is a woman's world, where knick-knack shelves satisfy the longings of women, who seek limited mastery over space. I am suggesting that Adichie's project of taking this space and magnifying it to occupy central stage is a radical feminist move. Stewart elaborates that 'the miniature becomes a stage on which we project ... a deliberately framed series of *actions*' (54, her emphasis). This explains this rather quaint word, 'étagère', that Adichie uses and repeats, underlining its significance. 'Étagère' is a French word for display shelves, and it is tellingly linked to an old French word for staging, as in a play. This small display unit becomes the stage upon which all the big events of the novel are played out. The smallness of the miniatures is enlarged by the sacredness of their being occupied by the spirits of tradition and the étagère looms large as the shrine, at the heart, at the centre, of all of the mother's survival, for all its deceptive, apparent smallness.

The ceramic figurines hint at other worlds and belief structures, reminiscent of the strategies and structures of other novels we have been discussing, such as Biyi Bandele's *The Street*. Stewart, referring to the toy, but applicable to Adichie's dancing figurines, suggests that the toy, as a fiction, as a fantasy, exposes the imagination to other worlds and opens up the boundary between the animate and the inanimate (1993: 56): 'once the toy becomes animated, it initiates another world' (57). The tiny, domestic and private world of the home, where these miniatures live, is not a microcosm of the bigger public forces at play in the country at large; the small is big in Adichie's world, where what happens on the tiny stage actually narrates, determines and demonstrates the nature of the corruption and degradation in Nigeria at the start of the twenty-first century. In this way, the novel also echoes Moses Isegawa's *Abyssinian Chronicles*, where dictatorship in the home actively constituted the nature of repression and deformed subjectivity in the country, rather than merely symbolising it. The daily life rituals and possessions, the special places in the home, in this view, are the basis and framework for political action. This is why the novel lovingly describes solid objects of everyday life in so much concrete detail. The medium is the message where small is big, the personal is political and ordinary daily life, embodied in the things that surround us, is where the sacred spirits live, and from which Nigerian culture should arise and grow.

The little stage and their ballerinas as shrine is foregrounded by a similar site associated with Papa-Nnukwu, who is a role model and a spiritual guide to the children, albeit that he is a 'traditionalist' and has not converted to Christianity. He carries the moral high ground in his sole, quiet and uncompromising refusal to be bullied by Papa, who tries to make him throw away 'the chi in the thatch shrine in his yard' (61). However, 'he would not throw away his chi' (61). His shrine is sacred and during their short visit to him in his compound, Kambili watches a grey rooster 'walk into the shrine at the corner of the yard, where Papa-Nnukwu's god was, where Papa said Jaja and I were never to go near' (66).

Like her mother, Kambili constructs her own sacred, comforting fetish, which her father similarly destroys. This is the unfinished painting of Papa-

Nnukwu, which her cousin, Amaka, had done and given her as a farewell gift when they left Nsukka. This painting is 're-enchanted', in that its solid layers of oil paint are porous, enabling the flesh and spirit of Kambili's ancestor, her departed grandfather, to meet. Kambili appears to find a way to her grandfather's chi through this painting, and she, like her mother, erects a shrine of a kind, a sacred object/space to comfort her. Kambili had obviously hidden the painting from her father and after Papa had burnt her feet, she reached for it, still hidden in her bag and still wrapped. However, she was too afraid of Papa to take it out, but she ran her finger over the wrapping, 'over *the slight ridges of paint that melded into the lean form of Papa-Nnukwu*, the relaxed fold of arms, the long legs stretched out in front of him' (196, my emphasis).

Through the ritual of touching this painting, Kambili is partially empowered to rebel against her father, the rebellion being of a passive nature. She does become more bold, and takes the painting out to show Jaja, knowing that Papa would discover her and Jaja caressing it: 'I knew Papa would come in to say good night, to kiss my forehead.... I knew Jaja would not have enough time to slip the painting back into the bag' (209). Papa indeed discovers them in this mode, snatches the painting and goes berserk. Like the figurines, he breaks the painting into bits, thereby dismembering Papa-Nnukwu's body, once again violating the sacred: 'I suddenly and maniacally imagined Papa-Nnukwu's body being cut in pieces that small and stored in a fridge' (210). Saving the pieces 'would mean saving Papa-Nnukwu' (210). Kambili, in an unprecedented rebellion, refuses to deliver the pieces of 'the body' to Papa and he beats her senseless. The tempo of the beating brings to her mind the fusion music that Amaka, her cousin, the author of the painting, loves so much. The rhythmic language of metonymy becomes a mantra distancing Kambili from the abusive, criminal behaviour of her father:

> Godlessness. Heathen worship. Hellfire. The kicking increased in tempo, and I thought of Amaka's music, her culturally conscious music that sometimes started off with a calm saxophone and then whirled into lusty singing. I curled around myself tighter, around the pieces of the painting; they were soft, feathery. They still had the metallic smell of Amaka's paint palette. The stinging was raw now, even more like bites, because the metal landed on open skin on my side, my back, my legs. Kicking. Kicking. Kicking. Perhaps it was a belt now because the metal buckle seemed too heavy. (211)

The violence is raw and relentless, written in the language of rhythm and repetition, of body and objects, which hurt and smell and touch. The pieces merge with the metal of paint and buckle. Kambili nearly dies, but we must leave her here, in a fetal state, and ask where does this implicit belief in the power of the old gods sit in a novel by a Catholic African author?

Catholic echoes of Igbo: language & the new religion

In an interview Adichie strongly asserts her Catholic identity:

> I'm not sure what secular Catholic means. I AM Catholic. It is an identity that, although

I didn't have much of a choice in, I have since taken ownership of. I am very much a Vatican II enthusiast, and think that the Church should make some more changes on its stance on a number of issues. Still, there is much I admire and love in the church, the rich rituals, the traditions, the commitment that some orders have to social justice and scholarship as well as the sort of outward-looking faith that holds to some of vision of a fairer world. (in Adebanwi, 2004: 1, emphasis in original)

We have already seen the respect the novel affords Papa-Nnukwu and his beliefs, including his devotion to the multiple spirits that inhabit the novel and play a crucial role in its unfolding. Papa-Nnukwu's age and frailty and his death, however, are indicators that his way of life is one that is passing and is not, by itself, the solution for the future. The future rests rather with Catholics like Father Amadi, the young priest in Nsukka, and Aunty Ifeoma and her family, who attempt to integrate the spirituality of Papa-Nnukwu, and his beliefs and rituals, into their Catholicism.

What the novel uncompromisingly rejects are narrow minded, Eurocentric, white priests, like Father Benedict, and the brand of Catholicism into which he has brainwashed Papa, who is a caricature in his over-zealousness. For Father Benedict, 'Igbo was not acceptable' and only Latin permissible for saying Mass. However, Igbo could be used in offertory songs: 'he called them "native" songs, and when he said "native" his straight-line lips turned down at the corners to form an inverted U' (4). The God of this priest, and of Papa is the one who could only make his invisible presence real by inflicting wounds on the human body, as described by Elaine Scarry (1985: 200). We begin to understand Papa's abuse of his own family, given that he was himself horribly abused as a child, in the name of a punitive Christianity. Papa explains to Kambili, after burning her feet, that he had once been caught masturbating: 'I committed a sin against my own body once' (196) and 'the good father', who had caught him, had asked him to boil water for tea and had proceeded to pour the water in a bowl and to soak Papa's hands in it: 'I never sinned against my own body again. The good father did that for my own good' (196). Papa then inflicts on his wife and children his own repressed sexuality and abuse, as so often happens.

Kambili breaks the cycle through the body and spirit of her grandfather and instead of thinking of, or learning from, Papa's burnt hands, 'I thought about the painting of Papa-Nnukwu in my bag' (197). She dwells not on the lesson of the harsh, so-called Christian punishment, but on the Igbo traditionalist, who is a kind and benevolent force. He is also recognised as deeply religious, making his son's rejection of him as a heathen quite outrageous. For example, one morning, during their visit to Nsukka, Aunty Ifeoma awakens Kambili and invites her to witness her grandfather's nakedness, as he enacts his own form of traditional prayer. In what would otherwise be a voyeuristic scene, we are made to understand the profound spirituality of Papa-Nnukwu as they watch him talking 'to the gods or the ancestors':

'Chineke! I thank you for this new morning! I thank you for the sun that rises,' His lower lip quivered as he spoke. Perhaps that was why his Igbo words flowed into each other, as if writing his speech would result in a single long word. (167)

The shape of the single long word, the metonymic chain of Igbo, signifies an alternative language, which Papa-Nnukwu, with his quivering lip, integrates into his body. His nakedness merges with his spirituality: 'Between his legs hung a limp cocoon that seemed smoother, free of the wrinkles that crisscrossed the rest of his body like mosquito netting' (169). He is made happy by his prayers, unlike Kambili after hers and 'he was still smiling as I quietly turned and went back to the bedroom. I never smiled after we said the rosary back home. None of us did' (169). The novel is unambiguous about his son's rejection of him on religious grounds as being an abomination. It is a disrespectful and illegitimate sacrifice of the past in the service of a distorted Christianity.

Papa-Nnukwu's aged body is both flesh and spirit, existing in the in-between space between life and death, between man and becoming god, an ancestor. This is the body that inhabits the painting after the death of the man. It also challenges the kind of somber Catholicism practised by Kambili's family, although not Aunt Ifeoma's, where Church rituals are integrated into older customs and language. What is clear is that after his death, the painting may be the spirit of Papa-Nnukwu, but it also is his body, his physical presence into which it melds. Like the wine and the wafer, which are literally perceived as the blood and the flesh of Christ, the painting is a metonym, part of the whole of Papa-Nnukwu. The overtones between Christ and Papa-Nnukwu, as both deeply religious beings, are faint but not far fetched, nor blasphemous in this novel of syncretisms and hybrids. In fact, Papa's 'murder' of his father by exorcising him from his life and ripping his painting cum embodiment into shreds, resounds with the crucifixion.

The novel's goal, however, is not to polarise Papa and Papa-Nnukwu, but to infuse Igbo customs into Catholic spirituality. The pathway to a more syncretic religion is via Igbo language, songs and rituals and these echo throughout the novel, much as Arabic does in Leila Aboulela's fiction, as we saw in Chapter Three. Adichie does not consistently adhere to the metonymic gap mode of leaving Igbo untranslated, in that she sometimes translates, sometimes makes the meaning clear in the context and only sometimes leaves the Igbo to speak for itself without clarification. These three different modes have been classified by Ismail S. Talib, in *The Language of Postcolonial Literatures* as 'overt cushioning', 'covert cushioning' or 'no cushioning at all' (2002: 128 & 129) or metonymic gaps, as Ashcroft would have it. In all cases, however, whether a translation is provided or not, the use of words from another language provides an alternative frame of reference outside of the dominance of English.

For example, there are times that the English is echoed into a sentence, as in "*Nne, ngwa*. Go and change,' Mama said to me, startling me although her Igbo words were low and calming' (8). The words may be explained, but the timbre of the language is what is metonymically communicated. Later, and likewise, Kambili says of Father Amadi that she 'did not fully comprehend his English-laced Igbo sentences at dinner because my ears followed the sound and not the sense of his speech' (135). And there is the '*atilogu*' dance, which is explained in terms of the yard being big enough 'for each dancer to do the usual somersaults and land on the next dancer's shoulders' (9). Again, the nature of the dance may be explained, but the metonymy is communicated by way of the rhythm of the dance, which is culturally specific.

There are times when less is explained, contributing to the overall effect of the mediating power of an alternative language and also knowledge base. The sisters from Our Lady of the Miraculous Medal prayer group are treated to *moi-moi*, an obvious delicacy because their gratitude is expressed as an insistence that they would have been content with *anara*, neither of which are translated (21). Local food and Igbo songs – senusal pleasure in taste and music – are chorused throughout and quite often the choruses are not translated, as in the repeated '*I na-asi m esonaya! I na-asi m esonaya!*' (179).

These songs, and their metonymic choruses, are crucial accompaniments to the growth of Kambili's identity and her ability to find her voice. For example, she and Father Amadi are driving together, after he has arranged to have her hair plaited, another cultural ritual, and 'as he drove, we sang Igbo choruses. I lifted my voice until it was smooth and melodious like his' (239). This was not always the case. Earlier on in the novel, before Kambili had found some courage, she had not joined in with the chorus response in a folktale recounted by Papa-Nnukwu. Later she wishes that 'I had joined in chanting the *Njemanze!* response' (161). Purging the folktales and oral stories is not a prerequisite for becoming a Christian, as her father would insist it was.

In fact, traditional culture is quite seamlessly incorporated into the Catholic ritual during prayer at Aunty Ifeoma's home: 'after we said the last Hail Mary' Amaka broke into Igbo song, to Kambili's enormous shock, causing her to snap back her head (125). The Igbo is not translated here: '*Ka m bunie afa gi enu...*' (125). Kambili, at this early stage, thinks censoriously, 'It was not right. You did not break into song in the middle of the rosary' (125). This family scene is emphasised and repeated and Kambili presses her lips together 'biting my lower lip, so my mouth would not join in the singing on its own, so my mouth would not betray me' (138–9). The body entwines with words, here contorted into biting her lip, so that treacherous words cannot escape from her mouth, reminiscent of the tight-mouthed bigoted priest, Father Benedict.

In other words, Kambili's upbringing gives her a very different, alienated kind of religion from that of her aunt and cousins in Nsukka. Kambili's religion in which 'sometimes I imagined God calling me, his rumbling voice British-accented. He would not say my name right; like Father Benedict, he would' place the emphasis on the second syllable rather than the first' (180). This is wilful ignorance, not like poor Bryan, protagonist in Aboulela's 'The Museum', who does not correctly pronounce Shadia's name, because she does not help him to get it right. In both cases, however, indigenous names are a powerful part of the metonymic portals into other religions and languages. This is why Amaka's refusal to take a European confirmation name is so important, with her resistance to joining the procession of young people 'with names written on them. Paul. Mary. James. Veronica' (273).

At the same time, Adichie does not essentialise or reify Igbo language, welding it as she does to other influences, and emphasising the point that it is the use to which language is put that counts. For example, Papa's use of Igbo is terrifying as it is the language of his most violent outbursts: 'the rage in his red-tinged eyes, the burst of Igbo from his mouth' (182). Equally, and cutting across race, Adichie describes a white woman as speaking Igbo fluently, tellingly giving us a metonymic gap through her European mouth, distancing this woman from the European priest with the tight lips: 'When she held my hand and said, '*Kee ka ime?*' I was stunned. I had never heard a white person speak Igbo, and so well' (215). This anticipates the white man, Richard, who will also become fluent in Igbo in Adichie's *Half of a Yellow Sun*, discussed in the next chapter. However, there we will see that the novel becomes conflicted and the living language transforms from a concrete tool to a symbolic marker of a whole culture.

Here we are left in no doubt regarding the novel's endorsement of Catholicism, albeit of a different kind. This is demonstrated by the pilgrimage Aunty Ifeoma takes them on to Aokpe, a little village in Benue, where the Blessed Virgin is supposedly appearing (99). In Aokpe, Kambili has this vision: 'And then I saw her, the Blessed Virgin: an image in the pale sun, a red glow on the back of my hand, a smile on the face of the rosary-bedecked man whose arm rubbed against mine. She was everywhere' (274–5). Kambili experiences a powerful confirmation of her Catholic spirituality, of the holy presence of the Blessed Virgin in every dimension of life, reflected here through the beauty of the sun. Once again, however, this Catholic 'miracle' is depicted as a hybrid one, which is Africanised in two ways. Firstly, it is in a remote village in Nigeria in which the Blessed Virgin has purportedly decided to appear, something that racists in more powerful places in the world are loath to accept. Amaka, Kambili's cousin, notes in a letter from America, after the family have emigrated, that a writer in a magazine there 'had sounded pessimistic that the Blessed Virgin Mary could be appearing at all, especially in Nigeria: all that corruption and all that heat' (300). Secondly, the Catholic experience is described through an intertext from the novel of another African writer, Ngũgĩ wa Thiongo's *Petals of Blood*. The ground underneath a big flame tree in Aokpe is 'covered with petals the color of fire' (274). This contributes to the red glow in which Kambili has her religious vision that the Blessed Virgin is everywhere. This brings us to the question of African and African American influences on this novel, and the growth of new symbols, of these flame petals redolent of Ngũgĩ, and to the nature of the purple hibiscus itself.

Finding a voice: tradition & the purple hibiscus

I think it pisses God off if you walk by the color purple in a field somewhere and don't notice it. (Walker, 1983a: 167)

What I have been emphasising throughout this book is the way in which postcolonial writers attempt to escape from Western culture's metaphors, which are steeped in racism and white, male colonial imaginaries, such as those of writers like Kipling, Conrad and Cary. The English language, into which these metaphors and symbols are deeply welded, refers to Africa using distorting images, such as a dark and savage. Young African writers, like Adichie, now have a wealth of alternative traditions from which to draw. Three powerful intertexts frame *Purple Hibiscus*: Chinua Achebe's *Things Fall Apart*, Ngũgĩ wa Thiong'o's *Petals of Blood* and Alice Walker's *The Color Purple.* These enrich Adichie's vision, but also contribute to the tensions within the novel, as her juggled agendas, on occasion, themselves slip and smash. This is unsurprising, given the differing politics and purposes of these different influences.

If *Things Fall Apart* charted the transformations wrought by colonialism, then *Purple Hibiscus* is a sequel, plotting postcolonial devastation, the demise of national liberation and the migration to North America of some of the best, most talented Nigerians, like Aunt Ifeoma. The opening words of the novel signal Adichie's indebtedness to Achebe: '*things started to fall apart* at home when my brother, Jaja, did not go to communion and Papa flung his heavy missal across the room and broke the figurines on the étagère' (3, my emphasis). Like the Europeans who violated the sacred shrines during Achebe's novel of colonialism, the new dictators are destroying the postcolonial, hybrid, but still holy spaces. Adichie signals the changes and also the brutal continuities by including, in a slightly different version, a folktale that Achebe also tells in *Things Fall Apart*. It is the story of how the greedy Tortoise cracked his shell (Achebe, 1958: 87–90; Adichie, 2004: 158–61). Inserting this adapted story from the oral tradition serves a double function here. It is both a metonymic gap, serving a similar function to that of including Igbo words in the novel, and an intertext referring to Achebe's novel. Both versions of the story focus on the greed of the Tortoise in a time of scarcity and famine. In Achebe's version, there are birds and in Adichie's there is a dog, but in both, the tricks of the Tortoise, who tries through his cunning to eat all the food at a feast in the sky, are turned against him. He ends up falling from the sky and cracking his shell. Achebe's story may be interpreted as a parable of the downfall of the greedy coloniser who steals wealth and resources from the indigenous population (Harlow, 1991: 75). Adichie is referring to postcolonial greed and corruption on the part of the powerful, which has continued to bedevil ordinary people.

Moreover, when Adichie tells the story of the greedy Tortoise, who is punished, through the lens of Achebe's novel, she is fulfilling more than one of her political agendas simultaneously. The story is part of the wealth of rhetoric comprising her novel; what we have are metonymies, metonymic gaps, songs, rhymes, drum beats, customs and Igbo words, which transform the English language in which the novel is written. Tortoise gobbles up all of the '*fufu* and *onugbu* soup and poured a full horn of palm wine down his throat' (160). Dog exacts revenge, narrated through a rhythmic chorus, repetition and metonymic gaps, which act subliminally on Kambili as part of finding her own voice and language:

Furious, Dog started to sing loudly. '*Nne, Nne*, Mother, Mother.'
   '*Njemanze!*' my cousins chorused.
   '*Nne, Nne*, it is not your son coming up.'
   '*Njemanze!*'
   '*Nne, Nne*, cut the rope. It is not your son coming up. It is the cunning Tortoise.'
   '*Njemanze!*' (160)

Dog's mother quickly cuts the rope, Tortoise falls and cracks his shell, which is cracked 'to this day' (160). We saw that the moral of this story, for Adichie's purposes, was that Kambili wished that she 'had joined in chanting the *Njemanze!* response.' The emphasis in this chapter has been on how Adichie's language arises out of her insistence upon the material, visceral level that fuels the spiritual lives of the everyday realities of aspects of life in Nigeria. This concreteness is critical to appreciate if we are to understand how the central images, such as that of the hibiscus, to which we will now turn, operates in the novel, given this book's questions regarding the search for a new language embedded in material cultural realities.

Kambili, at the outset of the novel, remembers how their lives changed with the visit to Nsukka and 'Aunty Ifeoma's experimental purple hibiscus', that 'began to lift the silence' (16), a silence behind which the terrible secret of family abuse lay hidden. This entwines the image of the purple hibiscus with language, with finding a voice out of the silence. This voice is both the liberation of Kambili, who is silent, or stutters and whispers, but also the voice of the young writer, Adichie, who finds her medium through the availability of literary traditions other than those of the Western canon.

While we will see that the meaning of the colourful hibiscus is linked to the influence of both Alice Walker's use of purple and Ngũgĩ wa Thiongo's of red, what is also clear is that any symbolic meaning of the hibiscus arises metonymically out of the minute detail of yards, houses and furniture. Where metaphors double up as metonymies, their symbolic function is grounded in concrete realities, happenstance and a torrent of mundane detail. The hibiscus bushes are described along with what happens to be contiguous with them in the yard and in relation to the house, the compound walls and other trees and plants. In other words, they mingle with their concrete environments in very ordinary ways. To substantiate this, some quite detailed quotations are necessary. The yard of the house in Enugu 'was wide enough to hold a hundred people dancing *atilogu*':

> The compound walls, topped by coiled electric wires, were so high I could not see the cars driving by on our street. It was early rainy season, and the frangipani trees planted next to the walls already filled the yard with the sickly-sweet scent of their flowers. A row of purple bougainvillea, cut smooth and straight as a buffet table, separated the gnarled trees from the driveway. Closer to the house, *vibrant bushes of hibiscus reached out and touched one another as if they were exchanging their petals.* (9, my emphases)

Wires, cars, the yard, the frangipani trees are all part of a big canvas, which includes the red hibiscus and later also the portentous, early budding purple ones, linked to the beginning of the children's rebellion against their father. The hibiscuses, in fact, are always described in their context, which is the ordinary objects, everyday activities and other plants that happen to be next to them. For example, there is the packing of the cars with the mountain of stuff to be taken to Abba Town for Christmas. Papa happens to stand beside the bushes, while everything is being loaded into the car:

> *Papa stood by the hibiscuses*, giving directions, one hand sunk in the pocket of his white tunic while the other pointed from item to car. 'The suitcases go in the Mercedes, and those vegetables also. The yams will go in the Peugeot 505, with the cases of Remy Martin and cartons of juice. See if the stacks of *okporoko* will fit in, too. The bags of rice and *garri* and beans and the plantains go in the Volvo.'
>   There was a lot to pack, and Adamu came over from the gate to help Sunday and Kevin. The yams alone, wide tubers the size of young puppies, filled the boot of the Peugeot 505, and even the front seat of the Volvo had a bag of beans slanting across it, like a passenger who had fallen asleep. (53–4, my emphasis)

Papa happens to stand by the hibiscus bush, which integrates it into the family's life and rituals. This dense description grows from being a bit of irrelevant detail to becoming part of the fabric of daily life. Note the metonymic gaps, mingling with similes and excesses of information about cars, their loads, the yams, rice, juice, and so on. Later in the novel, there is another incident of loading the car with stuff, this time for the children's journey to Nsukka:

> Kevin brought two full gas cylinders from Papa's factory and put them into the boot of the Volvo alongside bags of rice and beans, a few yams, bunches of green plantains, and pineapples. *Jaja and I stood by the hibiscus bushes*, waiting. The gardener was clipping away at the bougainvillea, taming the flowers that defiantly stuck out of the leveled top. He had raked underneath the frangipani trees, and dead leaves and pink flowers lay in piles, ready for the wheelbarrow. (108, my emphasis)

The old kerosene stove, gas cylinders, rice, beans and the Volvo, the hibiscus bushes as well as frangipani, dead leaves, pink flowers and bougainvillea, are all listed and mingle randomly and metonymically. The yard of the house, in which the children grow up in Enugu, then, is full of red hibiscus bushes. They visit their Aunt and cousins in Nsukka where Jaja is captivated by Aunty Ifeoma's garden and in particular by her purple hibiscus. Jaja brings back some cuttings from these purple bushes and plants them in the garden in Enugu. They take root and as they grow and flower, they act as a barometer, signifying the changes in the relationships within the family: 'the purple plants had started to push out sleepy buds, but most of the flowers were still on the red ones' (9). As such, they also grow in rhetorical function, becoming symbolic of changes within the family relationships. Kambili informs us that her memories go back to before the visit to Nsukka, to the time 'when all the hibiscuses in our front yard were a startling red' (16), that is to say, when Papa's Law was uncontested and absolute.

At this point, it appears as if a simple binary is being established between the blood red violence of home and the purple liberation of Nsukka. This polarisation is simultaneously interrogated, in that the red versus purple is undercut by the novel's consideration of the liberating potential contained also in the red. Ultimately, there will be the insistence on the necessity of red as well as purple, on Ngũgĩ wa Thiongo's petals of red, along with Alice Walker's purple fields. We have already seen that the red flowers make a connection between the Marxist Socialist politics of *Petals of Blood* and the ruby glow of the Blessed Virgin. This is crucial to Adichie's religious vision, where radical liberation theologians, like Father Amadi, create the possibilities for a politicised religion, what Adichie referred to in an interview as 'the commitments that some [Catholic] orders have to social justice' (Adebanwi, 2004: 1).

There are other traces of Ngũgĩ in the novel. In *Petals of Blood* there is the biblical warning to the new black leaders, who have inherited the mantle of power from the colonisers, that they will reap what they sow: 'Flowers for our land. Long live Nderi wa Riera. We gave him our votes: *we waited for flowers to bloom*' (Ngũgĩ 1977: 268, my emphasis). Flowers are also about to bloom in *Purple Hibiscus* as Papa's day of reckoning is drawing near. The day before Palm Sunday, when he did the unheard of thing and opposed Papa by refusing to go to communion, Jaja had said, echoing Ngũgĩ: 'See, the purple hibiscuses are *about to bloom*' (253, my emphasis). Ngũgĩ's insistence, moreover, that ordinary people 'would continue struggling until a human kingdom came ... so that flowers in all their different colours would ripen and bear fruits and seeds' (1977: 303) resonates with Adichie's search for a holistic vision of ordinary lives and people being incorporated in a just society, through the symbol of the many flowers. The problem with the multiple flowers, of purple and red, arises, however, in relation to the character of Papa.

Clashing symbols & agendas:
spirit ballerinas & a mixed bouquet of hibiscus

Adichie seems to be insisting that while Papa should be uncompromisingly condemned for the emotional and physical abuse he heaps on his family, he should also be appreciated, to some, albeit limited, extent, for the political stance he takes publicly. Papa struggles for national liberation, a struggle that has not terminated with independence. In this he is not dissimilar from Ngũgĩ's heroic characters. He is generous to the poor and a champion of democracy, to the extent of endangering his own life. This is part of the meaning of the red hibiscus with which he is associated. They are not only the red of blood that he spills in his family, but also the revolutionary colour of resistance. So, when government agents come to terrorise his family, Papa throws them out and the sinister 'men in black ... yanked hibiscuses off' (200) – red hibiscuses. As Adichie says in an interview:

> Kambili's father, for all of his fundamentalism, at least has a sense of social consciousness that is expansive and proactive and *useful*, so while his character may be seen as a critique of fundamentalism, the God-fearing public in Nigeria can learn a bit from him as well. (in Adebanwi, 1, emphasis in original)

Note the ambivalence expressed in the 'bit', rather than a lot, that one can learn. How can one learn anything from such a man, given his crimes in the home? And yet, the examples of Papa's brave politics abound. He owns a newspaper, the *Standard*, for which *Amnesty World* gave him a human rights award, as he uses the paper 'to speak the truth even though it meant the paper lost advertising' (5). Increasingly, not only does the newspaper lose advertising, but the publication of the misdoings of the thugs in power puts both Papa and his editor, Ade Coker, in severe danger and indeed, the latter is arrested, harassed and eventually blown up in a parcel bomb, to Papa's utter devastation (25, 38, 42, 146, 199, 206). Papa arranges everything for Ade Coker's funeral and takes on the care his family (207, 259). He is victimised by the soldiers, who close his factory. Papa is also generous, gives to beggars and hawkers, feeds his whole village at Christmas and is constantly handing over wads of money and writing cheques, but never towards corrupt ends (44, 54, 56, 90). Father Amadi, who is so opposed to Papa's religion and style of operating, and who has the novel's moral high ground, expresses great admiration for Papa's courage in publishing the truth in his newspaper (136–7).

In demonstrating Papa's true grit, Adichie potentially undermines the enormity of his crimes. It is possible that the tensions in her portrayal of Papa relates to Adichie's education in America and her belief in Alice Walker's 'womanism', as opposed to 'feminism'. 'A womanist', as coined by Alice Walker, is defined as 'a black feminist' (1983b: xi). She continues that 'womanist is to feminist as purple to lavender' (1983b: xii). The definition is bound up with 'the colour purple', which is also the title of Alice Walker's Pulitzer Prize-winning novel. A black woman writing fiction, especially while resident in North America and using 'purple' in the title of her novel, acknowledges Alice Walker's contribution as an alternative inspirational source to the Western canon. A crucial tenet of womanism is that it recognises the mutual suffering that black men and women together have endured, be it at the hands of the slavers or the colonisers. This it has to balance against the ways in which black men oppress black women, as patriarchs. And so, womanism is 'committed to survival and wholeness of entire people, male *and* female' (Walker: 1983b, xi, emphasis in original).

This balancing is successfully achieved in the character of Jaja, a young man, who is battling with issues not dissimilar from those of his sister and who is included in Adichie's vision of transformation in gender terms. He is sensitive, loves beautiful flowers and is a role model for the future. This accounts for the emphasis on the fact that the purple hibiscus is Jaja's rather than Kambili's passion, in a novel which focuses on the growth of Kambili's ability to develop a voice as a woman oppressed by her father. To foreground Jaja's simultaneous growth is why Adichie emphasises that Kambili is uninterested in the flowers: 'I wondered if [Aunty Ifeoma] was thinking that my voice lacked the enthusiasm of Jaja's when she talked about her garden' (143). The dilemma comes when women have to balance the reality that men have indeed also suffered the indignities of racism, colonialism and dictatorship, and with them they are struggling for a better world, but that the same men simultaneously abuse them at home.

This dilemma is manifested in the representation of Papa, which is where *Purple Hibiscus* gets caught in the crossfire of its own multiple agendas. There is no doubt that, at the deepest level, the novel is locating the stage centrally within the home, where men are judged politically in terms of their domestic relationships. At another, albeit more superficial level, it is examining the politics of Nigerian corruption and brutality, militarism and violence and suggesting that even patriarchal, wife-bashing men may somewhat redeem themselves in an African context, where struggle against colonialism and its aftermath involved both genders. Unfortunately, we will see this suppressed nationalist position surface more strongly, at the expense of gender issues when we focus on Adichie's next novel, *Half of a Yellow Sun* in Chapter Seven. Here, however, in Adichie's depiction of Papa as burning and beating his children and thrashing his pregnant wife into losing her babies, she goes too far to salvage him in any fundamental way. He is a demon, toxic to the family and we, as readers, feel only support for Mama and relief when she murders him. His obsession to root out any surviving remnants of his indigenous culture means that he also behaves abominably towards his own father, who he calls a heathen and disowns. He thereby infringes some of the most sacred traditions of respect for the elders. He is a sycophantic Anglophile, slavishly aping white ways and narrow Church doctrine.

Having said all of this about Papa, it was important for Adichie to insist that men as well as women are capable of working together, across religions and cultures, to achieve a better society. When this happens, purple and red hibiscus are not in conflict with each other: 'vibrant bushes of hibiscus reached out and touched one another as if they were exchanging their petals' (9). And Aunty Ifeoma's garden includes 'roses and hibiscuses and lilies and ixora' and these 'grew side by side like a hand-painted wreath' (112). The image of the wreath is important. These purple flowers are artefacts, a feat of science, the result of intensive experimentation on the part of Phillipa, Aunty Ifeoma's botanist colleague at the university. They are the result of scholarship and human endeavour and not essentialised as the involuntary gifts of nature. Jaja has to take cuttings and plant and tend them, hiding them and their meaning from Papa to enable them to grow. And grow they will, but only very uneasily beside the red hibiscuses of Papa's own struggles, both against the dictators and his own, terrible, blood-letting demons.

The novel ends with Jaja's and Kambili's plans to plant new orange trees, ixora and purple hibiscus. This reverberates with Alice Walker's *In Search of Our Mothers' Gardens*, where the child questions:

'Mama, why are we brown, pink and yellow, and our cousins are white, beige, and black?' Ans.: 'Well, you know the colored race is just like a flower garden, with every color flower represented.' (Walker, 1983b: xi)

Walker's description of her mother echoes Aunty Ifeoma, who was also a magnificent flower grower, reminiscent of Walker's memories of childhood, which 'are seen through a screen of blooms – sunflowers, petunias, roses, dahlias, forsythia, spirea, delphiniums, verbena' (241).

But Adichie is also aware that at times this harmony is difficult to achieve and elsewhere in the novel she shows an understanding that the 'big' politics of the public, national level are concerned with different freedoms.

> Jaja's defiance seemed to me now like Aunty Ifeoma's experimental purple hibiscus: rare, fragrant with the undertones of freedom, *a different kind of freedom from the one the crowds waving green leaves chanted at Government Square after the coup.* A freedom to be, to do. (16, my emphasis)

If you are fighting for freedom from domestic abuse, if you are searching for an individual identity and a voice without a stutter, liberated from terror at home, then a coup, or a rally in Government Square becomes less important, miniaturised by these bigger albeit purportedly smaller concerns. This per- ception is, however, muted when Adichie, simultaneously, even if partially, forgives Papa his crimes and portrays him as a brave fighter for democracy, standing shoulder to shoulder with women against the Nigerian state, red and purple entwined in an embrace. This sets up a polarisation between the 'public' and the 'private' in a novel that specifically and simultaneously contests this particular false binary through the other central image, that of the miniature figurines on the étagère, which Papa smashes. His domestic violence, in fact, interrogates the big picture and magnificently re-defines the political from within its standpoint.

Migrating writers & flying *aku:* conclusion

> I dreamed that the sole administrator was pouring hot water on Aunty Ifeoma's feet in the bathtub of our home in Enugu. Then Aunty Ifeoma jumped out of the bathtub and, in the manner of dream, jumped into America. (230)

Aunty Ifeoma migrates to America, at least in part because she is hounded out of the university by the dictatorial politics of the administration, signi- fied by the sole administrator, who doubles up in Kambili's dream as violent Father, the Law, the abuser, who scalded his children's feet in boiling water. This image entwines the domestic and national stages upon which Adichie is so bravely attempting simultaneously to perform. And when the pace is too heavy to maintain, the set changes to America, into which she, like her fictional Aunt, has jumped.

The novel is, of course, not entirely autobiographical. The character who probably most resembles Adichie is Amaka, Kambili's cousin. She is artistic, and, unlike Kambili, is a happy, articulate and feisty cultural mix between Igbo traditions, modern African music and American gadgets, magazines and fashion. Like Amaka's mother, Adichie's father was an academic at the Uni- versity of Nsukka, although he had more power there, given that he was a deputy vice chancellor. Both Adichie and her creation, Amaka, are creative artists and the painting of Papa-Nnukwu echoes the work on the novel we are reading. Like Adichie, Amaka continues her studies in North America. It is clear, however, that Adichie did not wish to write an autobiographical novel and Amaka is not the protagonist and Kambili is not Adichie.

Adichie is grappling with what it means to be Nigerian in the complex global world of cultural mixing and transformation, through the texture of daily life when she was growing up in Nsukka. Adichie's own sense, on a return visit to Nsukka, is that she is 're-seeing Nsukka with my Americanized eyes' (2003, 1). Authors such as Isegawa and Adichie, writing from Europe and North America respectively, unlike Bandele, set their fictions mainly in Africa and view their lives, their countries and cultures through the lenses of their experiences away from home. Adichie attempts to capture and hold the Nsukka in which she grew up, by focusing on the thick realities of its material culture. This is why Adichie is at pains, for example, to depict local food and its preparation, such as fufu and onugbu soup:

> Lunch was fufu and onugbu soup. The fufu was smooth and fluffy. Sisi made it well; she pounded the yam energetically, adding drops of water into the mortar, her cheeks contracting with the *thump-thump-thump* of the pestle. The soup was thick with chunks of boiled beef and dried fish and dark green onugbu leaves. ... I molded my fufu into small balls with my fingers, dipped it in the soup, making sure to scoop up fish chunks, and then brought it to my mouth. (11–12)

The 'thump-thump' of the pestle replicates the rhythm of the dance or the soothing tones of Igbo in Mama's voice and echoes the healing soup and its translations between cultures and languages in Aboulela's novel. Adichie emphasises how important this literal level is to the nature of her material, sensual vision. There is the discussion in the novel of how Jaja got his name. During a visit to Nsukka, Jaja's cousin, Obiora, plays metonymically with his name. He was:

> repeating the name Jaja slowly, placing the stress on both syllables, then on the first, then on the second. '*Aja* means sand or oracle, but *Jaja*? What kind of name is Jaja? It is not Igbo,' he finally pronounced. (143)

Jaja replies that his name is 'actually Chukwuka' and that Jaja is a 'childhood nickname that stuck' (143). According to Aunty Ifeoma, the nickname arose by happenstance: 'When he was a baby all he could say was Ja-Ja. So everybody called him Jaja' (144). But, there is also the story of Jaja of Opobo, a stubborn king who sold his people into slavery, and Aunty Ifeoma suggests that Jaja has inherited his rebelliousness (144–5). This suggests that Jaja did not take his name from epic stories, culturally inherited. We should take Jaja's name literally as the repeated rhythmic speech of baby learning language.

Adichie has an interesting exchange with Wale Adebanwi over this question of the literal as opposed to the figurative in her novel. They are discussing a little vignette, which describes the joy of the children, rushing about in the rain, trying to catch the flying *aku*. The scene is sensual; there is the rain, the sunlight through it and the smell of 'that edible scent the baked soil gave out at the first touch of rain', making Kambili imagine going into the garden and 'digging out a clump of mud with my fingers and eating it' (218). The corporeal delight of these smells, tastes and textures are contained within a metonymic gap in terms of the nature of *aku*. They seem to be a kind of winged termite, but this is not enlarged upon. The catching and eating them with anara leaves and red peppers (221) is part of the cultural specificity of this small moment in the novel. Father Amadi, however, points out that this is all a game because 'if you really wanted to catch them, you waited till evening, when they all lost their wings and fell down' (221). Wale Adebanwi says about this incident:

> I love the metaphor of aku, but I wonder if it is not a dangerous metaphor in the context of social change. After *aku* flies, it will still fall to the toad and you only have to wait till the evening when the *aku* would lose its wings and fall down. (2004: 1)

Adichie's response is to refute that she was constructing a metaphor:

> That will be left to the literary theorists. I wrote that scene out of a sense of nostalgia and nothing else. I wanted to capture the sense of rain-drenched innocence I remember so well from my childhood. *There was no intended metaphor.* (1, my emphasis)

We have seen how places, furniture, gardens and bodies interact with these material realities of daily life throughout the novel and this is what Adichie intended to capture with the flying *aku*. However, the interviewer is right and whatever her intentions, given the novel's framing of the corrupt state and the process whereby wickedness is punished, it does create the metaphor of the *aku*, whose day of reckoning, like the pre-coup leaders, like the sole adminis-trator, like Papa, will come. What Adebanwi is objecting to, is the politics of this metaphor, which uses the comparison with the inevitability of cycles of nature to describe what are really human endeavours and social and political processes. The *aku* will fall to the toad at night, inevitably, whereas Nigerians will have to work hard and struggle for their freedom from tyranny. While we saw Adichie go to some lengths to depict the purple hibiscus, as artefact, as science produced by the talent and inspiration of people, there is also the survival of the long tradition of the use of metaphors taken from the natural world inappropriately to describe social and political dimensions.

Overall, however, what stands out at the end of this reading is that *Purple Hibiscus*, with its visceral language and newly born symbols, is radical in its rhetoric, which is put to the service of an exploration of gender, however conflicted this exploration sometimes turns out to be. In the Introduction, we saw how new kinds of metaphors are called for within an understanding of the multiplicities of worlds, languages and knowledges making up these postcolonial migrant novels. We saw Lakoff and Johnson's concept of 'sym-bolic metonymies', which combine everyday experience with 'the coherent metaphorical systems that characterize religions and cultures' and which 'provide an essential means of comprehending religious and cultural con-cepts' (Lakoff and Johnson, 1980: 40). This becomes particularly potent in a novel in which the Catholic African author attempts to integrate her religion and her culture. The purple flowers and beige dancing figures stand as pow-erful symbolic metonymies. They breach the boundaries between the literal and the metaphoric, the solid object and the world of the spirits, between the modernist Christianity of Roman Catholicism and the traditional beliefs in the spirits of the Ancestors.

Towards the end of the novel, Kambili hopes that the silence between herself and Jaja will be broken; she hopes that they will be able eventually 'to clothe things in words, things that have long been naked' (306). *Purple Hibiscus* has given us many naked things, broken things, living things, things with the spirits of old gods still living in them. She has clothed them with the words appropriate to their concrete material realities, and transformed them into 'new "blended" mental spaces' (Turner and Fauconnier, 2000: 133). These new metaphors for a global world are constructed in America, in the Catholic Church and in the shrines of Igbo villages. Adichie found it difficult to hold these worlds together when she confronted the horrors of the Biafran war in her next novel, *Half of a Yellow Sun.*

7 An Abnormal Ordinary Chimamanda Ngozi Adichie's *Half of a Yellow Sun*

Successful fiction does not need to be validated by 'real life'; I cringe whenever a writer is asked how much of a novel is 'real'. Yet, I find myself thinking differently about the war novels I admire.... Perhaps it is because to write realistic fiction about a war, especially one central to the history of one's country, is to be constantly aware of a responsibility to something larger than art.
(Adichie, The Guardian, 16 September 2006)

What is the nature of the everyday in Chimamanda Ngozi Adichie's second novel, *Half of a Yellow Sun*, given her determination 'to write realistic fiction about a war'?

Her expressed sense of responsibility to something larger than art is what profoundly separates *Half of a Yellow Sun* from her first novel, *Purple Hibiscus*. While I could contest Adichie's implied fissure between art and the big, historical occurrences of 'real' life, including of war, what interests me here that she expresses an obligation to a degree of historical veracity in a fictional account of Biafra. And yet, in this novel she at times unwittingly falls back on dominant metaphors at the expense of depicting the concrete richness of material culture, which we saw her do so well in *Purple Hibiscus*. The focus of this chapter is to explore the context and the consequences of Adichie's increasing emphasis on the metaphoric in *Half of a Yellow Sun*.

Part One introduces the characters. Very briefly, there is Ugwu, who at the outset is the very raw village boy, who comes to work for the university professor, Odenigbo, in Nsukka. Odenigbo is in love with Olanna, who joins the household. Olanna has a strained relationship with her twin sister, Kainene, who is in a serious relationship with the rather awkward, sympathetic English character, Richard. More about all of them will emerge as the novel takes us down a tricky path. There is the portrayal of acts of untrammelled violence, of which a gang rape is one. This potentially plays into Western stereotypes of the African continent as a savage place of unnatural violence and blood letting. Ugwu, one of the gang of rapists, must atone for his crime, which he does by inheriting the white character, Richard's, role as the writer, who documents the realities of the atrocities of the war. Ugwu's writing echoes older forms of Igbo creativity as symbolised by the ancient roped pot and traditional Igbo words and wisdom, which pepper the novel. However, I will demonstrate that in providing a counter symbolism to the images of gratuitous acts of violence, Igbo material life begins to metamorphose into tropes of national pride. In so doing, as I will finally discuss, they detract from the concreteness of rape and compromise the novel's gender politics. In other words, we will see material objects, like the roped pot, and the use of Igbo words, mutate from being 'metonymic gaps' into quite essentialised and monolithic symbols of African culture, thereby falling into

133

the trap of what Eileen Julien has called 'ornamentalism' (2006: 669), as discussed in the introduction.

Yet, we saw that Adichie's stated purpose is to be as factually and literally faithful to the events of Biafra as they actually happened, as she can possibly manage. Although she indicates in the author's note that she has 'taken many liberties for the purpose of fiction' and that her 'intent is to portray my own imaginative truths and not the facts of the war' (434),[1] she qualifies this more than once in her comments on the novel and minimises the nature of those liberties. For example, she says in an exchange with Wale Adebanwi:

> *Half of a Yellow Sun* is fiction based on fact. I state in the author's note that I took some liberties for the purposes of fiction which means that *I played with small things* – I invented a train station in Nsukka, for example. *But I did not play with the big things.* I did not let a character be changed by something that did not actually happen. *All the major political events in the book are factually correct.* (email corresp., 2007, my emphases)[2]

And so, Adichie's second novel has no time for the exploration of the nature of Catholic belief hybridised with African spirits and animistic mind frames, which profoundly ordered events in *Purple Hibiscus*. The question this novel is asking is what happens to ordinary things, the smells, sights, sounds and possessions, when they are subjected to the horrors of war? The everyday will not shape shift into animation, but into another, demonic, version of what I am paradoxically calling the abnormal ordinary. This abnormal everyday is richly depicted, as Adichie is so skilled in doing. However, we will also see in this tense and conflicted novel that this abnormal ordinary will itself increasingly metamorphose into metaphor, as the novel develops. In the process, Adichie's stated purpose of confronting the horrors of the war in all their visceral reality is hijacked by being sucked into the tropes of dominant discourse, both with regard to representations of Africa and also in relation to portrayals of gender violence.

At the same time, one of the most interesting aspects of the novel is that it shows how devices of postmodernism may be employed in the interests of realism. These postmodern devices work in powerful ways to depict the abnormal ordinary. For example, time does not follow a linear path and the reader's perceptions of reality are distorted as we are invited to view the world through the prism of hindsight. Parts One and Two are chronological, being set in the early sixties and then the late sixties respectively. In Part Two, we get the escalation of violence and the depiction of the brutal atrocities of the war. When Adichie re-winds the reel in Part Three, back to the early sixties, when the peace is viewed by the reader through the lens of the realities of the war, which have already been portrayed in Part Two, our understanding of present realities is profoundly altered. In other words, when we observe characters involved in the minutiae of their daily lives before the war, char-

---

[1]   Page references to quotations in this chapter, unless indicated otherwise, are to *Half of A Yellow Sun* (London: Fourth Estate, 2004).

[2]   She repeats and emphasises this point in Peel, 2006, in *The Guardian*, 16 April, 2006 and in conversation with Bob Thomson of the *Washington Post*, 27 September, 2006.

acters who we have already seen brutally massacred during the war, the meaning of the everyday within its supposed ordinariness is de-familiarised. This is Adichie at her best. The novel produces confusion around authorship, stories within stories, time warps and the insistence on the existence of altered realities when life is viewed from different standpoints.

The different realms that Adichie captures are linked to her understanding of the distinctions between the affluent and the poor, in terms of how the war impinged on their everyday lives. In her Author's Note, Adichie explains that she was creating 'the mood of middle-class Biafra' in the novel and in a piece that she wrote for *The Guardian* newspaper, entitled 'Truth and Lies', Adichie expresses her admiration for Achebe's Biafra stories because of his depiction of 'the Biafran middle class who lived through the deprivations of war but were not completely flattened as were their poorer compatriots' (2006a). This is the angle that Adichie hopes herself to capture when she describes her wish to depict the war faithfully. This she accomplishes up to a point, until the contradictions that we saw her juggle with some difficulty in *Purple Hibiscus* career somewhat out of control in *Half of a Yellow Sun*. In other words, what Adichie wishes to understand is the thick texture of the everyday that people like her parents experienced at that time. This may only be grasped fully by juxtaposing their way of life before and during the war, and the novel begins by highlighting the material realities of the affluent class of the twins' parents, during peace time, which will be contrasted with their poorer relatives in the North:

> After dinner, they moved to the balcony for liqueurs. Olanna liked this after-dinner ritual and often would move away from her parents and the guests to stand by the railing, looking at the tall lamps that lit up the paths below, so bright that the swimming pool looked silver and the hibiscuses and bougainvillea took on an incandescent patina over their reds and pinks. (32)

The Lagos mansion, the dinners, the shady business deals involving sexual favours and gifts, like the latest European lace, are all meticulously conjured up. This affluent life is not only corrupt, it is also sensual and pleasurable and Olanna, who despises her parents' greed, lack of values and ill treatment of the servants, likes the beauty of the lit up, silvery pool and, significantly, the colourful plants in the garden.

The novel quite quickly takes us into the very different daily lives of the Kano branch of the family, which starkly highlights the class distinctions between them. Olanna adores her Aunty Ifeka, Uncle Mbaezi and her cousin Arize, who live a rural life where basic goods are a luxury, which Olanna provides as gifts on her visits. She brings 'bread, shoes, bottles of cream', which are received by her Aunt as great blessings (39). Over the course of seven pages, Adichie gives us details of the minutiae of life within this family, filtered through the privileged eyes of Olanna, who finds their basic existence something of a hardship, for all her love for them. It is necessary to reproduce the feel of those pages because these concrete realities provide the substance of Adichie's point. In other words, Adichie is operating at the level of these details of material culture in order to re-create how Biafra completely transformed these lives. We have to understand how important it is that her Uncle Mbaezi 'smelled of sweat, of the open-air market, of wares arranged on dusty wood shelves' (37). Aunty Ifeka has a modest kiosk selling 'cases of matches, chewing gum, sweets, cigarettes, and detergent' (39). Olanna tries hard to avoid 'looking at the cockroach eggs, smooth black capsules, lodged in all corners of the table' and she suffers from the choking smoke in the kitchen from the neighbour's wood fire (41). She also does not want them to know 'that the smoke irritated her eyes and throat or that the sight of the cockroach eggs nauseated her' (41–2).

Their small bungalow 'was unpainted' and worn out sofas have to be pushed aside for sleeping mats, mats on the floor on which her Aunt and Uncle insist on sleeping when the educated Olanna comes for a visit, so that she may have their bed. This bed is separated from the rest of the space by a 'thin curtain that hung on a rope attached to nails' and this rope 'was not taut, and the curtain sagged in the middle' (43) and Olanna, trying to sleep, imagines how her cousin, Arize, must have been privy to her parents' love-making through the threadbare curtain. This contrasts with how 'she had always been separated from them [her parents] by hallways that got longer and more thickly carpeted as they moved from house to house' until her parents chose separate bedrooms in their current, ten-roomed mansion (43). As she tries to sleep, Olanna smells the air 'thick with the odors from the gutters behind the house, where people emptied their toilet buckets' and she eventually falls asleep to the 'scraping sound of their shovels' as the 'night-soil men ... collected the sewage' (43).

Olanna, in fact, is like her creator when her old boyfriend, Mohammed, says to her after she expresses a desire to drive around and see some of the sights of the town: 'Sometimes you are just like the white people, the way they gawk at *everyday things*' (45, my emphasis). Unlike *Purple Hibiscus* where these everyday things are inhabited by spirits, by the *mmuo*, who animate and enchant them, all of this stuff is inanimate and un-enchanted and waiting to be metamorphosed, not by old beliefs, gods and ghosts, but by war. When Ugwu is persuaded to take Richard, the lover of Kainene, Olanna's twin, to his village to see 'the *ori-okpa* festival, where the *mmuo* paraded', what is emphasised about the trip is not those powerful and enigmatic spirits of *Purple Hibiscus*. Rather, the expedition provides Ugwu with the opportunity to impress everyone in his village 'with his English, his new shirt, his knowledge of sandwiches and running tap water, his scented powder' (86). Ugwu is disappointed by this outing only because Nnesinachi, on whom he has a lustful crush, was not present and all Ugwu hopes for is that when they get back there will be an Indian film on television (211).

The smells, sights, sounds and possessions, the sandwiches and scented powder will all metamorphose when they are subjected to the horrors of war. This is what Ugwu senses, well into Part Two, which is set in the late sixties of the war:

Change was hurtling toward him, bearing down on him, and there was nothing he could do to make it slow down.

> He sat down and stared at the cover of *The Pickwick Papers*. There was a serene calm
> in the backyard, in the gentle wave of the mango tree and the winelike scent of ripening
> cashews. It belied what he saw around him. (175)

In fact, when they heard Ojukwu make the auspicious announcement declaring *'Eastern Nigeria ... a sovereign independent Republic'* called *'The Republic of Biafra'* Olanna's response is that 'her mind [is] frozen in the present, on the cashew-juice stain on the front of Baby's dress' (162). What happens to Baby's dresses, her food and hair during the war provides us with a profound sense of the consequences of war on the everyday material realities of life. Dickens is code word for Ugwu's education in English and its canon, and *Pickwick Papers* becomes even more bizarre in this context, in the light of the uprooting of the familiar material anchors of plants, yards, trees and smells. The joys of silvery pools, glowing hibiscuses, mango trees and the heady scent of ripened nuts are not merely dissipating, but their reality is shifting into mirage; they are no longer material and real. Later, in Part Two, as the war escalates and the writing is full of foreboding, the laughter is incredulous and painful when Adichie caricatures Richard's servant, Harrison, the Anglophobe, boasting to the other servants: '"You are not knowing how to bake German chocolate cake?"' A cackle. "You are not knowing what is rhubarb crumble?" Another scornful cackle' (166).

While Olanna's difficulties in being deprived of face cream and her wig are given quite sympathetically throughout the novel, when time reverts, in Part Three, to the days before the war, but now seen through the lenses of the massacres, the moral decrepitude of the upper class of Olanna's parents becomes more grotesque. This critique is far more devastating than in the opening pages of the novel, which highlighted the pleasures to be had on a beautiful night with a glowing swimming pool and garden. Olanna's mother and her friends are now shocking with their gossip about 'who had bought local lace and tried to pass it off as the latest from Europe, and who was trying to snatch so-and-so's husband, and who had imported superior furniture from Milan' (217).

And yet, it is worth repeating that Adichie does not belittle middle-class hardships, which her own family would have experienced during the war. These are her people, and this is the class heritage to which Adiche is heir, and in which she has to find her bearings. As she puts it: 'I wanted to take ownership of a history that defines me' (Adichie, 2006a). Therefore, Olanna is not caricatured when she is depicted as being bitter about having left in Nsukka 'her books, her piano, her clothes, her china, her wigs, her Singer sewing machine, the television' (185) and we see throughout how she grieves for her possessions: 'her tablecloths with the silver embroidery, her car, Baby's strawberry cream biscuits' (262). The bathos rings true when she bewails the fact that her friend, Mohammed, could not know that Odenigbo was drinking too much, that Ugwu was conscripted and that 'she had sold her wig' (377). At the market, if Olanna buys the 'graying pieces of raw chicken' that would be all she had money for, so she buys 'four medium sized snails instead' (329). This is middle-class deprivation, given that she can still buy food and the family does not starve, albeit that Baby develops malnutrition. When Umuahia falls and they have to leave again and to go and stay in Kainene's house with her and Richard, we share in the sensuous pleasure that the sisters derive from the material luxury of 'a small pear-shaped vial of face cream' that someone brought for Kainene as a gift and which contrasts with 'that horrible Biafran-made oil' (388).

Here is the perch from which Adichie is attempting to tell her truth about Biafra, in the coded language of the material. Dickens, rhubarb crumble, all the vestiges of colonial aspirations inherited by the new elite are metamorphosing into an abnormal everyday life. To further our understanding of the Biafran war as transforming the very substance of daily life, and to see how this transformation in its turn swells up and becomes metaphorical, we have to return to Olanna's early visit to Kano and to the gift of a beautiful pair of leather slippers.

Slaughter, rape & the abnormal ordinary

> He opened his bag and brought out a pair of slippers and held them out to her, his narrow face creased in a smile, his teeth stained with kola nut and tobacco and whatever else Olanna did not know, stains of varying shades of yellow and brown. (40)

'He' is Abdulmalik, the family's Hausa friend and neighbour, and the slippers are perfect with their 'pleated red straps' which 'made her feet look slender, more feminine' (41). His teeth, stained with tobacco and kola, speak of rituals of civility and the colour of the earth, its yellows and browns. He wants Olanna to sample his wife's cooking, her 'very sweet *kuka* soup, made from the 'ripe gourdlike pods on the *kuka* tree' (40). The red leather, the pods from which sweet soup emanates, the sugarcane that Uncle Mbaezi provides for the two old friends to gnaw on and to revel in 'the juicy white pulp' (40) all contribute to the sensuality of food, friendship and family. Hausa and Igbo happily commune together and celebrate life's bounty, even within their somewhat straitened circumstances. This is the material culture of the time of peace. This is the reality that evaporates as if all that materiality had been mere mirage in the horror of what ensues during the Biafran war. He participates in the massacre of this same family with whom he broke kola, sucked sugarcane, offered sweet soup and for whom he made beautiful red leather slippers:

> 'We finished the whole family. It was Allah's will!' one of the men called out in Hausa. The man was familiar. It was Abdulmalik. (148)

At first Olanna cannot believe it. She looks closely at the killer:

> It *was* Abdulmalik. He had nudged another body, a woman's headless body, and stepped over it, placed one leg down and then the other, although there was enough room to step to the side. (148, emphasis in original)

As if we could not see that he has become a murderous brute, delighting in an orgy of slaughter, the novel has him step on the body of a decapitated woman. He has proudly confessed to what Olanna had already seen:

> Uncle Mbaezi lay facedown in an ungainly twist, legs splayed. Something creamy-white oozed through the large gash on the back of his head. Aunty Ifeka lay on the veranda. The cuts on her naked body were smaller, dotting her arms and legs like slightly parted red lips. (147)

This portrayal of Abdulmalik plays into dominant, Western stereotypes regarding African people, their wars in general and Biafra in particular. All of this contributes to what Mahmood Mamdani, writing about Darfur, terms a 'pornography of violence':

> Newspaper writing on Darfur has sketched *a pornography of violence*. It seems fascinated by and fixated on the gory details, describing the worst of the atrocities in gruesome details and chronicling the rise in the number of them. The implication is that the motivation of the perpetrators lies in biology ('race') and, if not that, certainly in 'culture'. (Mamdani: 2007, 26, my emphasis)

The newspapers to which Mamdani refers are American, and the image of Africa that is perpetuated in this reportage is of a level of violence that is innate and inevitable, assuming fixed biological or cultural characteristics of Africans. This critique had been Mamdani's focus in his book, *When Victims Become Killers*, published six years earlier, when the topic was Rwanda as 'a *metaphor* for postcolonial political violence' (2001: xi, my emphasis); Rwanda, for non-Africans, signifies Africa's inhumane Other-ness – 'the aberration is Africa' (7). Mamdani's gist is not that genocidal violence is 'rational', which it cannot be, but that that it is 'thinkable', which means we must be able to understand and to analyse it historically, as the outcome of 'political identities' (16) and therefore to understand it historically. Without this level of insight, depictions of Darfur, Rwanda, Mau Mau, or Biafra run the risk of reproducing knowledge about Africa that merely reinforces some of the worst stereotypes, whether the author is an ignorant American newspaper reporter or an original, young Nigerian voice.

It is true that Adichie's topic is cultural, vested in the quest to understand the changing nature of daily life. We as readers dictate the writer's obligations at our peril. Nevertheless, what cannot be avoided, once Adichie chose Biafra as her topic, is the danger of the novel being conscripted into the figurative arsenal of Western mis-representations of Africa. When families are butchered and cut up in the novel, when good men participate in gang rape, when a Hausa soldier guns down an Igbo man, Nnaemeka, at close range at the airport for no reason other than that he is an 'infidel', then what is added to our knowledge of Africa? The horrible sight of 'Nnaemeka's chest' which 'blew open, a splattering red mass' (153), adds to the archive of negative images of Africans. In this way, and within the terms that the novel itself sets up, certain fault-lines crack open, in the presence of the dominant images, tropes and metaphors through whose poor services Africa, and its violent wars, have always been depicted. Abdulmalik killed his neighbours for one reason only, which was that they belonged to the group, Igbo, and he was Hausa, and the frenzy of his violence went beyond the necessity, as he saw it, and became 'unthinkable'.

The same material manifestations of life are recalled, but are now utterly transformed into a different dimension of reality. Aunty Ifeka's kiosk is smashed: 'splinters of wood, packets of groundnuts lying in the dust' (147). Even the pod of the *kuka* tree has fallen down and is crunched under the wheels of the car (148). If these simple things have been crushed and smashed in reality, they have also shape-shifted in our perception of their previous lives before the war even began. And so, with these terrors still reflecting in our eyes, the novel winds back the clock in Part Three, and shows us this family before their annihilation. We are incredulous at the smallness of their concerns when we see Arize, who will be massacred along with her unborn child, passionately peruse 'sketches of bouffant wedding gowns' (225) in anticipation of her wedding.

Perhaps the most telling example of the abnormal ordinary, as I have called it, is the incident that recurs in the novel as a macabre motif, that of the grief-stricken mother with her child's decapitated head in her calabash. Olanna had just witnessed the murder of her family in Kano and had managed to get onto a train to take her back home. She sat next to a woman and bumped against 'a big bowl, a calabash' (148) that the woman had on her lap. We are given the calabash in all its material sensuality: 'she liked the firm feel of the wood'. Like the innocent time before the war, the calabash is soothing and solid and Olanna moved 'her hand forward until it was gently caressing the carved lines that crisscrossed the calabash' (149). However, the calabash, for all its solidity is horrifyingly metamorphosed when the owner beckoned Olanna to look inside it:

> Olanna looked into the bowl. She saw the little girl's head with the ashy-gray skin and the braided hair and the rolled-back eyes and open mouth. (149)

This terrible image begins to grow into part of the archive of unthinkably cruel African massacres and amputations, in the repeated reference to it:

> She thought about the plaited hair resting in the calabash. She visualized the mother braiding it, her fingers oiling it with pomade before dividing it into sections with a wooden comb. (149)

Hair, the part for the whole, is a metonymic device rendering the dead child in all her once flesh and blood reality. Olanna remembers this ghastly moment of revelation on the train over and over again in the novel. In this way, it becomes a blended metaphoric metonym, which stands for the irrational, vicious violence of Biafra. The still ornately plaited hair itself splits time into its sundered dimensions of pre- and post- war, as we imagine the mother lovingly plaiting the hair of her still-living, doomed child. In fact, Adichie will underline this point when, much later, Olanna is combing Baby's hair which is falling out. No longer the 'natural jet-black' of before the war, it reflects the malnutrition of the war child and is thin, wispy and 'a sun-bleached yellow-brown' 409). This contrasts with the thick hair on the decapitated head of the child, who no longer needs nourishment. Olanna remembers that head of hair minutely: 'it was very thick. It must have been work for her mother to plait it' (409). In fact the bereft mother, beside herself with grief, 'clearly remembered how it was plaited and she began to describe the hairstyle, how some of the braids fell across the forehead' (409).

The ordinary, everyday ritual of hair plaiting is demonically transformed. And nothing demonstrates this transformation more acutely than the normally gentle and kind Ugwu participating in a gang rape. Adichie does not flinch from portraying the rape in all its concrete detail. Ugwu enters the bar to find the brutalised, teenage character known as High-Tech raping the girl:

> The bar girl was lying on her back on the floor, her wrapper bunched up at her waist, her shoulders held down by a soldier, her legs wide, wide ajar. She was sobbing, 'Please, please, *biko.*' Her blouse was still on. Between her legs, High-Tech was moving. His thrusts were jerky, his small buttocks darker-colored than his legs. The soldiers were cheering. (365)

The cheering soldiers egg on the reluctant Ugwu to be next. He may have joined in the rape reluctantly, but he becomes a fully fledged participant. He is 'surprised at the swiftness of his erection' (365) and he manages to climax inside her:

> She was dry and tense when he entered her. He did not look at her face, or at the man pinning her down, or at anything at all as he moved quickly and felt his own climax, the rush of fluids to the tips of himself: a self-loathing release. He zipped up his trousers while some soldiers clapped. (365)

The question is whether the novel's mission to depict the concrete realities of the war faithfully provides any kind of explanation as to how it is possible that Ugwu could participate in a gang rape. While the Hausa Abdulmalik is slaughtering Igbos, the raping Igbo soldiers are simply criminalised by the war. Although it appears as if Adichie is being even-handed in the rape scene, given that she supports the Igbo cause, the danger, to which I have been pointing, is that the rape and slaughter buttress the trope of Africa's dark heart.

Having said this, the novel does indeed attempt an antidote to this view of Africa by invoking a different symbolic archive. This rebuttal begins promisingly with an historical account that emerges in Richard's books and newspaper articles, whose purpose is to document the culpability of colonialism in leaving a heritage of instability and disaster. He writes how 'in 1960, Nigeria was a collection of fragments held in a fragile clasp' (155). Adichie is aware of the danger of Western stereotypes of Africa, even though she is ultimately unable entirely to avoid reinforcing them. Richard is incensed by the British *Herald*, which describes 'the Nigerian pogroms' being as the result of 'Ancient tribal hatreds' (166). He responds with an article which points out that

> *If this is hatred, then it is very young. It has been caused, simply, by the informal*

> divide-and-rule policies of the British colonial exercise. These policies manipulated the
> differences between the tribes and ensured that unity would not exist ... (166–7)

Furthermore, the novel strives to deepen its understanding of the past, by surfacing an alternate archive of pre-colonial Igbo language and culture to buttress the suggestion of colonial culpability for the violence of the war. This brings its own pitfalls when symbols of national pride overwhelm the realities of male brutality against women.

Atonement, writing, roped pots & language

> He could not remember her features, but the look in her eyes stayed with him, as did the
> tense dryness between her legs, the way he had done what he had not wanted to do....
> *He would give himself time to atone for what he had done.* (397, my emphasis)

Ugwu works in the refugee camp during the day and whenever he can, he writes his book about the atrocities of the war under the flame tree. As in *Purple Hibiscus*, this tree with its red leaves echoes Ngũgĩ wa Thiong'o's *Petals of Blood* and the tradition of political writing that Adichie enables Ugwu to inherit from Ngũgĩ, and from Frederick Douglass, whose *Narrative of the Life of Frederick Douglass, An American Slave: Written by Himself* had inspired Ugwu. Ugwu was especially struck by Douglass's powerful insistence:

> *Even if it cost me my life, I was determined to read. Keep the black man away from the
> books, keep us ignorant, and we would always be his slaves.* (360)

An important narrative device in the novel is that there is confusion regarding the authorship of the writing. At first, it is unambiguously Richard who is writing books and by the end it is clearly Ugwu, but in between the reader is left in doubt, which echoes the communal nature of aspects of African art and orality. The 'in between' is made more complex by the further fracture in the temporal structure of the novel. We have already noted the splintering of time as the novel moves back and forth between the periods before and during the war, which alters the reader's understanding of both. In addition, quite a number of chapters end with a separate section in an entirely different style, which are extracts from a book that either Richard or Ugwu is writing.

In Part One, before the start of the war, in one such section at the end of the chapter, Olanna relates her encounter with the mother carrying her dead child's head in the calabash. She is talking to an unnamed writer, who we assume at this stage is Richard, as we have no inkling that the uneducated houseboy, Ugwu, is going to transform into a young intellectual. As always, we are given the visceral details, here for the first time:

> Olanna tells him this story and he notes the details. She tells him how the bloodstains
> on the woman's wrapper blended into the fabric to form a rusty mauve. She describes
> the carved designs on the woman's calabash, slanting lines crisscrossing each other, and

she describes the child's head inside: scruffy braids falling across the dark-brown face, eyes completely white, eerily open, a mouth in a small surprised O. (82)

The dried mauve blood on the fabric, the texture of the wood, the child's hair again and the whites of her dead eyes, are all metonyms for the war in the sense that they are a concrete part of their horrors. Again, the minutiae of material detail loom large in the style of Adichie's langue. But in the transformation of this incident into a part of Ugwu's atonement as he does the work of recording it, these concrete details develop symbolic importance. The evidence that it was not Richard who was the writer in Part One emerges in Part Four, when Kainene tells Richard about the head in the calabash and it is clear that he is hearing it for the first time (318). Only right near the end of the novel, however, is it unambiguously confirmed that it is Ugwu who is writing the book, and that it was he to whom Olanna was relating the story right at the beginning. Adichie attempts to turn this atrocity into the written word as part of Ugwu's atonement for his act of rape:

> Then she described the head itself, the open eyes, the graying skin. *Ugwu was writing as she spoke*, and his writing, the earnestness of his interest, suddenly made her story important, made it serve a larger purpose that even she was not sure of, and so she told him all she remembered about the train full of people who had cried and shouted and urinated on themselves. (410, my emphasis)

In serving this 'larger' purpose, it paradoxically becomes smaller; it is less a concrete experience of a mother driven insane with grief and more an opportunity for Ugwu to atone. At one point, both Richard and Ugwu are writing and assisting each other. Richard visits Ugwu in hospital, after he had been wounded, where Ugwu tells him about reading the autobiography of Frederick Douglass. Richard says he will use this anecdote in his book, the title of which is *'The World Was Silent When We Died'* (396). Richard takes the anecdote, but Ugwu is left with the title, which haunts him: 'It made him think about that girl in the bar; her pinched face and the hate in her eyes as she lay on her back on the dirty floor' (396). The title passes from Richard to Ugwu, who is healed and reinvented through recording the atrocities in his writing, which seems, at least in part, at the expense of the violated woman. And thus the novel ends:

The Book: The World Was Silent When We Died

Ugwu writes his dedication last: *For Master, my good man* (433)

Ugwu's blossoming creativity as a young Igbo man in the twentieth century is linked to the tradition of Igbo art, culture and technology through the image of the roped pot, which is hundreds of years old. I have been suggesting that the novel's weapon against the stereotype of Africa is its insistence that Africans have a complex tradition of art, culture and language that long pre-dates colonialism. It is also a tradition that has been communally forged and in this period of post-independence, white writing and education is part of the hybrid inheritance of Igbo artists and intellectuals in the novel represented by the Englishman, Richard. This creative endeavour, therefore, cuts across race. Richard's ill fated manuscripts may have been burnt or buried, but, like the roped pot, one is finally, symbolically, excavated by Ugwu in a stratigraphy of books reminiscent of the layers of inherited scholarship that we saw to be central to Jamal Mahjoub's archaeology of knowledge in Chapter Four. The entwinement of Richard and Ugwu's writing as Ugwu inherits the book could be captured by a line of a favourite poem of Olanna's, which is recited by Ugwu: 'Clay pots fired in zeal, they will cool our feet as we climb' (411). The image of clay pots as steps in the long climb towards knowledge is highly evocative of the ancient pot, so dear to Richard. And it is, in fact, Richard, who introduces knowledge of the pot into the novel, like the European archaeologist, who excavated it.

This explains the otherwise somewhat puzzling role of the 'magnificent roped pot' to be found 'in the land of Igbo-Ukwu art' in the southeast of the country, which was 'why he [Richard] had come to Nigeria' (56). The reason for Richard's obsession with this pot is not integrated into the logic of the narrative and can only be understood, I think, in the terms of shared authorship, which I have just outlined. Richard is neither archaeologist nor art historian, and yet his life seems to have become focussed on the pot made in a time and place that could not be further removed from his own. Richard's deep fascination, almost obsession, with the pot is a narrative moment of belief suspension:

> He was not sure where he first read about Igbo-Ukwu art, about the native man who was digging a well and discovered the bronze castings that may well be the first in Africa, dating back to the ninth century. But it was in *Colonies Magazine* that he saw the photos. The roped pot stood out immediately; he ran a finger over the picture and ached to touch the delicately cast metal itself. He wanted to try explaining how deeply stirred he had been by the pot ... (62)

And

> Richard sat there for a while, imagining the lives of people who were capable of such beauty, such complexity, in the time of Alfred the Great. He wanted to write about this ... (72)

The pot, and other unearthed treasures, function, then, if somewhat artificially, as part of Richard's refutation to the *Herald* of British perceptions of Africans. As Richard writes in his article, which was rejected as bland:

> *The notion of the recent killings being the product of 'age-old' hatred is therefore misleading. The tribes of the North and the South have long had contact, at least as far back as the ninth century, as some of the magnificent beads discovered at the historic Igbo-Ukwu site attest.* (166)

Adichie does not wish to imply that these skills have been lost in the present and so Richard is writing a piece about '*ogbunigwe*, the fantastic Biafran-made land mines' (316). The technologically advanced land mines are also symbolic of Igbo skills and specifically counter the notion of Igbos as primitive. In addition, they imply that the war and its atrocities were part of the colonial heritage which diverted people from their pre-colonial creative wellsprings.

This leads to the question of the purpose and consequences of the extensive use of Igbo words and sayings in the novel. In line with its tensions, in addition to the way in which it essentialises Igbo culture, *Half of a Yellow Sun* also produces metonymic gaps, which are woven into the texture of its language. For example, a reiterated device throughout is what could be called the English Igbo echo:

> Mama Oji started the song, '*Onye ga-enwe mmeri?*' and the other women responded '*Biafra ga-enwe mmeri, igba!*' ... Olanna joined them, buoyed by the words – '*Who will win? Biafra will win, igba!*' (332)

The words are translated for the benefit of the reader by being echoed in English, albeit that the women almost certainly did not sing them in both languages. The rhythm of the song is provided by the texture of the indigenous words. Sometimes the echo emphasises the inherited wisdom of the twins' grandfather, as in the following:

> 'Grandpapa used to say, about difficulties he had gone through, "It did not kill me, it made me knowledgeable." *O gburo m egbu, o mee ka m malu ife.*' (347)

And again Kainene says to Olanna:

> 'Grandpapa used to say that it gets worse and then it gets better. *O dikata njo, o dikwa mma,*' Kainene said. (390)

Other knowledges and wisdoms echo with the overtones of Spivak's resistant speech of her Echo referred to in the introduction, who seeks an alter-native to the toxic symbolic. 'Echo', remember, 'is obliged to echo everyone who speaks' in her opposition to the deep and meaningful language of the Law (Spivak, 1993: 27). The echo works again as an emphasis, as when Olanna is horrified to find that Odenigbo had brought home a gun: 'The double-barreled gun, long and black and dull, lay on the bed. '*Gini bu ife a?* What is this?' Olanna asked' (336). Or it is used to underline Olanna's desperation in her searching for her lost twin, Kainene. Note the slightly different way the echo is produced here, repeating Kainene's features:

> ... when [Richard] stopped to ask people on the roadside if they had seen anybody who looked like Kainene, [Olanna] would say, '*O tolu ogo, di ezigbo oji*'; as if repeating what Richard had already said, that Kainene was tall and very dark, would jog the people's memory better. (407)

And when she has given her sister up for dead, on the very last page of the novel, Olanna comforts herself with '"Our people say that we all reincarnate, don't they?" she said. "*Uwa m, uwa ozo.* When I come back in my next life, Kainene will be my sister"' (433). Sometimes we get a word here or there, which is not translated: Ugwu is referred to as '*Dianyi*' (93) or the '*nlacha* skin disease' is mentioned and not explained (184). Or, as a more conventional metonymic gap, we get a song, which is only partially translated, as when Olanna sings the song that the women at the relief centre sing:

> *Caritas, thank you,*
> *Caritas si anyi taba okporoko*
> *Na kwashiorkor ga-ana.* (283)

And the children sing a song given in Igbo while they sweep:

> *Biafra, kunie, buso Nigeria agha,*
> *Anyi emelie ndi awusa,*
> *Ndi na-amaro chukwu,*
> *Tigbue fa, zogbue fa,*
> *Nwelu nwude Gowon.* (337)

What I am suggesting is that this insertion of Igbo songs and chants of the women and children, whose spirits prevail under the intense suffering and duress, provides an alternative language to the ethnic glorification of pots and land mines. What I have been suggesting throughout this book is that the insertion of indigenous languages, or Arabic, into the English novel may serve the function of opening up the reader to the possibility of other concrete knowledges and worlds than the dominant European one. What we also discussed in the introduction is that this insertion of another language or of stories or wisdoms, could serve the opposite function if they became symbolic of an idealised and essentialised African pre-colonial culture. Eileen Julien's term coined for this is 'ornamentalism', which she identified, as discussed earlier, as arising out of the pressure on African writers to prove their credentials of authenticity (2006: 669). She further suggested that this pressure was particularly acute in the case of migrants (684). This makes sense, given that the migrant, who becomes increasingly distanced from the daily realities of African life, would feel this pressure even more powerfully. I would go further and say that what could catalyse this essentialised depiction is the African writer, who migrates to America, encountering the tradition of the African American search for African roots. The writer, newly arrived from Africa, carries a particular burden of authority and insiderness about the continent and would be pressed to capture its essence and its glory. I think that this pressure has quite profoundly mediated Adichie's second novel, in which its language and its characters move in contradictory directions. This is why Ugwu is both rapist and hope for the future, as we will discuss in a moment, and Richard is both quasi Igbo and also a typical white racist.

With regard to Richard, in foregrounding the enduring values of Igbo creativity, figuratively embodied in the roped pot and in the Igbo language, Adichie buys into a version of revived essentialism, which confusingly turns Richard, mid-stream in the novel, from being a reliable historical commentator and admirer of Igbo technological accomplishments and language, to a more stereotypical expatriat. Throughout much of *Half of a Yellow Sun*, he is a very sympathetic character, who increasingly identifies with the Igbo culture and community. He falls deeply in love with Kainene, Olanna's twin sister, learns the language and becomes a participant in the war on the side of Biafra, whose story he desperately tries to tell the world. His Igbo becomes 'near-fluent' (136) and he is even changing colour: 'he was browner' (137). With his new relationships and commitments, he is fundamentally trans-forming as a human being:

> Richard looked at his hazy reflection in the glass door. He had a tan and his hair looked fuller, slightly tousled, and he thought of Rimbaud's words: *I is someone else.* (307, emphasis in original).

Hair, skin colour and the uncertain reflection in the mirror, suggest that Rich-ard is capable of mutating into a different being. Adichie tells us that he is able to identify an Igbo person not by how they looked but by 'a fellow feel-ing' (319). He uses 'we' for Biafrans, with whom he fully identifies himself (372). This is able to be done by love, by learning a language, by appreciating a culture and taking on a politics. This is the Adichie of multiple worlds and gardens of mixed flowers. It is, therefore, perplexing when she changes direction. Towards the end of the novel, Richard is no longer writing his book because 'The war isn't my story to tell, really' (425) Yet, the depic-tion of Richard had been saying something else about his becoming an Igbo man, and the whole blurring of authorship was working towards a commu-nal ownership of narrative, where community of feeling cut across race and tribe. Adichie, however, withdraws from this understanding of culture as concrete and also performed and constructed, and returns to a more intrin-sic, ethnic view of it, where the pot, the beads and the land mines become the weighty symbols of authentic Igbo culture and where whiteness is denied access. In so becoming, the narrative can no longer sustain the position it had initially held that a white man, like Richard, could virtually become an Igbo. This is reflected in the unbelievable moment when Richard, in a jealous rage against Kainene's friend, Madu, reverts to stereotype. His racism has simply been repressed and Richard demands to know whether Madu 'ever laid *your filthy black hand* on her' (430, my emphasis). This is also contradictory, of course, given that Richard is grieving over the loss of the black Kainene, his true love.

All of this links to the references to slavery in *Half of a Yellow Sun*, by way of the Frederick Douglass autobiography. The history of slavery is often presented as a deeply unifying phenomenon for all black people everywhere – on the continent or in the Diaspora. This is a tradition which would, by definition, exclude the white man, Richard, on the basis of his racial catego-ry. And so, Adichie appears to change her portrayal of Richard as the novel becomes more steeped in its intra-figurative battles between Afro-centric ide-alisations of tradition and Western dark hearts. Both retain the paradigm of essences, which reduce multiple communities to homogenised and intrinsic qualities.

What I have been suggesting throughout, and need to elaborate now, is that Adichie has compromised her feminism in *Half of a Yellow Sun*. In her fissured attempt to exorcise her demons relating to Western representations of Africa, there are consequences for her depiction of gender violence.

War rape & gender tensions

In the discussion of *Purple Hibiscus* I demonstrated that Adichie does not ultimately redeem Papa and allow him to atone for his sins. His aberrations were too heinous and Adichie ensures that Mama has her revenge and that the poisoned Papa will never beat her, or her children, again. Furthermore, there is no hint that Mama has committed a crime at all, for which she will have to atone. The novel may attempt to redeem Papa in some small ways, but it cannot and does not, enable him to live after the crimes he has committed.

Adichie reproduces a version of this juggling dilemma again, but this time resolves her contradiction differently and adjudicates in favour of the penitent male subject, in the interests of an African cultural and national healing project. In many ways, Ugwu is reminiscent of the gentle Jaja. But in combining Papa and Jaja in the loyal and kind Ugwu, who participates in a gang rape, and is redeemed as the subject of the re-born nation after the war, Adichie suggests that betrayals, gender violence and all the passions of the personal in peace time shrink, become absurd and are swept into the abyss of public and distorted war realities. Ugwu is the African man that black feminists, womanists, recognise as also oppressed and in depicting his struggles they distance themselves from what they characterise as Western feminism's anti-male stance. This worked in the character of Jaja. The problem of ascribing this role of men as also oppressed by colonial racism to a character who participated in a gang rape is to sacrifice the abuse of women to some kind of bigger, male canvas of issues around colonial inheritances, war and soldiering. Of course, the novel does not condone rape, and we saw that Ugwu himself is horrified by his actions, but it does deflect it onto another, bigger, plane, in order for Igwu to emerge as the post-war hope of the nation. We do not find out what happens to the violated young woman in the bar, whether she survives her ordeal, or whether it destroys her. In its deflection, rape loses its visceral concreteness and becomes symbolic of the abnormality of war. What Ugwu participated in is thereby reduced to what Adichie calls, in email exchange with Wale Adebanwi, 'war rape' and her suggestion that it is 'in war situations' that 'our very humanity is in question' (2007).

This explains the lengths to which the novel goes to contextualise Ugwu's behaviour as atypical of him. While not playing down his role as a participant in the gang rape, Adichie does explain that he was drunk on an evil brew, the effects of which must have been lethal (365); he had been outside when the others had initiated the rape. Most importantly perhaps, he had been horribly provoked and enraged by the demonic character, High-Tech, who had torn out a page of his sacred book by Frederick Douglass in order to roll a joint. The novel also portrays other male characters as sharing a similar lack of control over their sexual urges. Responding to her mother's pleading,

Olanna, quite embarrassingly, has to urge her father to stop humiliating their mother with another woman. She comes to see him through new eyes and her disgust and loss of respect is portrayed by way of the metamorphosing material objects which surround him:

> She looked around his room and thought how unfamiliar his large bed was; she had never seen that lustrous shade of gold on a blanket before or noticed how intricately convoluted the metal handles of his chest of drawers were. He even looked like a stranger, a fat man she didn't know. (219)

This strange, fat man, grotesquely philandering and humiliating his family, is embodied, as Adichie is so adept in portraying, in the superficial glitz of his garish, no doubt ill-begotten possessions. He stands for his class of greedy, adulterous males of the new elite. However, it is not only men such as Olanna's father, who betray their families. Aunt Ifeka, whose voice echoes with the moral power of our prior knowledge that she will be brutally massacred in the war, bitterly refers to her husband's penis as 'that snake between his legs'. She had had to threaten to cut it off if he brought disgrace to her (226). It is she who explains to her niece, in Olanna's heartbreak at Odenigbo's betrayal of her with Amala, that 'Odenigbo has done *what all men do* and has inserted his penis in the first hole he could find when you were away' (226, my emphasis). This generalised male behaviour explains how the complex, and in many ways wise, Odenigbo, again a very different kind of man from Olanna's father or uncle, can love Olanna so deeply and yet allow himself to be seduced by Amala during peace and maybe by Alice during war. It explains how an Englishman like Richard, from a very different cultural background, can be seduced by Olanna, even though her twin sister, Kainene, is the love of his life. Adichie's feminism makes this critique of men, but in describing all men in this way, she contrarily appears to condone them by confirming that it is in their biological make-up to be sexually promiscuous. That is to say, it is the devil between their legs, which separates their bodies from their moral and spiritual selves.

In other words, this critique is double-edged. It both condemns and vindicates men, who may behave badly, but who cannot help themselves. They are further vindicated by what the novel rates as the even worse atrocities of the war. This is achieved by way of the splintering of time in the narrative structure of the novel. Throughout Part Two there are hints at some very bad betrayals between Olanna and Odenigbo, the details of which are withheld from the reader. This is a reversal of the convention whereby the omniscient writer colludes with the reader in ensuring maximum knowledge, not always shared by the characters. Throughout Part Two we, the readers, are aware of lacking information that the characters have, and which we gain only in the flashback. In Part Three only, we discover that Odenigbo had been unfaithful to Olanna and that Baby is his, but not her, biological child. We also find out that in a peculiar kind of irrational revenge, Olanna had had sex with Richard and thereby betrayed her twin sister, Kainene, whose lover he was. The effect of the delay in providing the reader with this information is that the narrative structure compels us to absorb it in the light of the unthinkable terrors of the civil war, with which we have been provided in Part Two. What this suggests is that issues of the domestic, of gender, of the everyday, are reduced, shrunken and brought down to size; like Dickens, like rhubarb crumble, they are a luxury during times of war. Kainene forgives Olanna the adultery that she engaged in with Richard because after the terrible war massacres, she re-thinks her values: 'There are some things that are so unforgivable that they make other things easily forgivable' (347).

To sum up, the contradiction with which Adichie is juggling here is her feminist critique of men in general – black, white, rich and poor – who are sexual predators, on the one hand, and her womanist insistence on including men in projects of national healing, on the other. Ugwu is both the male with the devil between his legs, which enables him to achieve an erection during his participation in a group rape and also a young intellectual and a citizen of a reconstituted Nigeria. It is in being both that the novel's gender politics come apart. We cannot begin to integrate this rape into the depiction of multiple realities engendered by war and peace times, on which the novel is based. It is a problematic position that says all men are potentially rapists, if pushed to extreme circumstances. This is a critique which both condemns, but also condones the rape and makes Ugwu a problematic role model for post-war Nigeria.

A maelstrom of competing currents: conclusion

What *Half of a Yellow Sun* palpably demonstrates is the maelstrom of competing currents which have buffeted its hugely talented young author. She is simultaneously, concretely, exploring her country's and her family's history, and also representing the Nigerian past to the world. She is outraged by the distorted representations of Africa and is sucked into the discourse which produces them. She is passionate about gender and the violation of women, and she is determined that men, who are also subjected to the aftermath of slavery and the existence of racism in the world, are not excluded from subjectivity. She lurches between her visceral and concrete feel for the daily realities of her characters and her pride in her Igbo community, which tempts her to symbolise and homogenise it. She understands culture as constructed and she also essentialises it. In the fanfare of the metamorphosis of the devil penis into the liberating pen, the violation of the woman in the bar, in all its stark reality, disappears from view.

8 Conclusion
The Rifle is not a Penis

'The rifle of the Senegalese soldier is not a penis but a genuine rifle, model Lebel 1916' (Fanon, 1970 [1952]: 75).

Frantz Fanon was insisting that issues of colonial exploitation, and resistance to it, were historically real and carried material consequences. These realities should not be concealed by trendy phallic metaphors of psychoanalysis. Fanon was prophetic in his cautions, given how fashionable the so-called linguistic turn, the focus on texts and tropes, has become. Harsh historical truths have been buried under infinite mediations, stories and representations. By contrast, this study has been an exploration of how material realities are evoked by writers, who are struggling to anchor themselves in their daily lives in new places and to make sense of their pasts. We saw how they often depicted these material realities in a concrete, a metonymic language, which potentially toys with, problematises and reconstructs, the figurative. This we saw it do as much by the music and texture of words as by returning the figurative, when it is potentially 'toxic', to its literal, material function. Many of the writers discussed in this book have been returning the phallus to the gun in their own ways and to suit their own fictional purposes. In the introduction I referred to the narrative politics of de-fetishising and restoring symbols their material ordinariness, as a way of confronting their power. This is a project that Ioan Davies refers to as 'decolonizing the fetish' (1998: 139), which he understands as a strategy to confront the old dominating metaphors (142). We saw tropes, myths and puffed-up fetishes, reduced to their mundane ordinariness, to their visceral fleshy body parts. These sometimes, magically, shape-shifted again into new metaphors, which blended the literal and the figurative in interesting ways. This demonstrated how the figurative is a fundamental part of the creative function of language, and is by no means always poisonous.

This confrontation with master metaphors ingrained in the English language is not new. From the beginning of African fiction written in English, pioneers like Achebe, Ngũgĩ and others, confronted the consequences of the fact that English is saturated with the metaphors and meanings linked to Imperialism. Africa has always tickled the imagination of Europe and been a reservoir for its images and tropes. Most recently, American movie stars have attempted to add lustre to their images by way of public performances of their adoptions of orphans 'rescued' from the African cauldron of hopelessness and death. The many African cultures and lives, in all their complex daily realities, of happiness and struggle, hope and routine, family and spirituality, are collapsed into frozen frames of AIDS orphans, eroded landscapes and irrational wars. I am not about to reify the concrete, but we saw how powerful these tropes are when a politically aware Nigerian writer, like Adichie, was herself sucked into the metaphoric force field of African savagery and blood-letting in *Half of a Yellow Sun*. What I have been suggesting therefore is that there are times, within this context, that the unfolding of material cultural realities, unadorned by stock symbols and images, may contribute to the de-toxification of the representations of Africa and, in the process, to a healthy purging of the English language itself. Binyavanga Wainaina's dripping irony in his 'How to Write about Africa' essay captures the importance of the con-crete and the everyday in depictions of Africa:

> In your text, treat Africa as if it were one country. It is hot and dusty with rolling grasslands and huge herds of animals and tall, thin people who are starving. Or it is hot and steamy with very short people who eat primates. Do not get bogged down with precise descriptions. (2005: 92)

And so, while there is a tradition of taking issue with the English language, begun by earlier generations of African writers, like Achebe, what I have been suggesting is that some young migrant African writers experiment with English, within the diaspora, in interesting, and sometimes novel ways. I have not been defining their experimentations in terms of their migrancy. Nor have I defined the language of this generation in monolithic terms, which is why it was so important to see how Adichie's devices and language usage changes from one novel to the next. However, what is true is that globali-sation has made a profound impact on African culture and its intellectual life. Material culture, and the language used to express it, are mediated and transformed by the fact that these writers are operating on a world stage and looking at their African homes from the vistas of Amsterdam, Aberdeen or London. This vantage point enables them to encounter the tropes of Empire viscerally as they are woven into their daily lives in Europe or America. In other words, unless these novels are read alongside what Davies refers to as 'other cartographies' (1998: 141), then there is the danger that 'the old meta-phors will continue to dominate and prevent the fetish from decolonizing itself' (142).

These other cartographies are themselves metamorphosing. The writers have transported worlds, cultures and knowledges, along with their suit-cases and boxes, curry spices and recipes. In so doing, they have transformed the new worlds that they encountered. What this means is that 'the abstract metaphor of the "Other" is now metamorphosed into concrete, histori-cal bodies' (Chambers, 1994: 70), into people with whom you queue at the supermarket or encounter in the bus or at work. What happens is that 'the urban script is rewritten' and the city moves 'according to *different rhythms*, making it move to a diverse beat' (Chambers: 23, my emphasis). These dif-ferent rhythms are inflected into the English language such that these new beats, mantras, metonymic gaps and material realities make up the language of those who, like the writers discussed, have to negotiate between different cultures and identities.

In other words, the journeys of these postcolonial writers and thinkers have established traffic in more than one direction, literally and figuratively.

As migrants are transformed, so Europe metamorphoses under their influence. And this has been so from the beginning of the colonial venture (See Gikandi, 1996). The narrative structures of the novels we have been reading, along with their language, often enacted the journeys, back and forth, in space and time. It is noticeable that most of the writers avoided linear narratives and played with flashbacks and forwards between places and historical moments. Mahjoub, Aboulela and Adichie swung us around from North America or Europe back to Nigeria or the Sudan or Algeria. Sometimes the past was childhood, or, as in the case of Mahjoub, it was thousands of years. Bandele ruptured his narrative by stopping time and by crashing into other planets and worlds and Isegawa began his novel with a time warp as Mugezi foresaw his father's death, which occurred much later than the main events of the novel. In these novels, the archaeology of time was that of disruption, rather than of continuity or the safe discovery of origins, ethnicities or nations.

At a more mundane level, possessions, homes, and all of the things one decides to take, and the stuff that one has to leave behind, are of particular importance to writers on the move. This is why Sam Selvon explains, when responding to an interviewer regarding 'why so many of his characters were keen to acquire things – houses, beds', that 'material things become very important when one gets out of one's land' (Sandhu, 2004: 159). Such objects, in the context of scarcity, act directly on bodies and contribute profoundly to identity, particularly in the aftermath of colonialism, which denigrated indigenous culture and cultural artefacts. The desire for these objects, in other words, should not be caricatured. These things, and their chequered journeys and biographies, (Appadurai, 1986: 42) constitute migrant language and subjectivity in profound ways. Elaine Scarry understands the allure of the merchandise of Manhattan on the part of 'less materially privileged cultures'. The fact that 'blue jeans are cherished in the Soviet Union, that a picture from a Sears Roebuck catalogue should appear on the wall of a hut in Nairobi, that Sony recorders are prized in Iran' are not evidence of 'incomprehensible corruption or an act of senseless imitation'. These material aspirations are, in fact, 'a confirmation and signal that something deep and transforming is intuitively felt to happen when one dwells in proximity to such objects' (Scarry, 1985: 243).

Isegawa captured this when the perplexed Mugezi both despised the priests and also understood that their golden pens, heavy watches and magnificent cars or boats, carried with them limitless possibilities of escape from the sordidness of his own daily life. Isegawa understood that for the average Ugandan, even for upright men like Mugezi's grandfather, the expulsion of the Asians mainly signified a unique opportunity to acquire their invaluable stuff. Leila Aboulela's Shamia, protagonist of her story, 'The Museum', was selling her soul by choosing to marry Fareed for his money, but the story has compassion for her conflicts and for the importance of her studies in Scotland, which Fareed sponsored and enabled. And the barometer for the extent to which Rashid, Mahjoub's carrier, overcame his slave, non-human condition was whether he owned, or was dispossessed of, his special treasures.

The relationship between these solid objects and identity is a complex one. James Clifford wonders whether there is 'a kind of kernel or core of identity' that travellers carry with them, presumably vested in some profound way in their possessions. 'What', he asks, 'is brought from a prior place? And how is it both maintained and transformed by the new environment?' (1977: 44). Migrants, arriving in London or Amsterdam, are in danger of losing their sense of place in the world. In other words, the journeys undertaken by writers are not only from one place to another, but from one way of being into new, global identities. May Joseph asks: 'How do immigrants, migrants, and nomads imagine, perform and invent themselves anew...?' (1999: 12). The profound difficulties involved in this re-invention relate to the deep and invisible systems of knowledge, language and practice that the newcomers often lack. When we saw Homi Bhabha quote V.S. Naipaul, in the introduction, as bemoaning the fact that he might have access to the English language, but that he profoundly lacked its tradition (Bhabha, 1984: 95), he was pointing to a gap, an abyss, in Naipaul's identity that is like the 'howling lacunae' that repeatedly threatened the trickster Mugezi in Isegawa's *Abyssinian Chronicles*. I have been suggesting that this abyss, this annihilating lack, confronts migrant parvenus, whose integration into their new homes is always partial, conditional and tense. The home the migrant seeks is as much a concrete place, as access to the archive of the dominant culture, to the unspoken, the ironic, the inflection, the symbolic meanings, the wink, and the nod.

This subterranean exclusion is the polite puzzlement of the Okking family, regarding who precisely Hassan was, and where he came from, in *The Carrier*. It is the bewildered absence of a level of subtle competence, of style and symbolic capital, that Leila Aboulela pinpointed in *The Translator* when Sammar walked the streets of the city, which were full of the 'surprise' of the citizens, who subtly communicated their distance from the stranger in their slightly sneering disingenuous bemusement, which even seeped into the solid granite of buildings. Sammar may have been trapped, at first, in the tentacles of the surprised citizens, but the novel enacted her struggles to break out of this entrapment. This she did by way of effecting a translation between the multiple worlds, knowledges, belief systems and languages in which she lived her daily life. It has been the inspiration of this study that writers have been shown to put their writing to the task of translating them from parvenus into citizens, who are no longer subject to the 'surprise' of the buildings and people around them, on the streets of Scotland or at dinner tables in Denmark. This involved infusing into their English the sounds and words and worldviews of the other languages into which they were born and socialised, such as Arabic, Igbo or Yoruba.

These different worlds, within which the writers functioned, were often parallel, simultaneous and equal, rather than polarities, binaries or hierarchies. They were both flesh, and also spirit, hope, soup and soap. This explains the recurrent doubling and twinning that often occurred in the novels. For example, there was Ossie's twin, who he sighted visiting from the land of the dead, in *The Street*. It was the ant in Britain, with the same surname as Mugezi in Holland in *Abyssinian Chronicles*. It was Rashid's half brother, born to a different mother on the same day in *The Carrier*. Rashid was as poor and clever as his brother was rich and slow, and yet for all their diametrically opposite lives, his brother determined Rashid's destiny. In *Half of a Yellow Sun* the potential for opening up the novel to other worlds and dimensions was present through the centrality of the twin protagonists, Olanna and Kainene. However, in closing down her vistas to shore up her defence of Igbo culture and tradition, this potential remains only a ghostly trace.

What I have resisted in this book is the woeful chorus of defeat in the face of the 'Master' language. I have not considered the route of the return to indigenous tongues, which could be the subject of another book. What has emerged is that the European language is both drenched in the dominant culture and its stubborn, self-reproducing tropes, and is simultaneously tactile, mobile, manoeuvrable and brimming with aesthetic and political potential. Or as Sukhdev Sandhu puts it, 'the language that Selvon's characters brought to London was a form of luggage, one considerably sturdier than the flimsy cases they hauled off the carriage racks at Paddington Station' (2004: 147). He elaborates on Selvon's language as a form of 'pavement poetry', which experiments with capturing the daily lives and culture of migrants on the streets of London (181). In fact, 'it was through his linguistic innovation that he [Selvon] made the quotidian vivid' (in Sandhu, 2004: 145). On these streets, in Brixton or Aberdeen, migrants are compelled to re-make themselves through manipulating the inherited language and so Selvon's 'life in London is composed of gerunds' (151), of the language of becoming, metamorphosing – 'his characters are always pursuing in vain: wandering the streets looking for a fiver they dropped weeks before, waiting for the day when they'll have a bed of their own to sleep in' (151). This language is the jazzy beat of Bandele's Brixton, or the craziness of Mugezi's multiple lives in Kampala or Amsterdam; it is the echoes of Arabic in Aboulela's novel and of Igbo in Adichie's *Purple Hibiscus* and the coded lists of the names of Arab scientists through the ages in Mahjoub's *The Carrier*. This infusion of other languages into English highlights the possibility of crafting a different and combative English, which echoes with other ways of understanding and being in the world.

What we have also seen is that this language is not by definition radical or transgressive. In Chapter Seven, for example, Adichie's extensive use of Igbo in *Half of a Yellow Sun* contributed to removing the material reality of Igbo life and transformed it into an essentialised metaphor. And if this study has seemed to privilege the material, the concrete and the rhetoric of metonymy, it has only been to emphasise the important role played by material culture and everyday life in the novels under discussion.

For example, in a rather lovely, pithy vignette, Ahdaf Soueif, in the title short story from her collection, *Sandpiper*, captures the nub of what I have been demonstrating throughout this book regarding how metonymy functions and to what purpose. Soueif's bewildered European protagonist intuits that the nature of the rhetoric of language is culturally significant but she is not sure how or why:

> The slatted blinds are closed against a glaring sun. They call the wooden blinds *sheesh* and tell me it's the Persian word for glass. So *that which sits next to a thing is called by its name.* I have had this thought many times and feel as though it should lead me somewhere; as though I should draw some conclusion from it, but so far I haven't. (27, my emphasis)

This contiguity, the metonymy of the concrete, in which the blinds and the glass are linked, anchors of the realities of the daily life, a world from which the protagonist is excluded, not least of all by her lack of understanding of how the language functions. It is part of the material reality of life in the hot climate of North Africa, from which the European protagonist, from her 'Northern land' (25) feels culturally dislocated. She cannot fathom the significance of this kind of language, which Soueif is foregrounding as the key to an understanding the existence of other knowledge bases and languages, alongside the English in which she writes.

What I have been suggesting throughout is that we need to read the language of these novels with an understanding of this aesthetic politics, otherwise Aboulela's or Adichie's lengthy pages full of long descriptions of furniture, cooking and yards, become inexplicable. Without reading the language and style of these novels within this purpose, we mis-read them, as does the writer and critic Hilary Mantel. Mantel expresses unhappiness with what she calls 'an Isegawa sentence' because it is 'ramshackle' and works against the language of the symbol, which 'everyone can understand' (2000: 28). I have been suggesting that Isegawa is quite consciously contesting the language of the European symbol. Mantel complains that his writing is like 'obscene graffiti on crumbling walls' (31). The politics of graffiti, with its slogans and wit and subversive dismantling of the great walls of the Law of private property, is precisely analogous to the wily Mugezi's defacing and exposing of the priest's boat *Agatha*, symbol of imperial wealth and power bonded to the Church, in *Abyssinian Chronicles*. Mantel elaborates that, for Isegawa, 'a myth is something to be dragged into full daylight' (30). Dragging the myths and symbols, the tropes and metaphors into the full sunlight of an Africa which is refusing European distortions and stereotypes, deeply soldered into its languages, is a profoundly political, postcolonial project, in which the writers studied have participated repeatedly. We saw how the rhetorical device of metonymy was brought into play in this attempt to portray the ordinary and the everyday, without recourse to fabulous myths, tales and imperial tropes buried deeply in the colonial library.

However, while this book has followed the writers' interrogation of the hegemony of some old, still powerful, metaphors, it has recognised that there is no language that is not blended, an amalgam of the literal and the figurative. We saw those tropes of Empire fight back, as Adichie found herself stranded between the rock of Primitive Africa and the hard place of Idyllic Africa, which turned out to be merely two sides of the same old figurative battle zone. Simultaneously, original and startling new tropes emerge behind the front line. The gun may have been a concrete weapon in the colonial wars and not a penis, but Dorobo's arrows in Isegawa's *Abyssinian Chronicles* shape-shifted into wily, witty words and in doing so they ceased to be only matter and wood.

The rifle *is* Dorobo's arrow: emerging metaphors & blended tropes

'but which word could I sharpen like Dorobo's monstrous arrows?' (Isegawa, 2000: 254)

I began this conclusion with Fanon's famous caution that political and material realities, with their consequences of war and suffering, should not become metaphors for psycho-sexual subjectivities. At the same time, we have seen that words are also weapons and that figurative language, with its poetry and coded meanings, has a powerful role to play in the continuing war against oppression. It is a war that is indeed about guns, but it is also about patriarchy, with its oppressive phallic significations.

The material always co-exists with the worlds of the spiritual and the figurative, blending and shape-shifting with them in multiple ways. Fanon's own pithy words about the rifle not being a penis have themselves metamorphosed into a counter-insurgent proverb, given how often they have been quoted. In this new guise, this proverb of guerrilla struggle has magnified and shifted into a symbol of resistance. Dorobo's arrows became metaphorics for the weapon of education, the library that the educated Mugezi harnessed as his own mechanism for confronting a hostile world. Dorobo's arrows were exemplary of the process through which Isegawa defetishised metaphorical objects of malevolent white, male power and then whittled arrows of wit and words in a new symbolic language for a young and militant generation of African writers. However, having returned the slippery sensual bobbin, redolent of the mother's sexuality and power, to the little sewing machine part it was, he demonised the mother and risked shooting himself with his own arrow. Like Adichie, we saw Isegawa gingerly negotiate the porous boundary between colluding with, and resisting, power. This symbiosis between old and new, literal and figurative, animate and inanimate is in constant flux, as stories never stop being re-told, invented and subverted.

Like Dorobo's arrows, Adichie's ceramic ballerinas, which became animated in their own way, also embodied new figurative territory. Adichie's ornaments occupied a universe of furniture and yards, flowers and gutters, bags of rice and tables, alive with ants embodying spirits. The ordinary was part of the world of the shrine and the church, as European ornaments housed the chi of the mother, who was violated by patriarchy and a deformed Catholicism. From the debris of the shattered ceramics, rose a new start for the girl, whose stuttering was transformed into voice, as she sang the rosary with the rhythm of an Igbo beat.

There were, in other words, multiple, original and arresting tropes, which repeatedly emerged from concrete and literal descriptions of the material realities surrounding migrant writers and their uprooted protagonists. There was Aboulela's coat, with the toggles instead of buttons, metonymic metaphor of translation between cultures, or Mahjoub's telescope, which in the bathos of its eventual emergence, symbolised the uselessness of science outside of society. These material objects, televisions and bobbins, tables and coats, coloured lights and perfume, occupied carefully delineated spaces. We saw the novels focus on these concrete spaces, which are the solid places of everyday life – a room, a shop, a house, a bus. These concrete places themselves began to slide into the metaphorical spaces of nomad metamorphosing into citizen. Ian Baucom calls such places 'blended mental spaces' in his analysis of the relationship between certain places and identity, within the historical context of Empire in his book, *Out of Place*. Certain privileged places, like 'a Gothic cathedral, the Victoria Terminus ... a cricket field, a ruined country house' have become 'apt metaphors for writers struggling to define what it means to be English' (1999: 4). The struggle for definition of the writers under discussion in this book was about what it means to be migrant, but with similar blending between the literal and the figurative that Baucom gestured towards. He may call these places metaphors, but he realises that this is not quite correct and suggests that the places he referred to, in addition to being metaphors of Englishness, are also '*material* places', which '*literally* shape the identities of the subjects inhabiting or passing through them', which means that these spaces are 'simultaneously literal and metaphorical' and have become 'synecdoches of the nation's space' (4, my emphases). As both figurative and literal, these spaces develop powerful capacities either to disorient or to anchor postcolonial writers and their migrating protagonists. Bandele's Brixton High Street or Aboulela's meagre flat in Aberdeen, compared with the family home in Khartoum, or the Aunt's flat and yard in Nsukka of Adichie's first novel, compared to the family mansion in Enugu, were all the detailed stages upon which the dilemmas and daily challenges of life were played out. They began to signify spiritual and moral positions, options for migrants and re-configurations of the world as global. In this way, these sites became blended metonymic metaphors of place in the novels.

The house in V.S. Naipaul's *A House for Mr Biswas* provides another example of such a blended site. Homi Bhabha rejects the interpretation 'of the House' as a metaphor, as 'the cumulative centre of the novel' (1984: 114). Instead, Bhabha suggests, working against the grain of the novel's aspirations to be included in the Canon of great British fiction, and its dominating modes, symbols and values, is a metonymic counter-insurgency:

> To demonstrate thematically how *House* resists its appropriation into the Great Tradition ... would not be difficult. It would be possible to see the *tropes of the text as metonymy and repetition instead of metaphor.* (115, my emphasis)

In place, then, of the metaphor of the house at the centre, we have 'the spectacle of Biswas's madness when he is haunted by the repetitive chaos and cacophony of "words", sliding, shifting, terrorizing, and the continual fear for his "fleshy parts"' (116). The house could better be described, I think, as a blended space. Emerging out of Biswas's mad words and fleshy body, it became symptomatic of the struggles over space and identity that Naipaul was grappling with in his early literary career. Biswas's discomfort links to Naipaul's plaintive complaint that he felt excluded from the deep meanings and unspoken codes of English language and culture already referred to. The overcrowded house, in all its corporeal claustrophobia, begins to symbolise Naipaul's own sense of ambivalence about home.

Going back once again to the Aberdeen of *The Translator* and those evocative, stern buildings that dwarfed and intimidated Sammar with their demonic 'surprise' built into their foundations, it becomes clear that they accrued meaning as part of the world of the stranger, the migrant, the parvenu, the person whose citizenship is contested. This is Zygmunt Bauman's point in his *Liquid Life*, in the chapter entitled 'Seeking Shelter in Pandora's Box'. Bauman examines the spatial repercussions of the situation that 'the elusive and mysterious strangers' have moved 'into the heart of the city' where they rub shoulders with the local inhabitants 'on the city streets' (2005: 73), streets like Brixton High Street. Surreptitiously, city designers attempt to barricade and protect the good citizens, to 'separate out strangers, keep them away and bar their entry', most commonly through 'gated communities' (73).

Bauman's shelter seekers in Pandora's box puts us in mind of the Pandora, used by Bruno Latour (1999) in defining his Science Studies as invested in all the messiness and ills of the world, that were released by opening the wretched box. This we found highly suggestive in unpacking Mahjoub's novel, *The Carrier*. Bauman envisages Pandora's box as the space enclosed by the perilous city, where migrant strangers – nomads and outsiders – are thrown into the maelstrom of their difference and their lack. Latour left us with the hope that Pandora finally encountered in the box. Our hope resides in the potential for African and other postcolonial writers to storm the gated city and establish spaces of their own making, sanctuaries richly described in all their concreteness. And let us not forget that the curious Pandora, who released all the ills of life onto our heads through her silly curiosity, has been re-written as the woman who refused to continue to be the carrier of the misfortunes of the world. She was Sammar and Shadia, Kambili and Aunty Ifeoma. When Aboulela ended *The Translator* with Dalia, Sammar's niece, negotiating her bike between the different plants in her landscape, she is hinting at the hope that a new generation of young women will successfully translate their curiosity into liberation rather than pestilence.

It has been a challenge to classify the world and its rhetoric into different dimensions, while recognising that these differences operate simultaneously, blend and syncretise. Lefebvre divided the world into that 'of everyday life (real, empirical, practical)' on the one hand, and on the other 'the world of metaphor' (1984 [1971]: 11). In reality, dealing with the world of the imagination, of language, of art, this division is, if at all, only analytically and momentarily possible. In a later argument, Lefebvre formulates a more complex interplay between the everyday, the political and the aesthetic when he talks about 'lived experience' as 'elevated to the status of a concept and to language' in order to bring about social transformation (1988: 80). And so, it is in the cracks of the monotony that 'spaces of freedom and *jouissance*' are to be sought and found (1988: 82). Jouissance, the sensual joy to which the female body is particularly attuned, is enmeshed in the everyday objects like soup and their transformation into stories.

However, perhaps more importantly the English language itself metamorphosed in the process, as metonymic gaps filled with the new, blended tropes of witty arrows and dancing ornaments, a coat and purple flowers. Lefebvre defines everyday life as 'sustenance, clothing, furnishing, homes, neighbourhoods, environment.... Call it material culture if you like' (1984: 21). However, he also suggests, as part of his attempts to define the quotidian, that the everyday is more than these objects and offers the potential for change, for making better lives; it is 'a half-way house, a halting place and a springboard' (1984: 14). It holds the potential for new discoveries, 'for the realization of the possible' (1984: 14), for the sighting of the snark as a new word and a new symbol, which occupies a new half-way house, albeit one perched on the edge of Isegawa's abyss. There will always be survivals, scars, remnants, tensions and contradictions. The purple hibiscus, which gave Adichie's novel its title, gave us pause for thought. The flowers and yards, which populated Enugu and Nsukka, were part of the concrete landscape of the author's memory. The purple flowers in particular became symbolic of the power of science, of hybridity and of transformation and resistance. Along the way, however, they picked up quarrelling, competing agendas and stand as a worthy image of the complexity and pitfalls of troping, and of the difficulties involved in inventing something new. This is nowhere more apparent than in the arena of gender.

Kitchens & streets: the blended spaces of gender

The sites available to female migrants seemed to remain the interior, domestic settings, which were linked to their gender strategies. These strategies are quite difficult to pinpoint, without reinforcing stereotypical divisions into public and private, male and female respectively. Kelwyn Sole refers to the ambivalence of feminists, like Rita Felski, who recognise the potential for women of the 'politics of everyday life' whose source is in 'the traditional linking of women with the domestic sphere and other sites of reproduction' (Sole, 2005: 195). Like the corruption of power, which Isegawa struggled so hard to contest, and by which he was partly contaminated, women battle to turn the kitchen into their stronghold, without being imprisoned by its tenacious stereotypes. The wonderful healing soup, lovingly prepared by Sammar, enabled her to express herself and to translate her knowledge, culture and religion into a language which would give her a voice and bring her life fulfilment. It hardly bears qualifying this, although we must, with the obvious pitfalls of associating Aboulela's Sammar or Adichie's Kambili with their spicy or *onugbu* soup.

At the same time, by using the material domestic site in this way, are these writers achieving the goal of creating a new language which would contribute towards making 'the Symbolic "feminine"'? (Spivak, 1993: 36). Elsewhere, Spivak calls for the infiltration of phallic metaphors and she uses concrete and domestic analogies in her response to the question: 'Can we clean up metaphor?' (Harasym, 1990: 41). 'No', she replies 'It's like cleaning teeth' and 'involves the same persistent effort' as 'housework' (in Harasym, 41). What does it mean when Spivak uses the metaphor of housework, most often done by women, to describe the persistent, necessary, unglamorous and ongoing hard work of combating metaphors that are exploitative? It is a strategy on a knife edge as feminist writers and scholars work within the stereotypes and attempt to overturn, infiltrate and re-constitute them in the project of 'reform(ulat)-ing the symbolic under new material and political conditions' (MacCannell, 1991: 183). What I have been emphasising throughout this book is that in addition to whatever postcolonial strategies are invested in the manipulation of language, there are also profound gender implications to these rhetorical choices. Emily Apter very suggestively refers to 'what a later generation of feminists (following Luce Irigaray) would characterize as the "homelessness of women in the symbolic order"' (Apter, 1999: 115). Apter enlarges, by reference to commentary on Irigaray that 'men continually seek, construct, create for themselves houses everywhere: grottoes, huts, women, towns, language, concepts, theory, etc.' ... this ... leaves women '"homeless" in the symbolic order' (Apter, 1999: 259). The strategies the women writers evoked in order to build themselves their own safe houses were not the intuitive, essentialised, emotional sites offered up to women as short change for language, rationality and intellect. The soup, the coat and perfume, the flowers and kitchens were all considered and constructed language strategies. Adichie most carefully crafted an image of gendered treasures in the little ceramic ballerinas. These became more potent and political than the more visible and public struggles for freedom. They did so doubly, on both gender terms and also through an adaptation of Igbo belief. It was a gentle, enlightened gender politics that struggled to include both men and women in its embrace, for all the contradictions that we saw this also generated. Adichie and Aboulela focussed on the daily lives of ordinary women and gave us visceral portrayals of the domestic, be it in the relationship between language, body and subjectivity, or the devastation of gender violence, wrought upon women in the home. When Adichie set her second novel, however, in the male zone of war, the home shrank from the centre stage, as the main action was focused on the devil penis, which became the pen in the hand of the male subject, who was able to atone for his violation of the woman's body.

Biyi Bandele's Brixton High Street was a public, male space. As Sandhu puts it, in relation to Samuel Selvon's London, he may have been determined 'not to overlook the seemingly mundane, to render the burr and plod of the lives of unexalted peoples' (2004: 145), but the burr and plod are gendered. Selvon's everyday, is that of the man's world of 'betting shops and local pubs' (146). It incorporates the 'enforced tunnel vision' of Selvon's female characters, who 'have even fewer opportunities for going out and scanning the capital than their husbands and partners' (152). I am not sure whether this is a criticism or a reflection of the reality. I think it is fair to say that Bandele takes the world he knows and interrogates and transforms its reality. *The Street* is certainly one of the very few novels that deals directly and sympathetically with gay sexuality and AIDS. More problematic, I think, are some of the gender images in Mahjoub's and Isegawa's fiction.

Mahjoub gave us a macabre and flawed, metaphoric portrayal of the white woman, Sigrid, who was transposed from the corporeal weightiness of her daily life and turned into a chimera, a source of light and symbolic incandescence. Sigrid burned and Rashid revelled in the light that was shed upon his understanding of the universe. This metaphor of spiritual light, like the mother and the goddess, appears to worship and adore women, but is its opposite. In removing her corporeal reality, Sigrid disappears from view in the fire that consumes her. She may have symbolised the light of new knowledge but she leaves Rashid as the subject, the carrier of that newness, albeit that she, too, had been a scientist and a thinker, who had taught Rashid many things. This reverberates with Adichie's figurative rape and her privileging of the male subject in *Half of a Yellow Sun*.

Likewise, Isegawa's portrayal of the mother, Padlock, who in her demonic anti-mothering may have contested the Mother Africa Trope, but in so doing came perilously close to being the femme fatale – dreaded female as vampire bat. We saw that Isegawa walked the narrow line between collusion with such stereotypes and resistance to them, as he sometimes teetered on the edge of his abyss. In many ways, *Abyssinian Chronicles* was a misogynistic novel, in which the mother is worse than the father and the son appears justified in his desire to destroy her. What is also striking is that Isegawa, in his devastating critique of the family, undermines the reverence with which an earlier generation of African writers regarded their elders and their ancestors. It is interesting, therefore, in winding up a book about younger African novelists, finally to contemplate the nature of the concept of 'generation', in terms of both its politics and its literary forebears.

Generation & the nation

Sweeping generalisations are always dangerous, but if understood as trends, carrying counter-currents within them, they can provide a useful mapping of developments in the field of African fiction writing. Harry Garuba, too, sounds a cautionary note on the dangers inherent in polarising the generations too rigidly: 'these transfers between the "generation" as a marker of age and as a signifier of poetic style ... create a slippery descriptive terrain in which nothing is conceptually or analytically certain' (2005: 52). Nonetheless, Garuba is prepared to attempt to map 'key defining moments', especially with regard to the generation of younger, emerging Nigerian poets (52). He suggests that while an earlier generation of poets believed firmly in the '"truth" of the "nation", a truth rooted in the people, their culture and traditions' (59), poets 'born after Nigeria's independence from colonial rule in 1960' had a quite different take on the world (62).

In other words, early African writers, who grew up during colonialism, were involuntarily drawn into the project of national liberation. Even when they were, almost as compellingly, forced to chart their disillusionment with their post-independence national power holders, they did so within the context of the priority of the project of nation-building and healing; they sought continuity with the cultural traditions of the past and wrote modern morality tales, using epic forms adapted from the oral tradition to express their visions. This was so for the generation of men, the giants, who constituted the African canon and who inspired their own, and subsequent generations. These are writers like Chinua Achebe, Wole Soyinka, Ayi Kwei Armah and Ngũgĩ wa Thiong'o, for all the significant differences in the substance of their proposed solutions, and also in their choice of the form and language in which to express them. While these early writers have all also migrated and re-located for different reasons and periods of time to the USA, they forged their reputations and published some of their key writings centring on questions of the state of the nation in Africa. These are the issues and the struggles that, by and large, still preoccupy them.

The differences between the generations of African writers are emphasised by Pius Adesanmi, a Nigerian intellectual of the younger generation. He confronts Ngũgĩ wa Thiong'o's 'clamour for a return to indigenous African languages in our literatures' (2002: 109) as having little to say to his generation. Adesanmi particularly resents the 'persistent attempts at inducing a feeling of guilt in African writers and scholars who continue to work in European languages' as somehow betraying 'the African cause' (109). The clarion call to this African cause is a form of cultural nationalism that Adesanmi passionately rejects, which he does on the basis of the generational gap between himself and Ngũgĩ (112).

This younger generation, 'born in the sixties and the youngest among us ... in the early seventies' (117) was born after independence and has, by necessity, become a generation of writers and intellectuals which has migrated away from Africa in large numbers. Adesanmi explains how as 'everywhere on the continent, bloodthirsty tyrants shot their way into the corridors of power' and as the infrastructure decayed and the universities were increasingly under-funded, there was 'an unprecedented emigration of African intellectuals' (106). And so, the difficult economic and intellectual climate of Nigeria 'drove some of the most productive members of our generation into exile in Europe and America in the late eighties and early nineties' (118). Among others, he mentions Biyi Bandele as a case in point.

Not forged in the fire of anti-colonial struggle, often working and writing within the institutions of Europe and North America, it is obvious, continues Adesanmi, that his 'generation writes predominantly in English, Nigerian English, and shall continue to do so in the foreseeable future' (126). The qualification regarding the kind of English – Nigerian English – is important, as it is precisely this kind of moulded language, which includes the rhythms of indigenous speech, words in Yoruba or Igbo and the language of the streets, which have been discussed in the preceding chapters.

This younger generation, which has been the subject of this study, celebrated a degree of freedom as roamers and adventurers and displayed less

pressure to commit themselves to the politics of the nation in their fictions than the earlier generation had done. For the moment, I am excluding
Adichie's *Half of a Yellow Sun* from this generalisation. We saw that Bandele, in particular, was adamant in his rejection of Achebe's injunction to
writers to be teachers. Writers such as Bandele and Isegawa manipulated the
transformations open to them, as they made London and Amsterdam their
own cities and quite clearly enjoyed the possibilities inherent in globalisation. For Bandele, this meant rejecting the super seriousness of his forebears
and we saw how he operated at the site of the surface, where word games,
play and nonsense powerfully characterised his language and constituted
a new politics of living in the here and now of the London he has made
his home. The contradictory trickster, Mugezi, enacted Isegawa's refusal of
moral or national still points. The Amsterdam, into which Mugezi forces his
way takes him into a realm of limitless possibility.

In the case of Aboulela, it was her insistence on Islam as the border beyond
which she would not travel, which enabled her protagonist to embrace other
cultures and to translate between them. On the whole, however, these writers, found affiliations based on race or nation distasteful. For Isegawa, and
in Adichie's *Purple Hibiscus* in particular, the family was metonymic of the
nation, and was the polar opposite of a loving and nurturing force. Demonic
subjectivities were spawned within unnatural nations torn by strife, corruption and violence. Both novels portrayed violent fathers, who abused
their children and damaged their psyches. While Aboulela, and Adichie in
her first novel, both contested narrow nationalist ties and insisted on the
personal as political, they were also both driven by religious belief. While
Aboulela's Islam travelled with her, Adichie forged a syncretism between her
Catholicism and traditional African spirituality. In both cases, their religious
affiliations were mediated by their gender project, which was grounded in
the desire to overcome the pessimism inherent in the belief that women have
no voice. Aboulela's Sammar and Adichie's Kambili lost and then found
their voices in various ways in the novels.

These multiplicities and contradictions exemplified the open-ended-
ness of Mahjoub's archaeology of knowledge, where his explorations of
the cosmos resulted in indeterminate outcomes for his protagonists, whose
views of the world were steeped in different paradigms. It was a world where
the twentieth-century protagonist had only partial access to the knowledge
of the past, a past which was ruptured. This anti-quest, this refusal of resolution, on the part of many of the writers, has overtones in the way Sukhdev
Sandhu describes Hanif Kureishi's characters, who seem to say 'Catch us if
you can' (2004: 274). They are slippery, floating, quick and street wise; they
know the language and the mores; they are second generation and no longer
entirely parvenus, even if they are equally not entirely settled, respectable
citizens. They stand for: 'escape not archaeology; discontinuity, not tradition;
self-gratification and elective affinity instead of unthinking communalism'
(Sandhu, 2004: 274).

'Elective affinity' stands out as echoing the new families and connections,
distinct from ties of blood or tradition, characteristic of the language and pre-

occupations of writers whose parents were born in Africa or Asia, but who themselves were born in Europe or North America. What Sandhu suggests is that hybridity conventionally characterises the earlier generation of migrants, who were not born in London. They occupy a state of 'in-between-ness', of double cultures where 'forever the twain shall meet' (2000: 142). By contrast, he poses a model of 'self fashioning' for second generation writers, such as Hanif Kureishi, and his characters, who 'can wear as many masks, create as many personae, explore as many new avenues' as they wish (142). Place, London in particular, is crucial in this 'potential for self-fashioning and the constant mutation and updating of the self' (143). What I have been suggesting, however, is that Bandele, and Isegawa and, perhaps to a lesser extent, the Adichie of *Purple Hibiscus*, do celebrate the capacity for self-fashioning, albeit that they are not second generation African writers, born in the diaspora. Writers like Mahjoub, Aboulela and Adichie, may have been more complicated than the playful Bandele and Isegawa, but hybridity, mongrelism, the belief in cultural fusions and patchwork quilts, rather than in master cultures, unified identities or national certainties, played a part in all of their fictions.

A similar rejection of the quest for the nation has been identified in the younger generation of Nigerian poets, as described by Harry Garuba in his analysis of Emman Shehu's poem, 'Folkland', which reverberates strongly with the vision and style of some of the novelists dealt with in this book. The poem is set in Nsukka, which is the folkland of its title. What Garuba highlights with regard to this poem is 'its refusal to cohere around a central organizing principle, *a deep structure* or motif of myth or ritual or *land or nation* of the kind that had often served as the generative force around which Nigerian poetry gravitated' (2005: 63, my emphases). This refusal of the deadly seriousness of their predecessors, linked to the dire urgencies of nation-building, characterises the rebellion of this younger generation. What is rejected is 'that unitary, monadic subject of the nationalist imaginary which was the major topos of Nigerian writing in the 1950s and 1960s' (64). Garuba emphasises the lack of modernist questing, the rejection of the search for the grail of national liberation that the anti-colonial struggle had promised: 'instead of plumbing the depths' this younger generation of poets acknowledge 'incoherencies, contradictions and multiplicities without seeking the resolution and coherence that a grand narrative provides' (65). Again the surface is preferred to the contaminated depths of symbol and meaning, and what they deem to be the outdated pressures on them to prove their political credentials.

Then again, Adichie's *Half of a Yellow Sun* prevents us from asserting these trends and generational differences too categorically. We saw earlier that this novel was torn in its desires. On the one hand, it provided that thick detail of material cultural reality that characterised *Purple Hibiscus*. On the other hand, this was undermined by its determination to symbolise the glories of traditional Igbo culture as a way of contributing to a new Nigerian nation of citizens cleansed of their more recent history of Biafran war atrocities. Cutting across generation, I suggest that Adichie's *Half of a Yellow Sun* has been influenced by the so-called new essentialism espoused by Nigerian intellectuals, who have migrated to the USA, like Isidore Okpewho, who is part of Adichie's father's generation. In his *Call Me By My Rightful Name* (2004) Okpewho insists upon the deep ancestral affiliations to Africa of Black people everywhere, including the African Americans he encountered in his new life. This reverberates in Adichie's key references in her novel to Frederick Douglass's slave narrative and her focus on glorious cultural roots in Africa. In constructing a symbolic Africa out of Yoruba or Igbo languages and worldviews, both Okpewho and Adichie are vulnerable to Eileen Julien's 'ornamentalism', which denies the multiple and changing histories and realities of different parts of Africa in its very attempt to capture them. It denies the constructedness of language and narrative and implies that there are intrinsic ways of telling African stories, directly transposed from African experience. This tendency could have arisen from the influence of African American politics in the USA, where Adichie studied and continues to spend a great deal of her time. The other writers under discussion all migrated to Europe – England, Scotland, Denmark and Holland, where the race politics are very different.

Furthermore, this generalisation regarding the earlier generation of writers' commitment to nationalist projects applies less to women and African Asian writers. For example, Buchi Emecheta reacted against what she perceived as the patriarchy invested in those traditions. As Eileen Julien observes, she 'found no novels by women that adhered to the traditional models' and noted the 'absence of an epic tendency among women writers' (1992: 47). Julien enlarges that 'the very act of writing for a woman, then, can be seen as transgressive against the order which the initiation story proper represents' (47). While this link between women writers and a transgressive urge is too sweeping, it is true that Emecheta views some of the structures of the oral traditions, which earlier writers were so committed to retaining, as profoundly inimical to the aspirations of African women. In *The New Tribe* (2000), Emecheta adapts an oral tale in order to expose its mythical distortions and gendered underbelly (Cooper, 2007).

Likewise, African Asian male writers of an earlier generation, such as M.G. Vassanji and Abdulrazak Gurnah, for different reasons, but linked to those of women writers, do not buy into the unified project of nation and continent-building. They battle with questions of their African identities and rights to citizenship. These writers, who have migrated to cities, like Montreal, London or New York, are hybrids, juggling the multiple identities – African, Asian and European – which both liberate and perplex them. See, for example, Vassanji's *The Gunny Sack* (1989), *No New Land* (1991) and *Amriika* (1999) and Gurnah's *Admiring Silence* (1996) and *By the Sea* (2001). May Joseph refers to 'inauthentic citizenship' in relation to these African Asians (2). She herself is a Tanzanian, whose family, eventually and sadly, felt it had to migrate. In response to the corrosive and exclusionary politics of ethnicity and so-called indigenous African nationalism, writers like Vassanji and Gurnah repeatedly construct families and affiliations which cut across race and nation (Cooper, 2004).

At the same time, what specifically unites the younger generation is that they write in a rich milieu of tradition that was unavailable to the first generation of writers of novels in English. When Adesanmi declares that 'Ngũgĩ's story has always been that of his generation and the one immediately preceding it' and 'the trouble is that I do not recognize myself and my generation in the picture which Ngũgĩ paints' (2002: 112), he is also rebelling against his literary forefather as part of the process of carving out a new set of tropes, language and canons.

Petals of purple: influences & traditions

As discussed earlier, Moses Isegawa called on tradition, on a fellow writer, one who made the journey to Europe and survived, and prospered – the Booker prize winning Nigerian writer, Ben Okri. Throughout his novel, Isegawa made subtle intertextual reference to Okri's *The Famished Road*. Biyi Bandele chose Amos Tutuola as his spiritual and aesthetic ancestor, in a distancing from the didactic tradition of Chinua Achebe, which had so powerfully influenced his earlier novels. Bandele travelled to other worlds, armed with Tutuola's animism, and in syncretising his African influences with Lewis Carroll's brand of nonsense, he created an entirely original work. Adichie paid tribute to Chinua Achebe's *Things Fall Apart*, alongside Ngũgĩ wa Thiongo's *Petals of Blood* and Alice Walker's *The Color Purple*. *Things Fall Apart*, in particular, has often been described as the founding text of African fiction written in English, an ur-text, which acted as an inspirational model for other African writers, as well as bringing African fiction in English into the consciousness of the world. Perhaps the founding text of migration, not written in English, but establishing its own powerful tradition, is the Arabic Sudanese novel, Tayeb Salih's *Season of Migration to the North* (1969). Salih's protagonist, Mustafa Sa'eed, as the title indicates, travels to Europe and in so doing he becomes an early postcolonial migrant. While Salih is not mentioned directly in their novels, echoes of the reverse journey from Africa to Europe reverberates in the younger generation of Sudanese writers, like Mahjoub and Aboulela, who use English to portray their own migrations to the North. What Salih demonstrated was the interdependence of identity and material culture in the process of migration. He graphically depicted the consequences on the psyche when a rift occurs between people and the realities of their daily lives. Salih charts Mustafa Sa'eed's ill-fated travels, and the disintegration of the identity of his beleaguered protagonist, quite profoundly, through the biographies of his possessions.

There is a key moment in the novel when Salih enacts the ritual disintegration of the cornerstones of Mustafa Sa'eed's being by way of the deranged white woman's destruction of his three most treasured possessions. He must sacrifice these possessions in return for sex with her. He will be selling his soul as he destroys the objects, which have given him protection and sustenance. The first, like Adichie's ceramic figurines, is a European artefact that is simultaneously part of his own mixed cultural history – a Wedgwood vase, which the vampire woman smashes and tramples (156–7). The objects she picks gain momentum and value and next to go is 'a rare Arabic manuscript', which 'she tore it to bits, filling her mouth with pieces of paper which she chewed and spat out' (157). The objects are extensions of Mustafa's flesh and are metonyms for him and therefore 'it was as though she had chewed at my very liver. And yet I didn't care' (157). She is devouring his body and soul, chewing his liver, along with his culture, his dignity and his traditions of knowledge, as embodied in the rare manuscript. This is a demonic version of Samar's coat or the model of the orbs of the universe, which become the orphaned Rashid's parents. Mustafa is obsessed with the white woman and with the European culture which has taken over his entire humanity; it has done so viscerally through dispossessing him of all he has. And so, finally, she is ready to destroy his most precious object, his 'silken Isphahan prayer-rug', which he gives her, and which she throws into the fire and she 'stood watching gloatingly as it was consumed, the flames reflected on her face' (156–7). These are the fires of hell into which Mustafa has been cast, as he has sold his birthright to the devil woman encountered on his migration to the North. *Season of Migration to the North* is a pioneering novel, anticipating many of the devices and preoccupations with which later generations of African migrant writers are grappling. Mustafa Sa'eed does not survive migration or the loss of subjectivity, linked to his possessions, his material life, that it entailed. However, it is problematic that a woman is the metaphoric device to represent the horrors of the season of migration to the North. Reminiscent of Astrid, who symbolised the light, this woman, who Mustafa desires, is darkness incarnate, is a symbol of what may await the unwary traveller. While it is important not to make too much of this, and to recognise that Mahjoub is writing from his own experiences and perspectives, it is the pessimism and trauma, linked to differences in material culture, which manifest in relationships across colour and belief, and resonate in both Aboulela's and especially Mahjoub's fictions. They profoundly echo the influence of the fictional pioneering journey to the North forged by Salih's doomed protagonist.

While this connection is highly suggestive, rather than overt, it is worth repeating the significance of the fact that this younger generation, on whom this book has focussed, has earlier generations of African writers to provide them with vital intertexts, which enable invention. This was not available to writers of the previous generations in the same way, writers who had to carve out their own inspirational sources, based most often on their re-constructions of their oral heritage and their love–hatred of their colonial literary fathers, such as Joseph Conrad. As for literary mothers, there were far fewer of those. Yet the younger writers tended to rebel against many of the issues and aesthetic devices of their forebears. Influence works in this paradoxical way, providing the grit against which those that follow may sharpen their tools of rebellion. A final question might be to ask again just how rebellious these writers were, given their distance from the life and death struggles against colonialism of the earlier generation.

'The darkened gaps between the frail flickers
of silent unspoken light'

Are the politics as serious and productive as I have been making out? There are perils in this politics of the surface, the fractured, happenstance and the sensual that avails itself of the gymnastics of postmodern pastiche and play-fulness. The hungry monsters of the road, or the boojums of the deep, are always ready to seize the unwary traveller at the surface. The continuing force of the global economic system, for all of the delights of mobility and mixing, demands that this fiction be read within the context of the continu-ing uneven distribution of wealth and privilege in the world. This is Sole's point when he cautions that we should be mindful of 'the manner in which macro issues impinge on the configurations of everyday life' (Sole, 2005: 188). I have been arguing, however, that the political has to be understood in a multi-faceted way, especially in this arena of fiction and the imagination. I would interpret the bold experimentations with language and style that we have seen throughout this study as evidence of the fact that writers are not engaging in trendy imitations of the latest European fashions, but that the opposite is true. They are attempting to break away from the symbiosis of the postcolonial, caught in the bind of re-living the past. They are attempting to write on their own terms and in their own way. That they do not always succeed does not detract from the endeavour.

Moreover, everyday material life, that we have seen so vividly reproduced, is political, determined as it is, by precisely where one is inserted in the unequal state of the world. When Sandhu suggests that 'the primary strug-gles for most black and Asian Londoners have been domestic, not political' (2004: xxvi), he misunderstands the politics invested in the struggle of his black Londoners to achieve 'a bed to sleep in, food on the table, friends with whom to banter, someone to cuddle up to at night, their kids to be safe and happy' (xxvi); they are waging a profoundly political battle for a better life in a London that has itself to metamorphose in order to accommodate them and to acknowledge its history of Empire, which brought them there in the first place. In this way, and however indirectly or unwittingly, they are contribut-ing to changing the balance of power in the world.

At the same time, in this complex, contradictory zone, in constructing new tropes, in perpetuating old symbols, in being arbiters of what is carried from Africa, in trunks and suitcases, these writers themselves develop power and the potential to become gatekeepers of a kind. Arjun Appadurai has an intriguing concept of the 'turnstile', which both enables and blocks. It is 'the interplay of knowledge and ignorance', which 'serves as a turnstile, facilitat-ing the flow of some things and hindering the movement of others' (1986: 56). Postcolonial writers as interpreters occupy a slippery slope, which faces in more directions than one. The writers and their novels come in their season of migration as 'culture brokers', who mediate 'the global trade in exotic – culturally "othered" – goods' (Huggan, 2001: 26). The writers have the privileges and the potential to gain symbolic capital and access to consumer goods, goods which become indicators and props and participate in rituals of their potential to become citizens rather than migrants or parvenu. It is the entanglement that Huggan demonstrates between 'the language of resistance' and 'the language of commerce' (264). Once in, like the wily Mugezi, these writers and intellectuals may well become new passport officials and arbiters themselves. But first they have to get inside the citadel. Some of their baggage gains entry; some items are refused or confiscated. What is admitted and who is excluded are open to change in what is a volatile political and cultural space. The writers also carry with them more than one language and knowledge base, with which they have transformed African fiction and the English language in which it is written. By perplexing our understanding, by being familiar and also strange, by sounding rather than signifying, by being visceral and carrying new meaning, their esoteric words, virtual and material objects, their possessions with spirits dancing within them, allow for the possibility of a contestation of received reality and its predictable meanings and power bases.

This is more partial and fragile than it might sound. And so, finally, the compelling last lines of Jamal Mahjoub's *The Carrier* stand as a fitting end to this book. Rashid, his seventeenth-century protagonist, has only a moment to take the dark gap, to avoid the abyss and make for home. This is an archetypal, perilous, postcolonial moment:

> The world tilts and he spills down the incline towards the patient, unassailable stars and the prayer on his lips is that he does not fall into *the darkened gaps between the frail flickers of silent unspoken light.* (278, my emphasis)

We have seen the danger of being sucked into the abyss, of falling into the gaps, as these migrants chart unknown terrain and juggle the complexities of their worlds. But those darkened gaps are illuminated by flickers of light. The momentary flickers and hesitations are also potent fleeting opportunities in the fiction, when the fetish is de-fetishised, the symbol is reversed and the metaphor is shod of its Emperor's imperial costume. And something new becomes possible. We have witnessed the writing of a new generation that scribbles its graffiti on the sacred myths, defecates on the accoutrements of power and most often refuses to be bogged down by the depths of the pessimism that surrounds thoughts of Africa. Those flickers of silent light have been seen to have the power to speak and to be heard, as they communicate in a strange, but familiar English language.

Bibliography

Aboulela, Leila (1999) *The Translator*. Edinburgh: Polygon.
— (2000) 'My Best Teacher', *Times Educational Supplement* (4389): 15.
— (2001) *Coloured Lights*. Edinburgh: Polygon.
Achebe, Chinua (1958) *Things Fall Apart*. London: Heinemann Educational Books.
— (1975) *Morning Yet on Creation Day*. London: Heinemann.
Adebanwi, Wale (2004) 'The Chimamanda Ngozi Adichie Interview', *Nigeria Village Square*, www.nigeriavillagesquare1.com/books/adichie-interview.html.
Adebanwi, Wale and Adichie, Chimimanda Ngozi (2007) 'My Book Should Provoke a Conversation', *Nigerian Weekly News Magazine*, January, http://www.thenewsng.com, accessed 2 April 2007.
Adesanmi, Pius (2002) 'Europhonism, Universities and other Stories: *How Not To Speak for the Future of African Literatures?*', in *Palavers of African Literature: Essays in Honor of Bernth Lindfors, Vol. 1*, Falola, Toyin and Harlow, Barbara (eds). Trenton, New Jersey: Africa World Press: 105–36.
Adichie, Chimamanda Ngozi (2001) 'You In America', *Zoetrope* (38): 1–7.
— (2003) 'Heart Is Where the Home Was', *Topic Magazine*.
— (2004) *Purple Hibiscus*. London: Fourth Estate.
— (2004) 'Half of a Yellow Sun', *Zoetrope* 7 (2): 1–11.
— (2006) *Half of a Yellow Sun* (Toronto and New York: Alfred A. Knopf).
— (2006a) 'Truth and Lies', *The Guardian*, 16 September, http://www.books.guardian.co.uk, accessed 2 April 2007.
Ahmad, Aijaz (1992) *In Theory*. London: Verso.
Anon (2002) 'Fear and Loathing: Special Report, Refugees', *Guardian Unlimited*, London: 1–3.
Anya, Ike (2003) 'In the Footsteps of Chinua Achebe: Enter Chimamanda Ngozi Adichie', *Sentinel Poetry*, 12 November.
Appadurai, Arjun (1986) 'Introduction: Commodities and the Politics of Value'. In *The Social Life of Things: Commodities in Cultural Perspective*, Appadurai, Arjun (ed.). Cambridge, Cambridge University Press: 3–63.
— (1996) *Modernity at Large: Cultural Dimensions of Globalization*. Minneapolis, London: University of Minnesota Press.
— (2001) 'The globalisation of Archaeology and Heritage', *Journal of Social Archaeology* 1 (1): 35–49.
Apter, Emily (1999) *Continental Drift*. Chicago and London: University of Chicago Press.
— (2002) 'Warped Speech: The Politics of Global Translation'. In *Beyond Dichotomies: Histories, Identities, Cultures and the Challenge of Globalization*, Mudimbe–Boyi, Elisabeth (ed.). New York, State University of New York Press: 185–200.
Armah, Ayi Kwei (1969) *The Beautyful Ones Are Not Yet Born*. Oxford: Heinemann African Writers Series.
Arteaga, Alfred (1994) 'An Other Tongue'. In *An Other Tongue: Nation and Ethnicity in the Linguistic Borderlands*, Arteaga, Alfred (ed.). Durham and London, Duke University Press: 9–33.
Asante, Molefi Kete (1989) *Afrocentricity*. Trenton, New Jersey: Africa World Press.
Ashcroft, Bill (1989) 'Is That The Congo? Language as Metonymy in the Post–Colonial Text', *World Literature Written in English* 29 (2): 3–10.
— (2001) *Post–Colonial Transformation*. London and New York: Routledge.
— (2003) 'Resistance and Transformation'. In *Resistance and Reconciliation: Writing in*

the Commonwealth, Bennett, Bruce, Cowan, Susan, Lo, Jacqueline, Nandan, Satendra and Webb, Jen (eds). Canberra: The Association for Commonwealth Literature and
Language Studies: 382–90.

Bandele, Biyi (1992 [1991]) *The Man Who Came in From the Back of Beyond*. Oxford, Portsmouth and Ibadan: Heinemann.

— (1993 [1991]) *The Sympathetic Undertaker and Other Dreams*. Oxford, Portsmouth and
Ibadan: Heinemann.

— (1999) *The Street*. London: Picador.

— (2001) 'Introduction'. In *Chinua Achebe: Things Fall Apart*, Penguin Books: vii–xiii.

Barcelona, Antonio (2000) 'Introduction: The Cognitive Theory of Metaphor and Metonymy'. In *Metaphor and Metonymy at the Crossroads: A Cognitive Perspective*, Barcelona,
Antonio (ed.). Berlin, New York: Mouton de Gruyter: 1–28.

Baucom, Ian (1999) *Out of Place: Englishness, Empire, and the Locations of Identity*. Princeton, New Jersey: Princeton University Press.

Bauman, Zygmunt (1997) *Postmodernity and its Discontents*. New York: New York University Press.

— (2005) *Liquid Life*. Cambridge: Polity Press.

Bender, Barbara (2001) 'Landscapes on-the-Move', *Journal of Social Archaeology* 1 (1):
75–89.

Benítez–Rojo, Antonio (1992) *The Repeating Island: The Caribbean and the Postmodern
Perspective*. Durham and London: Duke University Press.

Bhabha, Homi (1984) 'Representation and the Colonial Text: A Critical Exploration of
Some Forms of Mimeticism'. In *The Theory of Reading*, Gloversmith, Frank (ed.).
Sussex and New Jersey: The Harvester Press and Barnes and Noble: 93–122.

— (1994) *The Location of Culture*. London and New York: Routledge.

— (1996) 'Culture's In-Between'. In *Questions of Cultural Identity*. Hall, Stuart and du Gay,
Paul (eds). London, Thousand Oaks, New Delhi: Sage Publications: 53–60.

Bogue, Ronald (1989) *Deleuze and Guattari*. London and New York: Routledge.

Bourdieu, Pierre (1984 [1979]) *Distinction: A Social Critique of the Judgement of Taste*.
Cambridge, Massachusetts: Harvard University Press.

Bowker, Geoffrey C. and Star, Susan Leigh (1999) *Sorting Things Out: Classification and
Its Consequences*. Cambridge: MIT Press.

Boym, Svetlana (2001) *The Future of Nostalgia*. New York: Basic Books.

Britton, Celia M (1999) *Edouard Glissant and Postcolonial Theory: Strategies of Language
and Resistance*. Charlottesville and London: University Press of Virginia.

Butler, Judith (1993) *Bodies that Matter*. New York and London: Routledge.

— (1997) *Excitable Speech: The Politics of the Performative*. New York and London:
Routledge.

Carroll, Lewis (1992 [1876]) *The Hunting of the Snark: An Agony in Eight Fits*. London:
Wordsworth.

— (1998 [1865 and 1872]) *Alice's Adventures in Wonderland and Through the Looking–
Glass*. London and New York: Penguin.

Chakrabarty, Dipesh (1992) 'Postcoloniality and the Artiface of History: Who Speaks for
"Indian" Pasts?', *Representations* 37 (Winter): 1–26.

Chambers, Iain (1994) *Migrancy, Culture, Identity*. London and New York: Routledge.

— (1996) 'Signs of Silence, Lines of Listening'. In *The Post–colonial Question: Common
Skies, Divided Horizons*, Chambers, Iain, and Curti, Lidia (eds). London: Routledge:
47–62.

— (2001) *Culture after Humanism: History, Culture, Subjectivity*. London and New York:
Routledge.

Clayton, Anthony (1981) *The Zanzibar Revolution and its Aftermath*. London: C. Hurst
and Company.

Clifford, James (1997) *Routes: Travel and Translation in the Late Twentieth Century*. Cambridge, Massachusetts: Harvard University Press.

Cooper, Brenda (1998) *Magical Realism in West African Fiction: Seeing with a Third Eye*.

London: Routledge.

— (2004) 'A Gunny Sack, Chants and Jingles, a Fan and a Black Trunk: The Coded Language of the Everyday in a Postcolonial African Novel – M.G. Vassanj's *The Gunny Sack*', *Africa Quarterly*, 44 (3), November: 12–31.

— (2007) 'The Rhetoric of a New Essentialism versus Multiple Worlds: Isidore Okpewho's *Call Me By My Rightful Name* and Buchi Emecheta's *The New Tribe* in Conversation', *Journal of Commonwealth Literature*, 42 (2): 19–36.

Cooper, Frederick (2001) 'What is the Concept of Globalization Good For? An African Historian's Perspective', *African Affairs* 100: 189–213.

Cooppan, Vilashini (2000) 'W(h)ither Post-colonial Studies? Towards the Transnational Study of Race and Nation'. In *Postcolonial Theory and Criticism*, Chrisman, Laura and Parry, Benita (eds). Cambridge, D.S. Brewer: 1–35.

— (2004) 'Ghosts in the Disciplinary Machine: The Uncanny Life of World Literature', *Comparative Literature Studies* 4 (1): 10–36.

Cribb, T.J. (2000) '*Oroonoko* and *Happy Birthday, Mister Deka D*, by 'Biyi Bandele', *Research in African Literatures* 31 (1): 173–78.

Dash, Michael J. (1992) 'Introduction'. In *Caribbean Discourse: Selected Essays by Edouard Glissant* (ed.). Charlottesville: University Press of Virginia: xi–xlv.

Davies, Ioan (1998) 'Negotiating African Culture: Toward a Decolonization of the Fetish', In *The Cultures of Globalization*, Jameson, Fredric and Miyoshi, Masao (eds). Durham and London: Duke University Press: 125–45.

de Certeau, Michel (1984) *The Practice of Everyday Life*. Los Angeles: University of California Press.

Deleuze, Gilles (1990 [1969]) *The Logic of Sense*. New York: Columbia University Press.

— (1996 [1994]) ' 'Repetition for Itself, in *Difference and Repetition*'. In *Writing and Psychoanalysis: A Reader*, Lechte, John (ed.). London and New York: Arnold.

— (1997 [1993]) *Essays Critical and Clinical*. Minneapolis: University of Minnesota Press.

Deleuze, Gilles and Guattari, Felix (1983 [1972]) *Anti–Oedipus: Capitalism and Schizophrenia*. Minneapolis: University of Minnesota Press.

— (1986 [1975]) *Kafka: Toward a Minor Literature*. Minneapolis: University of Minnesota Press.

— (1987 [1980]) *A Thousand Plateaus*. Minnesota: University of Minneapolis Press.

Derrida, Jacques (1998 [1996]) *Monolingualism of the Other or The Prosthesis of Origin*. Stanford: Stanford University Press.

Diez-Tagarro, Rosa (1995) 'Biyi Bandele-Thomas talks to Rosa Diez-Tagarro', *Wasafiri* 22: 57–9.

Diop, Cheikh Anta (1991) *Civilization or Barbarism: An Authentic Anthropology*. New York: Lawrence Hill Books.

Douglas, Mary (1966) *Purity and Danger*. London and Henley: Routledge and Kegan Paul.

Douglas, Mary and Isherwood, Baron (1978) *The World of Goods: Towards an Anthropology of Consumption*. Harmondsworth: Penguin.

— (1996) *The World of Goods: Towards an Anthropology of Consumption* [New Edition]. New York and London: Routledge.

Duncan, Carol (1991) 'Art Museums and the Ritual of Citizenship'. In *Exhibiting Cultures: The Poetics and Politics of Museum Display*, Karp, Ivan and Lavine, Steven (eds). Washington and London: Smithsonian Institution Press: 88–103.

Durham, Deborah and Fernandez, James, W. (1991) 'Tropical Dominions: The Figurative Struggle over Domains of Belonging and Apartness in Africa'. In *Beyond Metaphor: The Theory of Tropes in Anthropology*, Fernandez, James, W (ed.), Stanford, CA: Stanford University Press: 190–210.

Elliott, Anthony and Frosh, Stephen (1995) 'Introduction'. In *Psychoanalysis in Contexts: Paths Between Theory and Modern Culture*, Elliott, Anthony and Frosh, Stephen (ed.). London and New York: Routledge: 1–11.

Emecheta, Buchi (2000) *The New Tribe*. Oxford: Heinemann.

Fanon, Frantz (1970 [1952]) *Black Skins, White Masks*. Frogmore, St Albans: Paladin.

Feyaerts, Kurt (2000) 'Refining the Inheritance Hypothesis: Interaction between metaphoric and metonymic hierarchies'. In *Metaphor and Metonymy at the Crossroads: A Cognitive Perspective*, Barcelona, Antonio (ed.). Berlin and New York: Mouton de Gruyter: 59–78.

Fisher, Philip (2001) 'Brixton Stories'. *The British Theatre Guide*, http://www.britishtheatreguide.info/review/brixton–rev.htm: 2 pages.

Fleck, Linda. L. (1998) 'From Metonymy to Metaphor: Paul Auster's *Leviathan*'. *Critique* 39 (3): 258–70.

Fleming, Kate (2000) 'Biyi Bandele's *The Street*', *World Literature Today* 74 3 (Summer): 572–3.

Foucault, Michel (1972 [1969]) *The Archaeology of Knowledge*. London: Tavistock Publications.

Freud, Sigmund (1977) *On Sexuality: Three Essays on the Theory of Sexuality and Other Works*. Harmondsworth: Penguin.

Frosh, Stephen (1995) 'Masculine Mastery and Fantasy, or the Meaning of the Phallus'. In *Psychoanalysis in Contexts: Paths Between Theory and Modern Culture*, Elliott, Anthony and Frosh, Stephen (eds). London and New York: Routledge: 166–87.

— (1999) *The Politics of Psychoanalysis*. London: Macmillan.

— (2002) *After Words: The Personal in Gender, Culture and Psychotherapy*. London: Palgrave.

Gallop, Jane (1985) *Reading Lacan*. Ithaca: Cornell University Press.

Garuba, Harry (2003) 'Explorations in Animist Materialism: Notes on Reading/Writing African Literature, Culture and Society', *Public Culture* 15 (2): 261–85.

— (2005) 'The Unbearable Lightness of Being: Re-figuring Trends in Recent Nigerian Poetry', *English in Africa* 32 (1): 51–72.

Gates, Henry Louis Jr (1988) *The Signifying Monkey*. Oxford: Oxford University Press.

Gikandi, Simon (1996) *Maps of Englishness*. New York: Columbia University Press.

Gilbert, Sandra M. and Gubar, Susan (1988) *No Man's Land: The Place of the Woman Writer in the Twentieth Century, Volume One: The War of the Words*. New Haven and London: Yale University Press.

Glissant, Edouard (1992 [1981]) *Caribbean Discourse: Selected Essays*. Charlottesville: University Press of Virginia.

Goodchild, Philip (1996) *Deleuze and Guattari: An Introduction to the Politics of Desire*. London: Sage Publications.

Gunew, Sneja (2004) *Haunted Nations: The Colonial Dimensions of Multiculturalisms*. London and New York: Routledge.

Gurnah, Abdulrazak (1996) *Admiring Silence*. London: Penguin.

— (2001) *By the Sea*. London: Bloomsbury.

Harasym, Sarah (ed.) (1990) *The Post-colonial Critic: Interviews, Strategies, Dialogues*. London and New York: Routledge.

Haraway, Donna J. (1991) *Simians, Cyborgs, and Women: The Reinvention of Nature*. London: Free Association Books Ltd.

Hardt, Michael (1998) 'The Withering of Civil Society'. In *Deleuze and Guattari: New Mappings in Politics, Philosophy and Culture*, Kaufman, Eleanor and Heller, Kevin Jon (eds). Minneapolis and London: University of Minnesota Press: 23–39.

Harlow, Barbara (1991) 'The Tortoise and the Birds: Strategies of Resistance in *Things Fall Apart*'. In *Approaches to Teaching: Achebe's* Things Fall Apart, Lindfors, Bernth (ed.). New York: The Modern Language Association of America: 74–9.

Hawley, John, C. (2003) 'Moses Isegawa's *Abyssinian Chronicles* as the Bildungsroman of Despair: AIDS and the Irrelevance of Reconciliation'. In *Resistance and Reconciliation: Writing in the Commonwealth*, Bennett, Bruce, Cowan, Susan, Lo, Jacqueline, Nandan, Satendra and Webb, Jen (eds). Canberra: The Association for Commonwealth Literature and Language Studies: 187–200.

Highmore, Ben (2002) *Everyday Life and Cultural Theory: An Introduction*. London and

New York: Routledge.

Holger–Ehling (2001) 'Biyi Bandele-Thomas, Coming out Grinning, Interview by Holger Ehling', *Matatu: Journal for African Culture and Society*, 23–4: 91–5.

Holland, Eugene, W. (1988) 'Schizoanalysis: The Postmodern Contextualization of Psychoanalysis'. In *Marxism and the Interpretation of Culture*, Nelson, Cary and Grossberg, Lawrence (eds). London: Macmillan: 405–16.

— (1996) 'Schizoanalysis and Baudelaire: Some Illustrations of Decoding at Work'. In *Deleuze: A Critical Reader*, Patton, Paul (ed.). Oxford, Blackwell Publishers: 240–56.

Holquist, Michael (1969) 'What is a Boojum? Nonsense and Modernism', *Yale French Studies* 43: 145–64.

Hoskins, Janet (1998) *Biographical Objects: How Things Tell the Stories of People's Lives.* London: Routledge.

Huggan, Graham (2001) *The Post-colonial Exotic: Marketing the Margins.* London: Routledge.

Hutcheon, Linda (1994) *Irony's Edge: The Theory and Politics of Irony.* London and New York: Routledge.

Isegawa, Moses (2000) *Abyssinian Chronicles.* London: Picador.

Jaggi, Maya (2001) 'Trajectories of Flight', *The Guardian*, London: 1–3.

Jakobson, Roman and Halle, Morris (1956) *The Fundamentals of Language.* The Hague: Mouton.

Jameson, Fredric (1981) *The Political Unconscious: Narrative as a Socially Symbolic Act.* London: Methuen.

— (1988 [1978]) 'Imaginary and Symbolic in Lacan'. In *The Ideologies of Theory: Essays 1971–1986* (ed.). London, Routledge. 1: 75–115.

— (1991) *Postmodernism or the Cultural Logic of Late Capitalism.* Durham, NC: Duke University Press.

Jeyifo, Biodun (1991) 'For Chinua Achebe: The Resilience and the Predicament of Obierika'. In *Chinua Achebe: A Celebration*, Petersen, Kirsten Holst and Rutherford, Anna (eds). Sydney: Dangeroo Press: 51–70.

Johnson, Barbara (1984) 'Metaphor, Metonymy and Voice in *Their Eyes Were Watching God*'. In *Black Literature and Literary Theory*, Gates, Henry Louis Jr (ed.). New York: Methuen: 205–19.

Jones, Jacqui (2000) 'Traversing the Abyss: Moses Isegawa – An Interview and Commentary', *English in Africa* 27 (2): 85–102.

Joseph, May (1999) *Nomadic Identities: The Performance of Citizenship.* Minneapolis: University of Minnesota Press.

Julien, Eileen (1992) *African Novels and the Question of Orality.* Bloomington and Indianapolis: Indiana University Press.

— (2006) 'The Extroverted African Novel'. In *The Novel, Volume I: History, Geography and Culture*, Moretti, Franco (ed.). Princeton and Oxford: Princeton University Press: 667–700.

Kanaganayakam, Chelva (1991) '"Broadening the Substrata": An Interview with M.G. Vassanji', *World Literature Written in English* 31 (2): 19–35.

Kaufman, Eleanor (2002) 'Solid Dialectic in Sartre and Deleuze', *Polygraph* 14: 115–28.

Kopytoff, Igor (1986) 'The Cultural Biography of Things: Commoditization as Process'. In *The Social Life of Things: Commodities in Cultural Perspective*, Appadurai, Arjun (ed.). Cambridge: Cambridge University Press: 64–91.

Lacan, Jacques (1977 [1966]) *Ecrits: A Selection.* London: Tavistock/Routledge.

Lakoff, George and Johnson, Mark (1980) *Metaphors We Live By.* Chicago and London: University of Chicago Press.

Lang, George (1996) 'Jihad, *Ijtihad*, and Other Dialogical Wars in *La Mère du printemps, Le Harem politique*, and *Loin de Medine*'. In *The Marabout and the Muse: New Approaches to Islam in African Literature*, Harrow, Kenneth, W. (ed.). Portsmouth and London: Heinemann and James Currey: 1–22.

Latour, Bruno (1999) *Pandora's Hope: Essays on the Reality of Science Studies.* Cambridge,

176 *Bibliography*

Massachusetts: Harvard University Press.

Lechte, John (1996) 'Editor's introduction to Gilles Deleuze's 'Repetition for Itself, in *Difference and Repetition'*. In *Writing and Psychoanalysis: A Reader*, Lechte, John (ed.). London and New York: Arnold: 19–21.

Lefebvre, Henri (1984 [1971]) *Everyday Life in the Modern World*. New Brunswick and London: Transaction Publishers.

— (1988) 'Toward a Leftist Cultural Politics: Remarks Occasioned by the Centenary of Marx's Death'. In *Marxism and the Interpretation of Culture*, Nelson, Cary and Grossberg, Lawrence (eds). London: Macmillan Education: 75–88.

Lemaire, Anika (1977 [1970]) *Jacques Lacan*. London: Routledge and Kegan Paul.

Lodge, David (1977) *The Modes of Modern Writing*. London: Edward Arnold.

Low, Gail Ching-Liang (1996) *White Skins, Black Masks*. London: Routledge.

MacCannell, Juliet Flower (1983) 'Oedipus Wrecks: Lacan, Stendhal, and the Narrative Form of the Real'. In *Lacan and Narration: The Psychoanalytic Difference in Narrative Theory*. Davis, Robert Con (ed.). Baltimore and London: Johns Hopkins University Press: 910–40.

— (1991) *The Regime of the Brother: After the Patriarchy*. London: Routledge.

Macey, David (1995) 'On the Subject of Lacan'. In *Psychoanalysis in Contexts: Paths Between Theory and Modern Culture*, Elliott, Anthony and Frosh, Stephen (eds). London and New York: Routledge: 72–86.

Mahdi, Muhsin (1995) *The Thousand and One Nights*. Leiden: E.J. Brill.

Mahjoub, Jamal (1993) 'The Cartographer's Angel', *New African*, March: 33–6.

— (1996) *In The Hour of Signs*. Oxford: Heinemann African Writers Series.

— (1996) 'Terra Ephemera'. In *Images of the West*, (ed.). Harare and Copenhagen: Baobab Books: 62–3.

— (1998) *The Carrier*. London: Phoenix House.

— (2002) 'Fiction, Reality and the Fear of Flying'. *Public Lecture given at Kolding Folkebiblioteket*, htpp://www.humaniora.sdu.dk/engelsk–kolding/mahjoub.htm: 1–12.

Mahjoub, Jamal (2003) *Travelling with Djinns*. London: Chatto and Windus.

Mamdani, Mahmood (2001) *When Victims Become Killers: Colonialism, Nativism and the Genocide in Rwanda*. Kampala, Cape Town, Oxford: Fountain, David Philip, James Currey.

— (2007) 'Darfur, the Politics of Naming', *Mail & Guardian*, 16–22 March: 22 and 26.

Mantel, Hilary (2000) 'Staring at the Medusa's Head: *Abyssinian Chronicles* by Moses Isegawa', *The New York Review of Books* 47, 19 November 30th.

Marks, Laura U. (2000) *The Skin of the Film: Intercultural Cinema, Embodiment, and the Senses*. Durham and London: Duke University Press.

Martin, Esmond, Bradley (1978) *Zanzibar: Tradition and Revolution*. London: Hamish Hamilton.

Mbembe, Achille (2001) *On the Postcolony*. Berkeley: University of California Press.

Mignolo, Walter D. (2000) *Local Histories/Global Designs: Coloniality, Subaltern Knowledges, and Border Thinking*. Princeton: Princeton University Press.

Miller, Daniel (1998) 'Why Some Things Matter'. In *Material Cultures: Why Some Things Matter*, Miller, Daniel (ed.). Chicago and London: University of Chicago Press: 3–21.

Minh-ha, Trinh T. (1989) *Woman, Native, Other*. Bloomington and Indianapolis: Indiana University Press.

Mohanty, Satya P. (1997) *Literary Theory and the Claims of History: Postmodernism, Objectivity, Multicultural Politics*. Ithaca: Cornell University Press.

Mudimbe, V.Y. (1988) *The Invention of Africa*. Bloomington and Indianapolis and London: Indiana University Press and James Currey.

Myers, Tony (2003) *Slavoj Žižek*. London: Routledge.

Ndebele, Njabulo (1991) *Rediscovery of the Ordinary: Essays on South African Literature and Culture*. Johannesburg: COSAW.

Negash, Girma (1999) 'Migrant literature and political commitment: puzzles and parables in the novels of Biyi Bandele-Thomas', *Journal of African Cultural Studies* 12 (1): 77–92.

Ngũgĩ, wa Thiong'o (1977) *Petals of Blood.* London: Heinemann Educational Books.
— (1998) *Penpoints, Gunpoints and Dreams: Towards a Critical Theory of the Arts and the State in Africa.* Oxford: Clarendon Press.
Okri, Ben (1991) *The Famished Road.* London: Jonathan Cape.
Okpewho, Isidore (2004) *Call Me By My Rightful Name.* Trenton NJ: Africa World Press.
Ola, Sheyin (1994) 'The Man who Came in From the Back of Beyond', *New African*, 325 (December): 26.
Parry, Benita (2004) *Postcolonial Studies: A Materialist Critique.* London and New York: Routledge.
Peel, Michael (2006) 'Love in the Time of War', *The Financial Times*, 9 September, http://www.ft.com, accessed 7 April 2007.
Rackin, Donald (1991) *Alice's Adventures in Wonderland and Through the Looking-Glass: Nonsense, Sense, and Meaning.* New York: Twayne.
Radden, Gunter (2000) 'How Metonymic are Metaphors?'. In *Metaphor and Metonymy at the Crossroads: A Cognitive Perspective*, Barcelona, Antonio (ed.). Berlin, New York: Mouton de Gruyter: 93–108.
Radhakrishnan, R. (1996) *Diasporic Mediations: Between Home and Location.* Minneapolis: University of Minnesota Press.
— (2000) 'Postmodernism and the Rest of the World'. In Afzal-Khan, Fawzia and Seshadri-Crooks, Kalpana (eds). Durham and London: Duke University Press: 37–70.
— (2002) 'Derivative Discourses and the Problem of Signification', *The European Legacy* 7 (No. 6): 783–95.
Ruegg, Maria (1979) 'Metaphor and Metonymy: The Logic of Structuralist Rhetoric', *Glyph* 6: 141–57.
Rush, Norman (2004) 'The Last Word on Evil: Snakepit by Moses Isegawa', *The New York Review*: 30–31.
Rutherford, Jonathan (1990) 'The Third Space: Interview with Homi Bhabha'. In *Identity: Community, Culture, Difference*, Rutherford, Jonathan (ed.). London: Lawrence and Wishart.
Said, Edward (1985 [1978]) *Orientalism.* Harmondsworth: Penguin.
— (1993) *Culture and Imperialism.* London: Chatto and Windus.
Salih, Tayeb (1991 [1969]) *Season of Migration to the North.* London and New York: Heinemann Educational Books.
Sandhu, Sukhdev (1999) 'Among the Undead: Biyi Bandele's *The Street*', *The Times Literary Supplement* (6 August): 23.
— (2000) 'Pop Goes the Centre: Hanif Kureishi's London.' In *Postcolonial Theory and Criticism*. Chrisman, Laura and Parry, Benita (eds). Cambridge: D.S. Brewer: 133–54.
— (2004) *London Calling: How Black and Asian Writers Imagined a City.* London: Harper Perennial.
Sarvan, Charles. Ponnuthurai (1991) 'M.G. Vassanji's *The Gunny Sack*: A Reflection on History and the Novel', *Modern Fiction Studies* 37 (3): 511–18.
Scarry, Elaine (1985) *The Body in Pain: The Making and Unmaking of the World.* New York, Oxford: Oxford University Press.
Schleifer, Ronald (1983) 'The Space and Dialogue of Desire: Lacan, Greimas, and Narrative Temporality'. In *Lacan and Narration: The Psychoanalytic Difference in Narrative Theory*, Davis, Robert Con (ed.). Baltimore and London: Johns Hopkins University Press: 871–90.
— (1990) *Rhetoric and Death: The Language of Modernism and Postmodern Discourse Theory.* Urbana and Chicago: University of Illinois Press.
Schwenger, Peter (2001) 'Words and the Murder of the Thing', *Critical Inquiry* 28 (Autumn): 99–113.
Seem, Mark (1983) 'Introduction'. In *Anti-Oedipus: Capitalism and Schizophrenia*, Deleuze, Gilles and Guattari, Felix (eds). Minneapolis: University of Minnesota Press.
Sewell, Elizabeth (1978 [1952]) *The Field of Nonsense.* London: The Arden Library.
Sévry, Jean (2001) 'Interviewing Jamal Mahjoub', *Commonwealth Essays and Studies* 23

(2): 85–92.

Shetty, Sandhya (1995) '(Dis)figuring the Nation: Mother, Metaphor, Metonymy', *differences: A Journal of Feminist Cultural Studies* 7.5: 50–79.

Sheyin, Ola (1994) 'The Man Who Came in From the Back of Beyond', *New African* (No. 325): 26.

Sole, Kelwyn (2005) '"The Deep Thoughts the One in Need Falls Into": Quotidian Experience and the Perspectives of Poetry in Postliberation South Africa'. In *Postcolonial Studies and Beyond*, Loomba, Ania, Kaul, Suvir, Bunzl, Matti, Burton, Antoinette and Esty, Jed (eds). Durham and London: Duke University Press: 182–205.

Sommer, Doris (1996) 'Who Can Tell? Filling in Blanks for Cirilo Villaverde'. In *Writing the Nation: Self and Country in Post–Colonial Imagination*, Hawley, John, C (ed.). Amsterdam: Rodopi.

Soueif, Ahdaf (1996) *Sandpiper*. London: Bloomsbury.

Spacks, Patricia Meyer (1961) 'Logic and Language in "Through The Looking Glass"', *International Society for General Semantics* 18 (part 1): 91–100.

Spivak, Gayatri Chakravorty (1993) 'Echo', *New Literary History* 24: 17–43.

Stern, Jeffrey (1982) 'Lewis Carroll the Surrealist'. In *Lewis Carroll: A Celebration. Essays on the Occasion of the 150th Anniversary of the Birth of Charles Lutwidge Dodgson*, Guiliano, Edward (ed.) New York: Clarkson N. Potter: 132–53.

Stewart, Susan (1993) *On Longing: Narratives of the Miniature, the Gigantic, the Souvenir, the Collection*. Durham and London: Duke University Press.

Stoltzfus, Ben (1996) *Lacan and Literature: Purloined Pretexts*. New York: State University of New York Press.

Suleri, Sara (1992) *The Rhetoric of English India*. Chicago: University of Chicago Press.

Talib, Ismail S. (2002) *The Language of Postcolonial Literatures: An Introduction*. London and New York: Routledge.

Thompson. Bob (2006) 'From Pages of Fiction. A Volume of Sad Truth: Young Novelist Preserves the Story of Biafra', *Washington Post*, 27 September, http://www.washingtonpost.com, accessed 2 April 2007.

Turner, Mark. and Fauconnier, Gilles (2000) 'Metaphor, Metonymy and Binding'. In *Metaphor and Metonymy at the Crossroads: A Cognitive Perspective*, Barcelona, Antonio (ed.). Berlin, New York: Mouton de Gruyter: 133–45.

Tutuola, Amos (1952) *The Palm-Wine Drinkard*. London: Faber and Faber.

Tymoczko, Maria (1999) *Translation in a Postcolonial Context: Early Irish Literature in English Translation*. Manchester: St Jerome Publishing.

Vassanji, M.G (1989) *The Gunny Sack*. Oxford: Heinemann, African Writers Series.

— (1991) *No New Land*. Toronto: McClelland and Stewart.

— (1999) *Amriika*. Toronto: McClelland and Stewart.

Vazquez, Michael C. (2000) 'Hearts in Exile: A Conversation with Moses Isegawa and Mahmood Mamdani', *Transition* 10 (86): 126–50.

Versi, Anver (1993) 'Charting A New Landscape: Anver Versi talks to Jamal Mahjoub', *New African*, March: 36–7.

Wainaina, Binyavanga (2005) 'How to Write About Africa', *Granta* 92 (Winter): 91–5.

Walker, Alice (1983a) *The Color Purple*. London: The Women's Press.

— (1983b) *In Search of our Mother's Gardens*. San Diego, New York, London: Harcourt Brace Jovanovich.

White, Hayden (1999) *Figural Realism: Studies in the Mimesis Effect*. Baltimore and London: Johns Hopkins University Press.

Woolf, Virginia (1964a [1925]) *Mrs Dalloway*. Harmondsworth: Penguin Books.

— (1964b [1927]) *To the Lighthouse*. Harmondsworth: Penguin Books.

Yan, Haiping (1999) 'Transnationality and Its Critique: Narrative Tropes of "Borderland" in *Our Sister Killjoy*'. In *Emerging Perspectives on Ama Ata Aidoo*, Azodo, Ada Uzoamaka and Wilentz, Gay, (eds). Trenton, New Jersey: Africa World Press.

Žižek, Slavoj (1991) *Looking Awry: An Introduction to Jacques Lacan Through Popular Culture*. Cambridge, Massachusetts: MIT Press.

Index

Printed and bound by CPI Group (UK) Ltd, Croydon, CR0 4YY

09/06/2025

14685778-0001